THE BUCK STOPS HERE

TO SALLY (1937-2007) AS ALWAYS.

— EDWIN KIESTER JR.

FOR ELIZABETH AND NATHANIAL VARDA, THE NEXT GENERATION OF PRESIDENTIAL HISTORIANS.

— THOMAS J. CRAUGHWELL

Text © 2010 by Thomas J. Craughwell and Edwin Kiester Jr.

First published in the USA in 2010 by
Fair Winds Press, a member of
Quayside Publishing Group
100 Cummings Center
Suite 406-L
Beverly, MA 01915-6101
www.fairwindspress.com

14 13 12 11 10   1 2 3 4 5

ISBN-13: 978-1-59233-427-8
ISBN-10: 1-59233-427-X

Library of Congress Cataloging-in-Publication Data
Craughwell, Thomas J., 1956-
 The buck stops here : the 28 toughest presidential decisions and how they changed history / Thomas J. Craughwell and Edwin Kiester, Jr.
     p. cm.
 Includes bibliographical references and index.
 ISBN-13: 978-1-59233-427-8
 ISBN-10: 1-59233-427-X
 1. Presidents—United States—History. 2. United States—Politics and government—Decision making. 3. Presidents—United States—Case studies. 4. United States—Politics and government—Case studies. 5. Political leadership—United States—Case studies. I. Kiester, Edwin. II. Title.
 E176.1.C879 2010
 321.8'042—dc22

2009052Y92

Cover design: Peter Long
Book design: Sheila Hart Design, Inc.
Book layout: Sheila Hart Design, Inc.
Cover images: Seal © Visions of America, LLC/Alamy; Truman © Bettmann/CORBIS

Printed and bound in Singapore

THE BUCK STOPS HERE

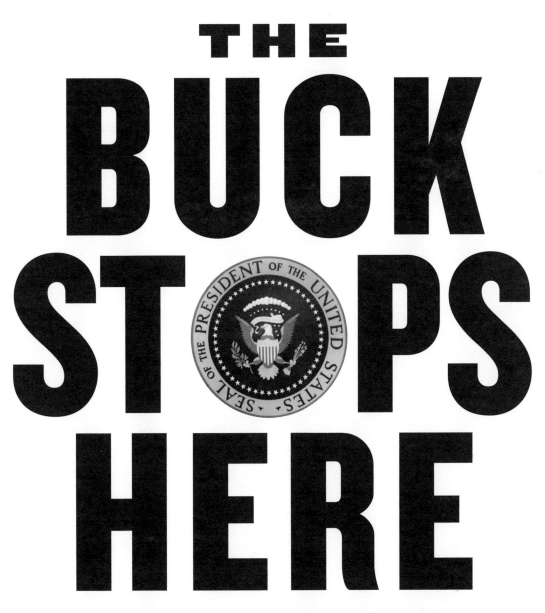

THE 28 TOUGHEST PRESIDENTIAL DECISIONS AND HOW THEY CHANGED HISTORY

THOMAS J. CRAUGHWELL
EDWIN KIESTER JR.

CONTENTS

INTRODUCTION

George Washington was in the saddle again, sitting majestically in buff and blue before a formation of 13,000 militiamen drawn up in Carlisle, Pennsylvania, in 1794. This time, however, the Revolutionary hero was not commanding troops into battle but delivering an emphatic statement. The infant United States, just five years old, was a strong government of strong principles, and the president was the established head of that government. He and that government must be accepted in that role. In times of crisis it was the president's responsibility—indeed, his duty—to make the tough decisions and provide leadership.

"The buck stops here." A century and a half later, Harry Truman kept that pithy slogan on his desk to remind visitors, and the world, of the president's pinnacle position under the U.S. Constitution. In 2006 another president stated the same position. "Under our system, I'm the decider," George W. Bush, no wordsmith, echoed his predecessors. "I hear all the voices and read all the opinions and then I decide."

October 1794 was one of those crisis times. America's western frontier was aflame with insurrection. To pay off huge debts from the Revolution, Congress, prodded by Secretary of the Treasury Alexander Hamilton with the president's backing, had imposed a ten-cents-a-gallon excise tax on rye whiskey, which frontier farmers distilled from grain and shipped as a major source of income. Protesting the tax, angry farmers had besieged the home of a federal official sent to collect the tax, set fire to it, and ignited a two-day clash in which two protestors were killed and five soldiers who were sent to quell the uprising were wounded. Such lawlessness and defiance of the new government's authority could not be permitted to continue. The mobilization at Carlisle was Washington's answer. Encouraged by Hamilton, he left the then federal capital in Philadelphia for Carlisle and prepared to lead a force over the mountains to enforce the government edict.

Himself a farmer, Washington was sympathetic to the farmers' plight. But in this first test of presidential authority he had to lay down the law. He quietly but firmly insisted that in conflicts between state and federal governments, the federal government took precedence, and that the president, as its agent, must be acknowledged as its leader.

Only someone of Washington's heroic stature and enormous prestige could carry off such a stance in such fractious times. Washington's decision to stand up for the presidential role was to resound through history and affect the nation for decades to follow. Though Washington's action was to doom the Federalist Party, historians agree that it was the defining moment of shaping the U.S. presidency. A decade later, in 1803, Thomas Jefferson, Washington's erstwhile opponent but now president himself, firmed up the presidential role. Almost unilaterally he initiated the purchase from France of the Louisiana territory, doubling with a stroke of the pen the size of the new country. Opponents argued that his "dictatorial" action was stretching the president's powers too much, the new acquisition was too big to be readily administered and governed, and that the purchase price would overwhelm the already overstretched budget. No matter. The presidential decision stood.

From Washington and Jefferson to the twenty-first century, presidents have made decisions that have re-stitched the fabric of American society and government and altered the nation's place in the world. These decisions were made by presidents who boldly confronted a national issue or problem, reacted to a crisis, responsed to the actions of others, or coped with problems not foreseen by the framers of the nation. This book explores twenty-eight critical presidential decisions and their legacy.

MONROE: HANDS OFF THIS HEMISPHERE

In 1823 the fifth president, James Monroe, looked southward and saw a continent in turmoil. One by one, Spanish and Portuguese colonial regimes had been overturned to be replaced by shaky and fragile self-governments. Greedy imperialists in Europe were eyeing the area as ripe for takeover and exploitation. The American president pronounced the "Monroe Doctrine," warning other nations that the young United States would not tolerate meddling in its neighborhood by any foreign nation. That doctrine has been the cornerstone of hemispheric relations ever since.

In the 1830s, 1840s, and 1850s, the central and most controversial issue in America was the expansion of slavery into new territory. Eight presidents in those decades did not make decisions about the conflicting aspects of that "peculiar institution;" they avoided them. Finally the inept Buchanan administration simply dumped the whole mess in the lap of the incoming Abraham Lincoln in 1861. When first seven and then four more Southern slaveholding states seceded from the Union, the Civil War began. Lincoln's decision to resist launched the Civil War.

Lincoln, of course, over the unanimous opposition of his "Team of Rivals" cabinet, issued the Emancipation Proclamation in 1863. It did not free a single slave, only those in states "in rebellion," which were part of the Confederacy and beyond Washington's control. But the landmark decision raised the banner of freedom and hope for millions in the enslaved South and gave the Northern armies a cause to fight for.

Not that those decades were bereft of decisions that affected U.S. history. President James K. Polk, rated by many historians as one of the nation's most effective presidents, wasn't ranked that way by many contemporaries, some of whom threatened impeachment. But Polk promised and made a series of tough, lasting decisions, and fought for them, that again greatly expanded the nation's borders. When Polk left office after one term in 1849, his decisions, including waging war with Mexico and the annexation of Texas, California, and the Oregon territory, had stretched the nation to the Pacific and northward to the present Canadian border.

Three decades later, Chester A. Arthur became known as the "Father of Civil Service" when he acknowledged the cries that the government was riddled with graft and corruption and instituted the first merit-based system for public employees, which now extends to all levels of government.

THEODORE THE DECISIVE

With the new century came Theodore Roosevelt and a cascade of critical decisions affecting virtually all areas of government. He decided to build a canal across the isthmus of Panama to link the two oceans. He hosted treaty discussions ending the Russo-Japanese War. He greatly enlarged and modernized the Navy, had the battleships painted a gleaming white, and sent the "Great White Fleet" on a globe-girdling "goodwill" tour that notified the world that the United States was now a world naval power.

Climaxing all these momentous decisions, he launched a conservation policy to protect the nation's natural resources and beauty, capstoned by setting aside national forests and a jeweled necklace of national parks.

Woodrow Wilson, an idealistic college professor turned politician, reluctantly decided to take America into "The Great War" of 1914–18 and then tried unsuccessfully to persuade the nation to join and anchor a League of Nations, a kind of international parliament, to deal with future international disputes. That, however, would have to wait for another war and a decision by another president, Theodore Roosevelt's cousin Franklin.

Franklin Roosevelt took office in March 1933 in the depths of the worst economic depression in American history and immediately rallied a dispirited nation with a stirring speech: "The only thing we have to fear is fear itself!" There then followed, as with his rambunctious relative, an outpouring of decisions that collectively became known as the New Deal. The Social Security Act constructed a safety net under struggling seniors. The Civilian Conservation Corps brought employment to young people, agricultural reform helped beleaguered farmers, and pro-union labor legislation put capital and labor on a new footing.

Then Roosevelt turned his attention from domestic issues to the war engulfing the planet. The Lend-Lease Act turned U.S. industrial might into "the arsenal of democracy," arming and supplying the Allies against Hitler's Germany and Imperial Japan. The United States then joined the Allies. When it became obvious that American armies would be victorious, Roosevelt signed the GI Bill of Rights, granting 11 million young men a college education and housing loans that would transform the postwar nation. His dream of a United Nations took shape in April 1945, but within a few weeks Roosevelt had died.

The buck then passed to Harry Truman. He had hardly entered office when he learned of the atomic bomb—and scarcely hesitated before deciding to drop the bomb on Japan and thus end the war. After the hostilities of World War II gave way to the Cold War between the United States and its wartime ally, the Soviet Union, he did not flinch in the face of crises in Korea and beleaguered Berlin, launching a round-the-clock airlift to keep the city fed and supplied.

Like Truman, John F. Kennedy inherited a crisis—the disastrous invasion of Cuba at the Bay of Pigs by exiles fashioned by the U.S. Central Intelligence Agency in the Eisenhower years. "How could we have been so stupid?" Kennedy ranted afterwards. A year later he faced—and faced down—another crisis in Cuba, when the Soviet Union installed missile launching sites on the island 90 miles from the United States. Ten tense days of international negotiation kept the world on edge before Kennedy persuaded the Soviets to remove the missiles.

Lyndon B. Johnson, assuming the presidency after Kennedy's assassination, faced decisions of a different sort. Following in the footsteps of his idol Franklin Roosevelt, he decided on his own version of the New Deal and had the political muscle to make it happen. He pushed through the Civil Rights Act, a century after the Civil War, at last bringing full equality including voting rights to blacks and other minorities. Then he supplemented Roosevelt's Social Security safety net with Medicare guaranteeing health care to all seniors.

Johnson was followed by Richard Nixon, who resigned the Presidency in disgrace but first made a critical decision that was to remake the world map: He visited China and recognized the Communist country, ending the isolation policy of the past. Seven presidents have followed Nixon (as of 2010), but the actions of Gerald Ford, Jimmy Carter, Ronald Reagan, George H.W. Bush and his son, George W. Bush, Bill Clinton, and Barack Obama are too recent for an unbiased assessment of their legacy. In the 1950s the Chinese Communist leader Zhou En-lai was asked about the long-term international impact of the French Revolution of 1789. "It's too soon to tell," he responded. Some similar verdict might apply to American presidential decisions of 1976–2010.

CHAPTER 1

GEORGE WASHINGTON PUTS DOWN THE WHISKEY REBELLION AND DOOMS THE FEDERALIST PARTY

1794

ONE OF THE MOST DRAMATIC—AND VIOLENT—EPISODES IN THE WHISKEY Rebellion occurred shortly after sunrise on July 16, 1794. Sixty-three-year-old John Neville had just finishing dressing when he heard a commotion outside his house. Neville was one of the richest men in western Pennsylvania. His estate, Bower Hill, covered more than 1,000 acres (4 km²) in the Chartiers Valley outside Pittsburgh. He owned eighteen slaves who worked his land.

In addition to being a man of property, he was a veteran of the American Revolution, a retired brigadier general of the Continental Army, and most recently the regional inspector for the collection of the whiskey tax. The previous day Neville had guided a federal marshal, David Lenox, to the cabins of his neighbors who were delinquent in paying the tax.

Standing in his doorway, Neville saw fifty or more armed men and boys crowded into his front yard. They were all poor farmers and backwoodsmen, the backbone of the Whiskey Rebellion, men who deeply resented the federal tax on their home-distilled whiskey and refused to pay it. Shouting, he asked what they wanted. The spokesman answered that David Lenox's life was in danger, and they had come to take him to a place of safety. Neville said he didn't believe them. Besides, Lenox was not in his house. Then he ordered the crowd to get off his land.

When they refused, he grabbed his musket and fired. The musket ball hit one of the mob's leaders, Oliver Miller, mortally wounding him. Enraged, every man raised his musket to fire on Neville, but the general slammed shut his heavy front door and bolted it. Seizing a signal horn, he gave a loud blast. A moment later the mob's flank was raked by shotgun blasts coming from the slave quarters. The skirmish raged for twenty-five minutes, with the mob firing on both the manor house and the slave cabins, yet all the casualties were on the frontiersmen's side. Finally they gave up, collected their six wounded, including Miller, and retreated back into the forest.

Certain that this was just the first scuffle, Neville sent his son Presley to Pittsburgh to summon the militia to defend Bower Hill. Whether they were afraid they would be overwhelmed at Neville's house or afraid to leave Pittsburgh undefended, the militia refused to come to Neville's rescue. But one major, James Kirkpatrick, as well as ten soldiers from Fort Pitt, volunteered to help Neville defend his home. Meanwhile, hundreds of frontiersmen had gathered in the forest, where they swore to avenge the death of Oliver Miller.

About 5 p.m. the next day, Neville, his family, and his little garrison heard the sound of drums approaching the house. Major Kirkpatrick convinced Neville to escape out the back and hide in a deep ravine behind the house. He had scarcely gotten away when an army of between 500 and 700 frontiersmen stepped out of the trees. One of them, James McFarlane, advanced carrying a flag of truce.

McFarlane ordered Neville to come out and bring the tax records with him. Kirkpatrick replied that Neville was not in the house, but he would permit McFarlane and six of his men to enter and confiscate the tax documents. This did not satisfy McFarlane, who changed his demands: Kirkpatrick and his men must come out and surrender their arms. Kirkpatrick refused. As some of the frontiersmen set fire to a barn and slave cabin, McFarlane made his final offer: Mrs. Neville and all other females in the house were free to go and no one would trouble them. Kirkpatrick accepted this offer, and all the women in the house left. When they were a safe distance from Bower Hill, the frontiersmen opened fire.

In the gun battle that followed, McFarlane was killed. Infuriated by the death of a second leader at the hands of the Nevilles, the frontiersmen set fire to the kitchen beside the manor house and the rest of the estate's outbuildings. Kirkpatrick and Presley Neville, realizing that within minutes the fire would spread to the main house, called to the crowd that they were ready to surrender.

In addition to McFarlane, two members of the frontiersmen army lay dead and several were wounded. Three or four of the soldiers from Fort Pitt had also been wounded. As for Kirkpatrick and Presley, they feared the frontiersmen would kill them, but they suffered nothing worse than being roughed up. As for the Neville family's fine house, it burned to the ground.

"THE STEEL CLAD BAND"

The attack upon and destruction of General Neville's estate outraged the federal government in Philadelphia. Urged on by his cabinet, President George Washington

A GROUP OF CITIZENS ATTACK A
FEDERAL EXCISE TAX COLLECTOR,
WHOM THEY'VE TARRED AND
FEATHERED AFTER BURNING
HIS HOME, IN THIS NINETEENTH-
CENTURY ENGRAVING. MANY
SETTLERS, ESPECIALLY IN WESTERN
PENNSYLVANIA, DEPENDED ON
THE SALE OF HOMEMADE WHISKEY
TO SURVIVE.

called out an army of 13,000 militiamen to enforce the law and crush the Whiskey Rebellion. On October 4, 1794, Washington arrived in Carlisle, Pennsylvania, to review the troops. The president was sixty-two years old, yet he had not lost his military bearing. Dressed in the blue uniform of a general of the U.S. Army, surrounded by a staff of officers, Washington surveyed approximately 13,000 men—a larger force than he had commanded at Yorktown.

One Pennsylvania militiaman who was clearly overwhelmed by the sight left an anonymous description of what he saw that day. Washington, he wrote, "The Man of the People, with a mien as intrepid as that of Hector, yet graceful as that of Paris, moved slowly onward with his attending officers." The commander in chief looked upon his army with "his eagle eye," taking in "the dazzling effulgence of the steel clad band." It was a scene, the Pennsylvanian wrote, that was both "augustly picturesque and inspiring."

Five days later, two local government officials from the western counties of Pennsylvania, where the most serious disturbances had occurred, called upon the president to assure him that peace and order had been restored in their part of the state. But Washington was not convinced; he informed the delegates that he required "unequivocal proof of [the rebels'] absolute submission" before he would disband the army.

Unable to supply such evidence, the two men went away, anxious and distressed. Once his visitors were gone, Washington confided to an aide, "I believe they are scared."

If the frontiersmen who had fomented the uprising were frightened, Washington reasoned, they would be much less likely to put up a fight, and might even surrender their ringleaders. To give this fear a chance to spread, Washington kept his army in camp until October 20. Then, after handing over command to General Henry Lee, Washington returned to the capital in Philadelphia.

Washington's reliance on the fear factor worked. No army of frontiersmen came out to fight the militia. Angry citizens lined the road to mock and harass the troops as they marched by, but no one took potshots at them. The rebels seemed to have vanished.

THE PRESIDENT'S MISGIVINGS

It was Alexander Hamilton, secretary of the treasury, who had first suggested taxing whiskey. After the American Revolution, the thirteen states struggled to pay off the debts they had incurred to keep their governments operational and to outfit and provision the troops they sent to the Continental Army. Making these debt payments was crippling the state economies, so Hamilton proposed that the federal government assume responsibility for the states' debts. But although Hamilton's plan liberated the states, it saddled the federal government with an $80 million obligation (approximately $1.820 billion in today's money).

Toward the end of 1790 Hamilton examined the finances of the federal government and concluded that the current level of income was insufficient. If the government did not find other sources of revenue, it would see a shortfall of $826,624 in 1791. But he had a solution: a ten-cents-per-gallon tax on domestically produced whiskey. Hamilton estimated such a tax would bring in an additional $975,000, thereby enabling the federal government to cover its expenses, service the national debt, and remain comfortably in the black.

The type of tax Hamilton proposed is known as an *excise tax*, sometimes called an *inland* or *interior tax*, because it is levied on goods produced domestically rather than on those imported from over seas. The government could collect the tax at the place where the product was manufactured, at the point when it was sold to a distributor, or when it was sold to the consumer. Such taxes had always been unpopular with shopkeepers and consumers in Great Britain and the United States. In 1643, for example, mobs rioted in the streets of England's cities and towns when Parliament placed an excise tax on beer and beef.

Washington was uneasy about taxing whiskey. He knew that every settler in the backwoods distilled his own whiskey, and that it was vital to the settler's personal economy. Most pioneer families grew corn, but they had no way to get their grain to market: There were few roads through the forests, and shipping grain by riverboat was prohibitively expensive. The solution was to distill the corn into whiskey, load the casks on mules and horses, and transport it to towns and cities where it could be sold for as much as one dollar a gallon. The cash the frontiersmen earned from selling the whiskey enabled them to purchase goods they could not make for themselves, such as guns and farm implements.

If the government had only taxed the whiskey they sold, the frontiersmen might have tolerated it, but Hamilton's plan called for a tax on every gallon of whiskey distilled, even the whiskey the settlers kept for their own consumption. Washington understood that in an average year most frontier families saw only a few dollars in hard money; they did not have reserves of cash to pay the ten cents on every gallon of whiskey they made. If the government demanded those dimes anyway, these independent-minded, volatile, well-armed, hard-drinking individuals might respond violently. Despite his misgivings, Washington endorsed Hamilton's plan—the government needed the money—and a few weeks later in March 1791 Congress passed an excise tax on domestically distilled whiskey.

THE NEW SONS OF LIBERTY

When Robert Johnson took the job as collector of the whiskey tax for Washington and Allegheny counties in western Pennsylvania, he was aware that the settlers in the backwoods would resent his visits, but he felt confident that the worst he would experience were foul looks and probably a few harsh words.

On September 11, 1791, as he rode through the woods toward the town of Canonsburg, about a dozen men dressed in women's dresses stepped out from behind trees and bushes and surrounded Johnson. They pulled him off his horse and dragged him into the forest, to a clearing where a cauldron of hot tar bubbled over a fire and a sack of feathers stood nearby. Johnson's panic mounted as his abductors stripped him naked and hacked off his hair. He screamed in pain as they ladled the hot tar over his body, and he struggled to get away as they dumped the feathers over him. Then the men took Johnson's horse and disappeared into the woods.

Tarring and feathering was not only cruel and humiliating, it was also an American memory strongly linked to the years leading up to the Revolution: Men who attempted to collect the stamp tax, tea tax, or any of the other taxes the British Parliament imposed upon the colonists had been ambushed in the streets or dragged from their homes and tarred and feathered. The gang that tarred and feathered Johnson was sending an unmistakable message to the federal government: The whiskey tax collectors were enemies of the common man, the vigilantes were a new incarnation of the Sons of Liberty, and the government in Philadelphia would be wise to repeal this unjust tax.

The attack on Johnson was not an isolated incident. In the western districts of Virginia, North Carolina, South Carolina, and Georgia, gangs of backwoodsmen attacked excise collectors, beating them up, flogging them, and of course tarring and feathering them.

At first glance the settlers' response to the whiskey tax may appear excessive, but in fact they viewed the tax as the last straw after decades of what they regarded as mistreatment. Time and again they had asked for the construction of roads and canals so they could get their produce to market, troops to protect their settlements from Indian attacks, and surveyors who would establish clear boundaries so they could obtain legal title to their land. The colonial governors had ignored these petitions; so had the state legislatures. When the people of the backwoods petitioned for the right to split off the western lands into new states so they could elect representatives who would respond favorably to their concerns, members of the East Coast political elites, such as John Adams, dismissed such ideas as "utopian schemes."

And the government was just as stubborn about the whiskey tax: In spite of three years of almost nonstop violence on the frontier, neither George Washington nor Congress would consider repealing it.

A TIMELY GIFT

Invariably, grassroots protest movements attract agitators, and David Bradford was a born rabble-rouser. Although a rich man, he got on well with his poor, backcountry neighbors, perhaps because he could be as irascible as they were. In the days after the destruction of Bower Hill, some settlers were saying that the situation was getting out of hand, that it was time to hold open discussions with representatives of the federal government regarding the whiskey tax and their other grievances.

But Bradford mocked the moderates as little better than cowards who fretted about personal property at a time when the government was trampling upon their liberties. Then Bradford surprised his neighbors by producing a handful of letters supporting his position, which were written by three citizens of the nearby town of Pittsburgh. They had come into his possession when he and a gang of thugs had ambushed the mail carrier. Exactly what Bradford and his men hoped to find in the mailbag is unknown—perhaps cash or other valuables. From Bradford's perspective the letters were useful: In them the correspondents condemned the frontiersmen for burning the Neville place and attacking excise men and other government officials. Brandishing these letters, Bradford characterized the inhabitants of Pittsburgh as enemies of the freedom-loving people of the backwoods. In August 1794 he called upon his neighbors to arm themselves and prepare to attack Pittsburgh.

When word of the planned assault leaked out, the people of Pittsburgh panicked. They banished the three letter writers. Then while they were still scurrying about trying to find hiding places for their silver, jewelry, and other valuables, an armed mob of about 7,000 men and women appeared outside the town. (Pittsburgh at this time had a population of about 1,400.)

A delegation of very frightened men ventured out to meet the rebels. They announced that the letter writers who had been so critical of the uprising had been driven from the town; this news was well received. The delegates said they had brought barrels of whiskey, a gift from the people of Pittsburgh; this news was well received, too. As the crowd tapped the whiskey barrels, the delegates slipped back to the safety of the town, where, like everyone else in Pittsburgh, they waited to see what would happen next.

Sending whiskey to the mob had been a masterstroke: Within a few hours everyone was drunk and had lost all interest in attacking Pittsburgh. By sundown the 7,000 drunken men and women were staggering back to their homes in the woods.

AN AFFRONT TO THE GOVERNMENT

In Philadelphia it was apparent to everyone in the federal government that the situation in the western districts was spinning out of control. Alexander Hamilton viewed the uprisings not as a protest, but as sedition and a real threat to the stability of the government. He urged Washington to call out the militia to crush the rebellion.

John Jay, chief justice of the United States, argued against a military response to the uprising—not because he was a pacifist or sympathized with the frontiersmen, but because he had no confidence in the militia. Jay was convinced the backwoodsmen could drive the militia from the field. It was humiliating enough that the government could not collect a legal tax from these people, but being defeated by them on the battlefield would make the American government an international laughingstock. Jay did not even want the government to threaten reprisals. "No strong declarations should be made," he said, "unless there be ability and disposition to follow them with strong measures."

As for Washington, he told his cabinet plainly that he believed the new Democratic Clubs that were springing up around the country were to blame for the unrest: Led by unprincipled men, the clubs filled the heads of the uneducated with the radical principles and violent methods of the French Revolution.

Ultimately, Washington sided with Hamilton and called out the militias of Virginia, Maryland, New Jersey, and Pennsylvania. Hamilton urged Washington to target the rebels in western Pennsylvania. He chose Pennsylvania because, given its proximity to the capital in Philadelphia, the unrest there was a particular affront to the government. Washington agreed.

"A PERFECT SENSE OF THEIR MISCONDUCT"

No army of angry backwoodsmen ever appeared to face the militiamen, nor could the militia find David Bradford or any other leader of the uprising—they had fled, along with about 2,000 of their followers, deep into the mountains. In their frustration, the militia's officers sent detachments into the countryside to round up suspected rebels. They seized about 200 men, but because the evidence against them ranged from slight to nonexistent, in December when the militia was called home, the officers released all but twenty of their prisoners—these they took to Philadelphia to stand trial.

On Christmas Day the army marched into Philadelphia, where it was greeted by cheering throngs. Standing amid the crowd was Presley Neville; watching the handful of bedraggled prisoners limp by, he said that he "could not help feeling sorry for them."

Soon afterward Washington boasted to Chief Justice Jay that thanks to the army, the rebels had been brought "to a perfect sense of their misconduct without spilling a drop of blood." It was true that there had been no battle between the militia and the army, but whether the rebels repented their rebellion was open to debate.

As for the twenty suspected rebels, all were acquitted but two—John Mitchell, a poor farmer who did not own a still, and Philip Wigle (or Vigol) who was even poorer than Mitchell. Although there was no damning evidence against the two men, William Paterson, justice of the Pennsylvania Supreme Court, instructed the jury to find Mitchell and Wigle guilty of treason; after three years of violence along the western frontier, and the expense and trouble of sending an army of 13,000 men to quell the rebellion, someone must be found guilty of treason. The jury did as Paterson instructed, but Washington pardoned Mitchell and Wigle and released them—by then the two men had already spent more than a year in Philadelphia's city jail.

As for the whiskey tax, it remained on the books for eight more years, and it remained nearly impossible to collect. During the presidential election of 1800, Thomas Jefferson pledged to repeal it, and in 1802 the hated tax was finally abolished. But the memory of the whiskey tax and the rebellion it sparked lingered on: In the 1830s, when the French political observer, Alexis de Tocqueville, toured the United States, time and again he heard ordinary American citizens say that the quickest way to start a revolution in America was for the government to tax whiskey.

George Washington, John Adams, Alexander Hamilton, and their fellow Federalists regarded the suppression of the Whiskey Rebellion as the triumph of law and order. Men like Thomas Jefferson, James Madison, and Herman Husband saw it as an attempt by the Federalists to stifle popular participation in the national government. Writing to James Madison, Jefferson characterized the army of 13,000 as an outrage, "an armament against people at their ploughs."

Jefferson even went so far as to claim that Washington had become "dazzled by the glittering crowns and coronets" and longed to wear one himself. The charge was not true, but it does reveal the extent to which Washington and Jefferson's views of the nature of government were at odds. Jefferson and his supporters believed Washington was trying "to suppress the friends of general freedom." Washington and the Federalists believed they were trying to keep the peace.

The Federalist model of government concentrated the lion's share of political power in the hands of the federal government at the expense of the state and local governments. The philosophy may have been antithetical to the ideals of the American Revolution, but the fact that it was espoused by George Washington, the greatest hero of the Revolution, made it palatable to most Americans. It was Washington's response to the Whiskey Rebellion that turned many small farmers and artisans against the Federalists.

Thomas Jefferson and the members of his political party, the Democratic-Republicans, cast the Federalists as power-hungry absolutists and presented themselves to American voters as "the friends of liberty" who safeguarded the principles of 1776. And the voters believed it. In 1800 Jefferson was elected president; the Democratic-Republicans would maintain control of the White House for the next twenty-five years. As for the Federalists, by 1820 they had died out, their support of the whiskey tax being a major factor in the extinction of their political party.

The Democratic-Republicans' zeal for states' rights, and eventually even regional rights, at the expense of the power of the national government became the dominant political philosophy for much of the nineteenth century. The Civil War not only settled the question of slavery in the United States, but it also resolved the question whether power rested with the states or the federal government. After the Union victory in 1865, the federal government assumed primacy and the states saw their independence of action diminish (although the issue of states' rights was fought over again during the civil rights era of the 1950s and 1960s).

George Washington never could have foreseen that by raising an army against backwoods insurgents he would destroy his political party and constrict the power of the national government for decades. Yet that is how his decision played out, in what has become a classic case of unintended consequences.

CHAPTER 2

THOMAS JEFFERSON BUYS THE LOUISIANA TERRITORY AND DOUBLES THE SIZE OF THE UNITED STATES

1803

TECHNICALLY, PRESIDENT THOMAS JEFFERSON HAD NO RIGHT TO ENTER INTO a treaty with France to purchase the Louisiana Territory. He admitted as much in a letter he wrote in August 1803 to Senator John C. Breckinridge of Kentucky. "The treaty must of course be laid before both Houses [of Congress], because both have important functions to exercise respecting it." Furthermore, the U.S. Constitution had no provision for, as he put it, "incorporating foreign nations [i.e., the Louisiana Territory] into our Union." Yet he expected that the American public would forgive him for reaching beyond his authority, and he believed Congress would ratify the treaty with France and agree to purchase Louisiana. He rationalized it to Breckinridge this way: "It is the case of a guardian, investing the money of his ward in purchasing an important adjacent territory; and saying to him when of age, 'I did this for your good.'"

FRANCE ON THE BACK DOORSTEP

In spring 1801 Jefferson received troubling news—Napoleon had entered into a secret agreement with the Spanish king, Charles IV, to return the Louisiana Territory in North America to France. France had lost almost all of its possessions in North America at the end of the French and Indian War: According to the provisions of the treaties of 1762 and 1763, the British received Canada, and France was forced to cede the Louisiana Territory to Spain. (As a token, France was permitted to keep the islets of St. Pierre and Miquelon south of Newfoundland.)

After the United States won its independence from Great Britain in 1783 it had some trouble with British garrisons, which dragged their feet about quitting their forts in the Great Lakes region, but by and large the Americans got on well with the Spanish government based in New Orleans. In 1795 the two nations signed a treaty that permitted American goods to be shipped down the Mississippi to be deposited temporarily in New Orleans until they were sold and loaded onto ships bound for foreign or domestic ports.

For Jefferson, the idea that Napoleon would take possession of the Louisiana Territory was deeply disturbing. Jefferson had been an enthusiastic supporter of the French Revolution, even after it spun violently out of control. From his perspective, France's abolition of the monarchy, aristocracy, and privileges of the Catholic Church and its establishment of a republic outweighed all the atrocities and judicial murders of the Reign of Terror. But Napoleon was something different. Although he claimed to be exporting the principles of the French Revolution—liberty, equality, brotherhood—to all of Europe, Jefferson recognized Napoleon for what he was, an imperialist who was transforming the continent of Europe into his personal empire. Jefferson's assessment was correct—in 1804 Napoleon proclaimed himself emperor.

If France should appear suddenly on the United States' back doorstep, Jefferson would be faced with a practical and political dilemma. The French were under no obligation to respect the trade treaty the United States had made with Spain. If Napoleon denied Americans access to the port of New Orleans, overnight three-eighths of the produce and other trade goods of the United States' western territories would have no outlet. It would be a severe economic blow to the country as a whole, and an economic disaster for the settlers west of the Appalachians, who had no other way to get their goods to market.

To neutralize the French threat, the United States would be obliged to ally itself with Great Britain, which had the greatest navy in the world and had already gone to war against Napoleon. An Anglo-American alliance, however, would be an extremely bitter pill for Thomas Jefferson to swallow. Even before he wrote the Declaration of Independence in 1776, Jefferson had denounced the British monarchy as tyrannical. To be compelled to put aside America's political convictions and "marry ourselves to the British fleet and nation" would have been hard on Jefferson's conscience and almost certainly would have alienated a significant segment of the American public, which, twenty years after the American Revolution, was still anti-British.

After Spain transferred the Louisiana Territory to France, but the French did not take possession of New Orleans immediately, and during the interim the Spanish made a few concessions to their former treaty partners: Americans could offload their goods directly onto the trade ships in the port; if it was absolutely necessary to deposit their goods in New Orleans warehouses for a brief period of time, the Americans would be permitted to do so in exchange for paying port fees. Meanwhile, Jefferson prepared to send his friend and protégé, James Monroe, to Paris as minister plenipotentiary. Monroe was to offer Napoleon $2 million for New Orleans; if necessary, he was authorized to raise the price to $10 million. Jefferson's objective at this point did not extend beyond purchasing New Orleans.

"THE NOBLEST WORK OF OUR WHOLE LIVES"

James Monroe arrived in Paris on April 12, 1803. He was forty-five years old, a Virginia planter like his friend and mentor, Thomas Jefferson. He had fought for American independence, crossed the Delaware with George Washington, and been wounded during the Battle of Trenton. (In Emanuel Leutze's iconic painting, *Washington Crossing the Delaware*, Monroe is the young officer clutching the American flag.) He was fluent in French, and had contacts in the French government—Monroe had been America's minister to France (as ambassadors were termed at the time) from 1794 to 1796. He felt confident that he could persuade the French to part with New Orleans. When Monroe met with Robert Livingston, America's minister in France, however, he learned that the French had a different deal in mind.

Napoleon's minister of finance, François de Barbé-Marbois, had convinced Napoleon that Louisiana was virtually worthless. It was so vast that no French army could secure it, and in the absence of a large French force in the country, it would almost certainly be seized by the British coming down out of Canada. Only recently Napoleon's campaign to reconquer the island of St. Domingue, comprising modern-day Haiti and the Dominican Republic, had failed, costing the lives of 40,000 French soldiers. This calamity reinforced Barbé-Marbois's point—that establishing France in the New World required great sacrifice with no guarantee of success. Why not sell the territory to the Americans?

Napoleon agreed. The day before Monroe arrived in Paris, French foreign minister Charles Maurice de Talleyrand informed Livingston that France was willing to sell not only New Orleans to the United States but also the entire Louisiana Territory.

Initially Monroe and Livingston were stunned by Talleyrand's offer, but they recovered quickly and leapt at this unexpected opportunity. Within a matter of days, representatives of the French and American governments had hammered out a deal: France would sell the entire Louisiana Territory, including New Orleans, to the United States for $15 million. The United States had just acquired approximately 827,000 square miles (2,141,920.2 km²) of territory, effectively doubling the size of the country at the bargain price of fewer than five cents per acre (4,046.9 m²).

There was one small difficulty—neither Livingston nor Monroe had been authorized to make such an agreement on behalf of the United States. Yet neither man hesitated. They understood immediately what such a land purchase would mean to their people. As Livingston said upon signing the treaty, "We have lived long, but this is the noblest work of our whole lives . . . The United States take rank this day among the first powers of the world."

When he received word of what Monroe and Livingston had done, Jefferson was euphoric. With a stroke of a pen, the territory that might have been a great threat had suddenly become America's greatest blessing. Now the trick would be getting Congress to overlook the unorthodox manner in which the Louisiana Territory had been acquired and convince it to ratify the treaty.

THIS PAINTING DEPICTS THE SIGNING OF THE LOUISIANA PURCHASE BY MARQUIS FRANCOIS DE BARBE-MARBOIS, NAPOLEON'S MINISTER OF FINANCE, ROBERT LIVINGSTON, AMERICA'S MINISTER IN FRANCE, AND JAMES MONROE, ACTING ON PRESIDENT JEFFERSON'S BEHALF, IN PARIS ON APRIL 30, 1803. DE BARBE-MARBOIS HAD CONVINCED NAPOLEON THE TERRITORY WAS WORTHLESS AND TOO LARGE TO BE SECURED BY THE FRENCH ARMY.
The Granger Collection, New York

DOWN TO THE WIRE

Ever since George Washington led 13,000 troops into western Pennsylvania to put down the Whiskey Rebellion, the Federalist Party's political influence had been dwindling. In the election of 1802 the Federalist Party had won only twenty-nine seats in the House of Representatives (the Democratic-Republicans held one hundred and three) and nine seats in the Senate (the Democratic-Republicans held twenty-five). But the unauthorized—or as they read it, unconstitutional—treaty Monroe and Livingston had made to purchase the Louisiana Territory gave them a new stick with which to beat Jefferson and his fellow Democratic-Republicans. This outrageous defiance of the Constitution might be the scandal that would loosen the Democratic-Republicans' grip on political power and sweep the Federalists back into office.

The Federalists were correct in one respect: There was nothing in the Constitution that empowered Congress or the president to acquire a portion of another nation's empire.

Even Jefferson suspected that before the treaty could be ratified, the Constitution must be amended (although he feared it would be impossible for such an amendment to be ratified by the states before the October 30 deadline stipulated in the Louisiana Purchase treaty).

Sensing that they had the upper hand, the Federalists tried to rally various constituencies to their cause. They warned the antislavery people that Southern slave owners would undoubtedly extend the notorious institution into the new territory. They frightened the wealthy merchant families of New England by claiming that their economic influence would be eclipsed by the throngs of settlers who would pour into the western lands and use the Mississippi River as their main outlet, rather than seaports such as Boston and Portsmouth, New Hampshire. And they reminded Americans who were anti-Napoleon that they were about to contribute $15 million to Bonaparte's war chest.

Another Federalist newspaper editor derided the Louisiana Territory as "a great waste, a wilderness unpeopled with any beings except wolves and wandering Indians.

We are to give money of which we have too little," he concluded, "for land of which we already have too much."

But the Federalists' arguments did not resonate with most American voters. By now settlers had moved as far west as the eastern bank of the Mississippi River, and some were chafing to cross into the Louisiana Territory. Some had already made the journey, most notably that great American trailblazer, Daniel Boone, who in 1799 received permission from the Spanish government to acquire land in what is now St. Charles County, Missouri.

As for Jefferson, for nearly twenty years he had been advancing his dream of what he called "an Empire of Liberty," which extended from the Atlantic to the Pacific Ocean. For the many thousands of Americans who were always eager to move to new land in unsettled territory, Jefferson's vision was irresistible.

Ultimately, the Democratic-Republican-controlled Congress opted to waive a constitutional amendment and move straight to a vote. The treaty came at last to the floor of the U.S. Senate on October 20, ten days shy of the deadline. By a vote of 24 to 7, the Senate ratified Monroe and Livingston's treaty with France and authorized the purchase of the Louisiana Territory.

LEWIS AND CLARK

On October 15, 1803, twenty-nine-year-old Meriwether Lewis climbed up the steps of General George Rogers Clark's home in Clarksville, Indiana, to meet his partner, the general's thirty-three-year-old brother, William Clark. Historian Stephen Ambrose described the scene:

"Each man was about six feet (1.8 m) tall and broad-shouldered. Each was rugged in the face, Clark somewhat more so than Lewis, who had a certain delicacy to his profile. Their bodies were rawboned and muscled, with no fat. Their hands—sunburned, like their faces, even this late in the season—were big, rough, strong, capable, confident . . . And who can doubt that, as they stuck out their hands to each other, both men had smiles on their faces that were as broad as the Ohio River, as big as their ambitions and dreams."

Now that the Louisiana Territory belonged to the United States, Thomas Jefferson was eager to learn what marvels it might contain. In January 1803 he convinced Congress to appropriate $2,500 to fund a small military expedition to explore the vast new land. It would be captained by two men, both Virginians, both Revolutionary War veterans, both experienced frontiersmen—Meriwether Lewis and William Clark.

Meriwether Lewis was still a boy when he first met Thomas Jefferson (their plantations were only ten miles (16.1 km) apart). Years later, when Jefferson was elected president, he invited Lewis to serve as his secretary. The two men had much in common: They were both Virginia aristocrats, they were both college graduates (Jefferson from the College of William and Mary, Lewis from what is now Washington and Lee University), they were both lifelong students of plant life, wildlife, and topography. But while Jefferson made only occasional forays into the deep woods, Lewis spent long periods in the wilderness and was perfectly at ease there.

William Clark came from a family of ten children, and all five of his older brothers had fought for America's independence from Great Britain. Unlike Lewis, Clark's education had been spotty—he never learned how to spell or write a grammatical sentence (at one point in his journal he describes setting sail "under a jentle brease"). But he had other skills: At age nineteen he had joined the Kentucky militia, where he learned how to build forts, draw maps, and even spy on the enemy. He had a knack for learning the languages of the Indian tribes and a natural talent for befriending strangers. Because part of the expedition's mission was to establish good diplomatic relations with the tribes in the West, Clark was a natural choice to share the leadership of what came to be called the Corps of Discovery.

THE CORPS OF DISCOVERY

Lewis and Clark recruited twenty-five men to join them, three with the rank of sergeants, as well as others who were not members of the military, according to historian Stephen Ambrose. Among the nonmilitary members of the Corps of Discovery was William Clark's slave, York, about thirty-three years old. York and Clark had grown up together. When Clark's father died, he bequeathed York to his son as his personal servant. As the Corps traveled westward they would recruit other members, most famously Toussaint Charbonneau, a French-Canadian fur trader, and his seventeen-year-old Shoshone wife, Sacagawea. This couple joined the Corps as guides and interpreters through what is now North Dakota all the way to the Pacific. Three months after joining Lewis and Clark's expedition, Sacagawea gave birth to a son; she and Toussaint named the child Jean Baptiste, but Clark, for reasons known only to him, nicknamed him "Pompy," sometimes abbreviated to "Pomp."

The Corps brought along an enormous amount of equipment: mathematical instruments such as sextants, surveyor's compasses, and a chronometer to calculate

longitude; gifts for the Indians, including silk ribbons, vermilion face paint, 33 pounds (14 kg) of colored beads, and 4,600 sewing needles; and of course weapons, including fifteen muzzle-loading .54 caliber rifles, 420 pounds (190.5 kg) of lead to make bullets, and 176 pounds (78.9 kg) of gunpowder packed in fifty-two waterproof lead cans.

They set out from St. Charles, Missouri, the last outpost of civilization on the Missouri River, on May 14, 1804, traveling in two small boats known as *pirogues* and a keelboat that measured fifty-five feet (16.8 m) long and eight feet (2.4 m) wide. On a good day, a stiff wind propelled the keelboat upriver; otherwise, the men rowed, or poled her, or if there was no other alternative, scrambled ashore and dragged the keelboat along with ropes. They rarely covered more than fourteen miles (22.5 km) in one day, and often, because of conditions on the river, much less.

LEWIS AND CLARK MEET A GROUP OF NATIVE AMERICANS ON THE COLUMBIA RIVER IN THIS 1905 WATERCOLOR BY CHARLES M. RUSSELL. THE PAINTING IS BASED ON A TRUE ENCOUNTER. CLARK IS STANDING IN THE CANOE, HOLDING HIS RIFLE, WHILE THE GROUP'S GUIDE, SACAGAWEA, ATTEMPTS TO SPEAK TO THE TRIBE USING SIGN LANGUAGE.

Amon Carter Museum, Fort Worth, Texas

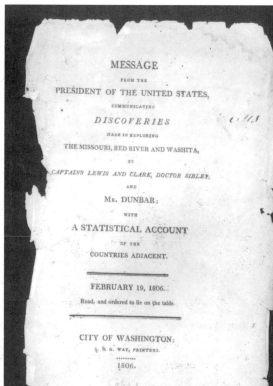

MESSAGE

FROM THE

PRESIDENT OF THE UNITED STATES,

COMMUNICATING

DISCOVERIES

MADE IN EXPLORING

THE MISSOURI, RED RIVER AND WASHITA,

BY

CAPTAINS LEWIS AND CLARK, DOCTOR SIBLEY,

AND

MR. DUNBAR;

WITH

A STATISTICAL ACCOUNT

OF THE

COUNTRIES ADJACENT.

FEBRUARY 19, 1806.

Read, and ordered to lie on the table.

CITY OF WASHINGTON;

A. & G. WAY, PRINTERS.

1806.

THE ORIGINAL FEBRUARY 19, 1806, MESSAGE FROM PRESIDENT THOMAS JEFFERSON TO CONGRESS COMMUNICATED THE DISCOVERIES MADE BY LEWIS AND CLARK DURING THEIR EXPEDITION OF THE WEST. LEWIS AND CLARK WROTE EXTENSIVELY OF THE NATIVE AMERICAN TRIBES THEY ENCOUNTERED AND SENT SAMPLES OF MINERALS AND PLANTS THEY DISCOVERED, AS WELL AS MAPS OF THE NEW TERRITORY, TO THE PRESIDENT.

Library of Congress

During the first four months the Corps had killed, collected, or described 178 plants and 122 animals that were unknown to botanists and zoologists, including the grizzly bear, the pronghorn antelope, and the prairie dog. Periodically, Jefferson received packages from Lewis or Clark containing plant and mineral specimens, buffalo robes, or other artifacts. Meanwhile, Lewis and Clark were carefully charting their course and the land through which they traveled—these were the first accurate maps of the region.

On November 7, 1805, the Corps reached what they took to be the Pacific. Clark wrote in his journal, "Ocian in view! O! the joy." In fact, they were about twenty miles (32.1 km) short of their goal—they were looking on Gray's Bay in what is now Washington State. After wintering nearby, on March 23, 1806, the Lewis and Clark expedition began the long journey home, arriving in St. Louis on September 23; they had been away two and a half years.

Their return was celebrated across the country, but nowhere with more enthusiasm than in Washington, D.C., where they were feted almost nightly. Congress, in an exuberant mood, voted double salaries for every man in the Corps of Discovery, then granted the two captains 1,600 acres (6.5 km²) of land apiece and 320 acres (1.3 km²) to each of their men. Furthermore, Lewis was named governor of the Louisiana Territory and Clark was made superintendent of Indian Affairs in the West.

The Lewis and Clark expedition dispelled the myths that the far West was the last habitat of wooly mammoths, unicorns, and seven-foot (2.1 m)-tall beavers, and that there were tribes of Welsh-speaking Indians, descendants of a Welsh prince who had sailed to America in the twelfth century. One of Thomas Jefferson's books on American geography claimed that California was an island. Another declared that out West there were entire mountain ranges of erupting volcanoes, and that the Blue Ridge Mountains in Virginia, at 6,500 feet (2 km), were the highest in North America. Lewis and Clark found no volcanoes, but they did find mountain peaks in the Rockies that were more than twice as high as the Blue Ridge. And they assured the president that California was not an island.

Jefferson was frustrated to learn from the captains that there was no Northwest Passage, no quick water route across North America to the Pacific Ocean that would give American manufacturers and merchants more direct access to the markets of Asia. The hostility of the Sioux worried him—they would get in the way of the settlement of the new lands. And Lewis's report that the Great Plains did not have enough water to become an agricultural paradise also disappointed the president.

THE LEGACY OF THE LOUISIANA PURCHASE

Only eighteen years after it had come into existence, the United States had doubled in size—without going to war or shedding one drop of American blood. The Louisiana Purchase set the precedent that would enable the U.S. government to purchase other western lands and thereby achieve Thomas Jefferson's dream of an America that stretched from the Atlantic to the Pacific.

The land acquired in the treaty comprised what are now the states of Arkansas, Missouri, Iowa, Oklahoma, Kansas, Nebraska, most of North Dakota and South Dakota, Minnesota, Montana, Wyoming, Colorado, New Mexico, and of course, Louisiana. Included in the purchase were the great port city of New Orleans and the up-and-coming city of St. Louis. Furthermore, the Mississippi was now an American waterway.

In the decades following the purchase, the Louisiana Territory proved to be an immensely rich prize. In these new lands settlers would discover vast forests for lumber, pastures for grazing livestock, endless prairies for farms, and copper, lead, coal, gold, and silver. Many of the Indian tribes of the region resisted the encroachments of newcomers, but nothing could stop the settlement of the West.

In many respects, for the Indian nations of the American West, the coming of the settlers was a disaster. By 1837 recurring epidemics of whooping cough and smallpox had reduced the Mandans to only 125 people. The Shoshone, Sacagawea's people, fought a series of wars throughout the 1860s in a futile effort to keep white settlers off their lands. They suffered a terrible defeat in 1863 when the U.S. Cavalry attacked their camp at Bear River, massacring approximately 400 men, women, and children. The Arikaras, the Nez Perce, and the Hidatsas suffered a similar fate. Within thirty years, due to disease and warfare, many of the fifty tribes Lewis and Clark had encountered on their journey west were teetering on the verge of extinction.

CHAPTER 3

JAMES MONROE CREATES THE "MONROE DOCTRINE," KEYSTONE OF U.S. INTERNATIONAL POLICY

1823

AFTER SPAIN SUFFERED DEFEAT IN ITS 1793–1795 WAR AGAINST THE revolutionary French republic, the Spanish king abdicated in favor of Napoleon Bonaparte's brother, Joseph, who was widely scorned by the Spanish people as the puppet that he certainly was. In 1808, a popular Spanish uprising led to the Peninsular War, which not only contributed to the final defeat of Napoleon but, leaving Spain economically devastated and politically unstable, also loosened its grip on its longtime Latin American colonies. Beginning in 1815, the very year of Napoleon's final downfall, José de San Martín led Argentina, Chile, and Peru to independence from moribund Spanish rule, and Simón Bolívar became instrumental in creating the Republic of Colombia out of several former Spanish colonies.

Many people and politicians in the United States were as mesmerized by these developments as they had been by the Napoleonic wars so recently concluded in far-off Europe. The uprisings in Latin America embodied the very political values that had given birth to the United States less than half a century earlier. Little wonder that the fledgling Latin American republics looked to the United States for endorsement of their struggles, and little wonder that many citizens of the United States were eager to give them just what they wanted.

Yet James Monroe, newly inaugurated in March 1817, and his secretary of state, John Quincy Adams, were not so sure that the United States could afford to give the infant republics much of anything. Monroe's predecessor, two-term President James Madison, had allowed a hawkish Congress to goad him into leading the nation into the War of 1812, ostensibly provoked by British violations of American sovereignty but really driven by an insatiable American hunger to push the nation into Florida and the West. Instead of expanding the country and enriching it, the war resulted in the burning of most of the public buildings in Washington, D.C.; killed in combat 2,260 American soldiers (some eight times this number died from disease and privation); nearly cost the country great swaths of its western territory; and broke the fragile American economy, dragging the still-new nation into a ruinous depression that would last long after the war ended in 1815.

Yet because an outnumbered American army under Andrew Jackson had spectacularly defeated a much larger British force at the Battle of New Orleans— fought during December 1814 to January 1815, *after* the Treaty of Ghent had ended the war but before word reached the United States—to most Americans the war felt like a glorious triumph.

Not only was Madison's fellow Democratic-Republican Monroe elected in 1816, but he was also elected by a landslide, claiming 183 electoral votes to the 34 for his Federalist opponent, Rufus King. The fact was that the Federalist Party, the party of Washington and John Adams, was all but dead by 1816, having been mortally wounded by Thomas Jefferson, principal architect of the Democratic-Republican Party, whose presidency propelled both Madison and now Monroe into office. With so solid a mandate, Monroe could afford in 1817 to be magnanimous and pay a goodwill visit to Boston, last bastion of Federalism, as a gesture of conciliation. Writing in the *Columbian Centinel*, a local newspaper, journalist Benjamin Russell remarked (with tongue firmly in cheek) that the visit had initiated in American political life an "era of good feelings." For some reason the phrase caught on as both a contemporary and a historical label for the two terms of James Monroe.

Yet anyone with political, social, or economic savvy could tell that any "good feelings" were more apparent than real. The nation was wallowing in economic hard times, and despite the Democratic-Republican Party's victory, the party was in the throes of an internal split. The so-called "old party" members adhered to a strict Jeffersonian interpretation of the Constitution, which held that the only legitimate governing powers were those actually *enumerated* in the Constitution, not those *implied* by it. They clashed with the reformers—called the National Republicans—who sought to exploit a host of "implied powers" to multiply the authority of the federal government.

It was more than an ideological difference of opinion. Speaker of the House Henry Clay, one of the new Nationalist breed, led a congressional initiative to use federal funds to finance what he called "national" projects. These included major highways and canals to open up commerce between the East and—Clay's constituency—the developing West. Monroe, an "old party" man, countered that the federal funding of such "internal improvements"

29.

It was stated at the commencement of the last Session, that a great effort was then making in Spain and Portugal, to improve the condition of the people, of those countries; and that it appeared to be conducted with extraordinary moderation. It need scarcely be remarked, that the result has been, so far, very different from what was then anticipated. Of events in that quarter of the Globe, with which we have so much intercourse, and from which we derive our origin, we have always been anxious and interested spectators. The Citizens of the United States cherish sentiments the most friendly, in favor of the liberty and happiness of their fellow men on that side of the Atlantic. In the wars of the European powers, in matters relating to themselves, we have never taken any part, nor does it comport with our policy, so to do. It is only when our rights are invaded, or seriously menaced, that we resent injuries, or make preparation for our defense. With the movements in this Hemisphere we are of necessity more immediately connected, and by causes which must be obvious to all enlightened and impartial observers. The political system of the allied powers is essentially different in this respect from that of America. This difference pro-
                                                          -ceeds

THE MONROE DOCTRINE WAS, IN FACT, NOT A STAND-ALONE POLICY, BUT A SET OF REMARKS DEEPLY EMBEDDED IN THE PRESIDENT'S ANNUAL MESSAGE TO CONGRESS, SHOWN HERE, WHICH HE DELIVERED ON DECEMBER 2, 1823. IN SHORT, MONROE VOWED NOT TO INTERFERE IN EUROPEAN AFFAIRS, BUT WARNED THAT ANY EUROPEAN ATTEMPT TO MEDDLE WITH THE AMERICAN REPUBLICS WOULD BE REGARDED AS A DIRECT THREAT TO THE UNITED STATES.

National Archives

was not enumerated in the Constitution and would therefore require not merely a law, but a constitutional amendment. Clay replied with outright defiance of the president—de facto leader of the party—by pushing the Democratic-Republican congressional caucus to pass a bill to improve the old Cumberland Road, the nation's principal east-west artery. Monroe responded to it with a veto, which seemed to underscore an *absence* of good feelings in the national leadership.

With the nation economically weak and politically divided, Monroe and John Quincy Adams worried that taking a stand in support of the new Latin American democracies, no matter how philosophically appealing a gesture, risked provoking some European powers to a reprise of the War of 1812, which the United States literally could not afford to fight. What is more, who even knew whether the new republics would survive?

IN THE WAKE OF A BRITISH MAN-OF-WAR

And thus in this tentative and uncomfortable posture did the nation and its foreign policy stand from Monroe's inauguration in 1817 until 1822. During this period, the president refused to respond to the situation in Latin America as Secretary of State Adams went about the delicate process of negotiating a treaty with Spain to settle a border dispute by purchasing Florida from the Spanish crown. The Adams-Onís Treaty was concluded in 1819, but it was not ratified by the United States until 1821. Only after Florida had been safely acquired did the Monroe government finally announce its diplomatic recognition of the Latin American republics. The United States acknowledged Argentina, Chile, Colombia, and Mexico in 1822, adding Peru four years later.

The very next year, however, France offered to support Spain in the restoration of a Bourbon king to imperial power. This immediately led to speculation that France and Spain would unite in conducting war against the Latin American republics to reestablish them as Spanish colonies for a new emperor to rule. Moreover, the two nations would almost certainly enjoy the support of the so-called "Holy Alliance," a pro-monarchy, anti-republican league consisting of Russia, Prussia, and Austria. Suddenly, it was no longer a question of Spain and her former colonies being left to fight it out among themselves. The four major powers of continental Europe—known collectively as the *Allies*—appeared to be inviting one another to preside over and participate in the recolonization of the entire American hemisphere.

DURING MONROE'S PRESIDENCY, THE DEMOCRATIC-REPUBLICAN PARTY WAS TORN BY AN INTERNAL SPLIT. SPEAKER OF THE HOUSE HENRY CLAY, PICTURED IN THIS 1843 PAINTING, WAS CONSIDERED A PARTY REFORMER, WHILE MONROE, AN "OLD PARTY" MEMBER, WAS HIS IDEOLOGICAL OPPOSITE.

Getty Images

The monarchies of Europe, it seemed, had tossed the gauntlet at the feet of the United States. Yet this call to action did not immediately move the American president or his secretary of state. It was rather the government of another monarchy, Great Britain, the enemy of 1812 no less, that first took alarm. There were two reasons: First, much English blood had been spilled in the North American wars of the seventeenth and eighteenth centuries, culminating in the French and Indian War of 1754–1763, to evict France from the Americas. All of a sudden, there was a real threat of France returning to the region as a power to be reckoned with. Second, although the United Kingdom was certainly a monarchy and therefore philosophically opposed to republican government, it was first and foremost an empire built on trade, and there was far more money to be made in trading with the separate republics of the Americas than if they were lumped together as colonies of a Spanish (or French, Prussian, Austrian, or Russian) empire.

Would the British crown bow to political philosophy, or would it yield to trade? The question was answered quickly and without ambiguity. When the governments of Russia and France invited the United Kingdom to join an alliance to restore Spain's New World empire, Britain declined, and instead of joining arms with the other monarchies, its foreign minister, George Canning, reached out to the United States. He proposed an Anglo-American alliance to wave off and, if necessary, actively resist any Franco-Spanish attempt to curtail the independence movement in the Americas.

Both of Monroe's most recent White House predecessors, Thomas Jefferson and James Madison, urged the president to embrace the offer, even though both Jefferson and Madison were by temperament and inclination Francophiles and Anglophobes. John Quincy Adams was not nearly so enthusiastic about the prospect. First, he noted that both Britain and the United States laid claim to a large portion of the Oregon country, which encompassed the present-day states of Oregon, Washington, and Idaho, as well as parts of Wyoming and Montana, and extended north into British Columbia, Canada. Adams worried that an alliance with the United Kingdom would both weaken and complicate U.S. claims in the region and might even encourage both Mexico and Russia to assert their own claims there.

More important, however, was Adams's fear that the United States would deliberately cast itself in the shadow of Great Britain, in effect relinquishing a portion of the sovereignty for which it had fought both a revolution and the War of 1812. As the secretary of state put it in a cabinet meeting of November 7, 1823: "It would be more candid, as well as more dignified, to avow our principles explicitly to Russia and France,

than to come in as a cockboat in the wake of the British man-of-war." It was John Quincy Adams, therefore, not James Monroe, who initiated the independent policy that would result in the doctrine history has named after the fifth president of the United States.

A MESSAGE TO CONGRESS

George Washington, John Adams, Thomas Jefferson—they were all the proverbial men bigger than life, in their bearing, speech, thought, and deed entirely fit to do and declare great things. James Monroe and Adams's son John Quincy were, in contrast, hardly suited to high political drama.

Although he had fought and fought well in the Continental Army during the American Revolution, Monroe was, in the words of a Virginia lady who once met him, "quiet and dignified," his "dress plain and in the old style." Tall and slender, with a handsome face, he was nevertheless a self-conscious figure, his manner halting and deliberate. The best that could be said of him was said by his mentor Jefferson: He was a man "so honest that if you turned his soul inside out there would not be a spot on it."

PRESIDENT JAMES MONROE, AT GLOBE, IS SHOWN WITH HIS CABINET IN THIS PAINTING ENTITLED "THE BIRTH OF THE *MONROE DOCTRINE*," PAINTED BY CLYDE O. DELAND CIRCA 1823. THE POLICY THAT RESULTED IN DOCTRINE NAMED AFTER THE FIFTH PRESIDENT OF THE UNITED STATES WAS ACTUALLY THE BRAINCHILD OF MONROE'S SECRETARY OF STATE, JOHN QUINCY ADAMS, SHOWN HERE AT LEFT.

Getty Images

KEEP OFF!
The Monroe doctrine *must* be respected.

UNCLE SAM IS PICTURED AS AN
ARMED SOLDIER STANDING BETWEEN
EUROPEAN POWERS AND NICARAGUA
AND VENEZUELA IN THIS LITHOGRAPH,
WHICH APPEARED IN THE FEBRUARY
15, 1896, ISSUE OF THE WEEKLY
MAGAZINE *JUDGE*. IN THE LATE 1800S,
THE U.S. GOVERNMENT EXTENDED
THE MONROE DOCTRINE AS A WAY OF
BRINGING LATIN AMERICAN NATIONS
VOLUNTARILY INTO LINE BEHIND
U.S. POLITICAL AND ECONOMIC
LEADERSHIP AND THROWING OPEN
CENTRAL AND SOUTH AMERICAN
MARKETS TO BIG U.S. TRADERS.
Library of Congress

As for John Quincy Adams, although he was if anything even more brilliant than his father—under whose tutelage he had also become a man thoroughly prepared for public service—he was so remote in manner that critics described him as a "chip off the old iceberg." Even the man himself admitted to being possessed of such austerity and reserve that he could not understand how anyone might have affection for him—though his marriage, to Louisa Catherine Johnson Adams, whom he met while serving as a foreign diplomat in George Washington's administration, was long and happy and produced four children.

It is not surprising, then, that neither of these men created in the so-called "Monroe Doctrine" an eloquent, profound, or even remotely stirring document. The pronouncement was, in fact, not a stand-alone "doctrine," but a set of remarks deeply embedded in the president's Annual Message to Congress, which he delivered on December 2, 1823.

"In the wars of the European powers in matters relating to themselves we have never taken any part," Monroe observed. "It is only when our rights are invaded or seriously menaced that we resent injuries or make preparation for our defense. With the movements in this hemisphere we are of necessity more immediately connected. . . ." He explained that the "political system" of Spain and the other imperial monarchies "is essentially different . . . from that of America. . . . We owe it, therefore, to candor and to the amicable relations existing between the United States and [the European] powers to declare that we should consider any attempt on their part to extend their system to any portion of this hemisphere as dangerous to our peace and safety." Monroe had no intention of interfering with "the existing colonies or dependencies of any European power," but "with the Governments who have declared their independence and maintain it . . . we could not view any [European] interposition for the purpose of oppressing them . . . in any other light than as the manifestation of an unfriendly disposition toward the United States."

In short, Monroe vowed not to interfere in European affairs, including in the Old World's *existing* New World colonies, but warned that any European attempt to meddle with any of the American republics would be regarded as a direct threat to the United States.

THE DOCTRINE AND ITS LEGACY

Monroe's proposal was not an ultimatum to the European powers, but a proposed quid pro quo: You leave our part of the world alone, and we'll do the same with yours. Nevertheless, the American president put the emphasis on the quid rather than the quo: The "American continents," he said, "by the free and independent condition which they have assumed and maintain, are henceforth not to be considered as subjects for future colonization by any European powers."

Under the circumstances that existed at the time, Spain, France, Prussia, Austria, and Russia could readily be forgiven for taking the "Monroe Doctrine"—this is the name the policy only later acquired—as just so much hollow talk. The United States had little more than an embryonic navy and almost no army. It had fought the War of 1812 mainly with short-term militia forces, not a standing national army, and it had come close to losing badly.

But in persuading President Monroe not to ride in the wake of a British warship, John Quincy Adams did not mean to discourage him from taking less direct advantage of British military might. Ever since the Duke of Wellington had defeated Napoleon at Waterloo in 1815, much of the world had been under the influence of a so-called "Pax Britannica," a state of relative peace created by the Royal Navy's unchallenged control over the post-Napoleonic seas. Because Britain had no desire to see France and its allies return to influence in, let alone possession of, any part of the Americas, its government tacitly backed the otherwise empty threat of the Monroe Doctrine. Nobody said a word, but the Royal Navy effectively sailed under the flag of the American president, a banner unseen, but apparent nevertheless.

Yet if for many years the Monroe Doctrine was enforced by the presence of British men-of-war, it also drove developing U.S. policies that eventually built America's own military into the most formidable in the world, transforming the United States first into a genuine world power, then a superpower, and, by the end of the twentieth century, the world's *only* superpower.

Thanks to the Monroe Doctrine, the United States came to be seen—and came to act as—the central power in its hemisphere. During the 1880s, James G. Blaine, secretary of state to three presidents, James A. Garfield, Chester A. Arthur, and Benjamin Harrison, promulgated what the press called the "Big Sister" policy, which extended the Monroe Doctrine as a means of bringing the nations of Latin America voluntarily into line behind U.S. political and economic leadership by throwing open Central and South American markets to big U.S. traders, such as the companies that joined together as United Fruit.

President James Monroe's proposal was not an ultimatum to the European powers, but a proposed quid pro quo: You leave our part of the world alone, and we'll do the same with yours.

Little more than two decades later, in 1904, President Theodore Roosevelt returned to the Monroe Doctrine to justify his assertion of the right of the United States to intervene in cases of "flagrant" or "chronic wrongdoing or impotence" by a Latin American nation, particularly any nation that failed to pay its debts to European lenders, thereby inviting intervention from European powers.

As the president explained to Congress, "All that this country desires is to see the neighboring countries stable, orderly, and prosperous. If a nation shows that it knows how to act with reasonable efficiency and decency in social and political matters, if it keeps order and pays its obligations, it need fear no interference by the United States." But, Roosevelt warned, if a country fails in any of these respects, "the Monroe Doctrine may force the United States . . . to the exercise of an international police power."

This so-called "Roosevelt Corollary to the Monroe Doctrine" has been criticized both at home and abroad as nakedly imperialist, yet it has repeatedly served as precedent in a long history of U.S. intervention in Central and South America as well as the Caribbean. In 1928, President Calvin Coolidge's undersecretary of state,

J. Reuben Clark, issued a memorandum (now known as the "Clark Memorandum"), which used the Monroe Doctrine and the Roosevelt Corollary only to step beyond both. The memorandum concluded that the U.S. government had no need to cite the Monroe Doctrine to justify its interventions in Latin America because these were acts of self-defense, to which any nation has an inherent, self-evident right.

In 1954, at the height of the cold war, Dwight Eisenhower's secretary of state, John Foster Dulles, chose not to rely on the self-evident when he explicitly based his denunciation of Soviet influence in Guatemala on the Monroe Doctrine. Less than a decade later, in 1962, addressing the Tenth Inter-American Conference, President John F. Kennedy denounced the intervention of Soviet communism in Cuba by framing his policy toward the island nation in terms of the Monroe Doctrine, which, he told reporters, "means what it has meant since President Monroe and John Quincy Adams enunciated it, and that is that we would oppose a foreign power extending its power to the Western Hemisphere." That is why, Kennedy explained, "we have cut off our trade . . . to isolate the Communist menace in Cuba."

Throughout the cold war, U.S. presidents have used the Monroe Doctrine to justify a variety of interventions in Latin America, but they have also enlarged the implications of the doctrine to define the United States as the world's chief defender of democracy, an interpretation of Monroe and Adams that reaches far beyond Latin America and even the Western Hemisphere. Thus interpreted, the long shadow of the Monroe Doctrine can be seen in Woodrow Wilson's justification for U.S. entry into World War I (which Americans in 1917 still referred to as the "European War"): "to make the world safe for democracy."

The doctrine bolstered Franklin Roosevelt's entry into both the Pacific and the Atlantic theaters of World War II, and in the postwar world it prompted the policy of intervening globally to "contain" the spread of communism—the "*Truman* Doctrine," named for FDR's successor, Harry S. Truman. The Korean War, the Vietnam War, the two wars in Iraq, of Bush father and son, and the Afghan war are all rooted in the collective political and popular mind-set created by a few paragraphs, somewhat verbose, indirect, and excessively ornate, in President James Monroe's annual message to Congress for 1823.

CHAPTER 4

JAMES K. POLK DECLARES WAR AGAINST MEXICO AND GAINS WESTERN STATES AND CONTROL OF TEXAS

1846

WHEN JAMES K. POLK DECIDED TO ENTER TENNESSEE STATE POLITICS IN 1820, according to a campaign biography, he went first to the state's most powerful political figure, Andrew Jackson, for guidance. What advice could "Old Hickory," the war hero who would go on to become a two-term president of the United States, give the fledgling office seeker who had just set up a law practice in Tennessee?

Jackson ruminated for a minute. His answer was characteristically blunt. The young man should find a good wife and marry her.

"What?" Polk's face lit up. "You mean Sarah Childress, sir?" Polk asked, naming the vivacious, dark-haired, sixteen-year-old daughter of one of the state's leading families, whom he avidly admired. "I shall ask her right away!" And off the young man rode to follow Jackson's advice. He asked, Sarah accepted, and her father eventually consented. In 1824 the young couple was married in one of frontier Tennessee's most glamorous weddings. Sarah became her politician husband's most trusted adviser and speechwriter, and even sat in on cabinet meetings when he was president.

The details of Polk's courtship and marriage to the redoubtable Sarah are disputed, but one element of the story stands out. It reflects Polk's early qualities as a man of strong decisions, who sought advice, set firm goals, formulated plans to achieve them, and then carried them out—qualities that made him one of the most influential presidents of the nineteenth century, whose actions stretched America's boundaries from coast to coast and turned the young nation into a major player on the world stage. Many historians rate Polk among the ten most effective U.S. presidents, right up there with Washington, Lincoln, and the faces on Mount Rushmore.

"YOUNG HICKORY"

James Knox Polk, one of ten children, was born on a small hardscrabble farm in western North Carolina in what may have been a log cabin—another detail of his history in dispute. He was named for John Knox, the Scottish father of Presbyterianism, his churchgoing family's faith. His parents, with other members of the Polk clan, moved to the more inviting soil of middle Tennessee. The young James attended the University of North Carolina, studied law, was admitted to the bar, and argued his first case, defending his father on a charge of public fighting. (He paid a one dollar fine.)

The young lawyer advanced to his first political position. He was chosen clerk of the Tennessee State Senate, receiving six dollars a month. (The legislators got four dollars.) Polk was so proficient at keeping the senators abreast of legislative bills and mastering their details that he was brought back for a second two-year term without competition. In 1824, he joined the populist wave backing the Democratic Jackson for president. He became so close to Jackson personally and politically and copied his speaking style so precisely that he was known as "Young Hickory."

Wearing the Jacksonian mantle, he was elected to the Tennessee House of Representatives, winning two two-year terms before moving up to the U.S. House. He served in Washington as a congressman from 1825 to 1839, the last four years as Speaker. In 1839, he was elected governor of Tennessee. Clearly, James K. Polk was a young man on the way up, and in a hurry. Then his sky's-the-limit career hit a roadblock. He ran for reelection in 1841 and lost. He tried again two years later and lost again. It looked like his political star might have set, at age forty-six. Instead, Polk set his sights higher. With the encouragement of Jackson, he began to think about becoming president of the United States.

"TIPPECANOE AND TYLER, TOO"

The Whigs had won the presidency in 1840 behind William Henry Harrison, known as "Old Tippecanoe" for his victory over Tecumseh's American Indian federation at the Tippecanoe and Wabash rivers in the Indiana Territory in 1811. John Tyler, a Democratic senator from Virginia who left the party to ally with the Whigs, was nominated for vice president. The memorable campaign slogan "Tippecanoe and Tyler, Too" carried the Whigs to victory. But Harrison, sixty-eight, caught a cold on inauguration day, contracted pneumonia, and died after only a month in office. Tyler became the first vice president in U.S. history to be elevated to the presidency.

"His Accidency" promptly antagonized both his new party and his former one. He vetoed Whig bills, proposed legislation, and demonstrated that he planned to be more than a chair warmer. Although he hinted strongly that he expected to run for a full term in 1844, the Whigs were having no part of such an apostate. The aging Jackson saw an opportunity for his protégé.

So did Polk. With the same canniness, foresightedness, and preparation that he had shown in proposing to Sarah, he mapped out a future to make it happen. He ignored the implorings of Jackson and Sarah and decided he would not run for president in 1844. He would run for *vice* president.

Normally, no political aspirant ran for vice president. The candidate was usually anointed by party leaders to bring regional balance to the ticket or to satisfy an aggrieved party faction. Sometimes the presidential candidate chose his own running mate and the party simply rubberstamped the choice. To most politicians, the ostensible number two position in the government was considered a dead-end job.

The Democrats got together in Baltimore for their nominating convention in May 1844 with no clear front-runner. Former president Martin Van Buren, whom Harrison had defeated for reelection in 1840, was the favorite, but he was still tarred by the Panic of 1837 and the subsequent depression. Besides, as a free-state New Yorker opposed to the expansion of slavery, he was unpopular in the slaveholding South. "Van, Van, he's a used-up man," opponents chanted.

Polk announced that he and his supporters backed Van Buren, who had been vice president under Jackson and had succeeded him in the presidency. His move, Polk indicated, had the endorsement of "Old Hickory." Jackson was now in failing health at his "Hermitage" home in Nashville, but his populist views were still a power in the party. Shrewdly, Polk let it be known that he would be open to a vice-presidential nomination on a Van Buren ticket, thus rallying Southern support for Van Buren. That would put him at the head of the line to follow Van Buren whether he won or lost.

THIS SATIRE IN SUPPORT OF PRESIDENTIAL CANDIDATE HENRY CLAY SHOWS HIM ON THE SOLID "PEOPLE'S BRIDGE." HIS OPPONENT, JAMES POLK, IS SEEN FOLLOWING IN THE FOOTSTEPS OF HIS MENTOR, ANDREW JACKSON, ACROSS THE "LOCO FOCO" BRIDGE. *LOCOFOCO*, SPANISH FOR "MATCHES," WAS THE TERM USED TO DESCRIBE THE MORE RADICAL PART OF THE DEMOCRATIC PARTY. THE LITHOGRAPH, SIGNED H. BUCHOLZER, WAS PUBLISHED IN 1844.

Library of Congress

On the first ballot, Van Buren received the greatest number of votes but lacked the two-thirds majority of the delegates required for nomination. John C. Calhoun was next, with the remaining votes split among other candidates. On the second ballot, Van Buren increased his lead, but only slightly. The deadlock went on for eight ballots without a victor.

But on the seventh ballot, a new name had appeared in the vote count. James K. Polk, the erstwhile vice-presidential candidate, received one vote for president. On the eighth ballot, the number increased to twenty-two. On the ninth ballot, after some

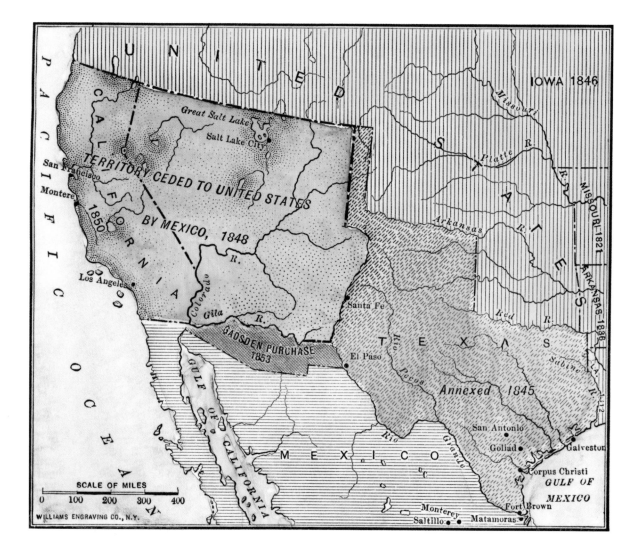

THE UNITED STATES RECEIVED FROM MEXICO 1.2 MILLION SQUARE MILES (3,107,985.7 KM²) OF TERRITORY, INCREASING THE SIZE OF THE NATION BY ONE-THIRD, AS SHOWN IN THIS HAND-COLORED WOODCUT OF A NINETEENTH CENTURY ILLUSTRATION. THE SO-CALLED MEXICAN CESSION COMPRISED THE PRESENT-DAY STATES OF CALIFORNIA, NEVADA, UTAH, AND ARIZONA, AS WELL AS PARTS OF NEW MEXICO, COLORADO, AND WYOMING.

prodding from Jackson men, state after state went for Polk. The Van Buren supporters switched to Polk and "Young Hickory" was nominated by acclamation.

WHO IS JAMES K. POLK?

Polk's surprise nomination made him the first "dark horse" candidate in U.S. history—the racing term for an unknown outside entry who lags almost unnoticed in the back of a race field, letting others set the pace and exhaust themselves, then suddenly bursts to the outside in the homestretch and sweeps to victory. Although a state governor and former house speaker was scarcely a true political outsider, Polk remained an unknown to the public at large.

Polk and his running-mate, George Mifflin Dallas of Pennsylvania, were greeted with derision, not to say sarcasm, by the rival Whigs. "Who is James K. Polk?" hooted the Nashville *Republican Banner*. "Who is James K. Polk" became the Whig mantra throughout the campaign. ("They will find out in November," the Democrats responded.)

The Whigs then picked a candidate with name recognition—the party stalwart Henry Clay. He was known as "the Great Compromiser" for engineering the Missouri Compromise of 1820, settling a free-states-versus-slave-states controversy that threatened to split the youthful Union. It would be Clay's third try for the presidency. Democrats—and some Whigs—portrayed him as shopworn. Meanwhile, Tyler, rebuffed, entered the race as an Independent. James Birney complicated matters further by running as the standard-bearer of the abolitionist and anti-immigrant American Liberty party, which was popular in the Northeast.

Two hot-button issues dominated political wrangling in 1844—the ongoing and thorny question of slavery and that of expanding the young country's territory. The two were almost inextricably intertwined, especially in the matter of Texas.

In 1820, Mexicans along the Rio Grande had risen up and overthrown the Spanish colonial regime. Coaxed by the new government with the lure of free land, Americans flocked by the hundreds across the boundary. By 1835 "gringos"—English speakers—outnumbered locals in the territory three to one. When they began to agitate for political rights, the Mexican strongman Santa Anna sent in troops to quell the disturbance. A hastily assembled militia fought back. After the fabled and heroic siege of the Alamo, the Texans came back to defeat Santa Anna's army in a series of ambushes and surprise attacks, often striking when the Santa Anna forces were observing siesta.

Led by Sam Houston, a settler who had once been a Tennessee congressman, the Texans petitioned Congress for admission to the Union as a slave state. Congress demurred. Texas was, after all, a Southern agricultural society dependent on bent-back slave labor to tend the crops. Admitting a slave state without an offsetting free state would tip the political balance toward the slaveholding South. Additionally, a parcel of land the size of a whole Mexican province would be a huge amount to take in at one gulp. So, should "Texas" be admitted as a single state, or perhaps carved into several, presumably slaveholding, states? And much of the territory was only sparsely populated, seemingly not settled enough to qualify for statehood. With so many choices, Congress punted, kicking the question down the field for the future to solve.

Polk won a narrow victory. The electorate split over the Texas issue; Polk received 1,337,243 popular votes; Clay, 1,299,062. The difference lay with New York State, where

U.S. GENERAL STEPHEN KEARNY IS
SHOWN CAPTURING NEW MEXICO
FROM MEXICO IN THE SUMMER
OF 1846 IN THIS HAND-COLORED
WOODCUT OF A NINETEENTH
CENTURY ILLUSTRATION.
© North Wind Picture Archives /
Alamy

the abolitionist Birney received a surprising 15,812 votes, enough to swung the state's 36 electoral votes into the Polk column, giving him 170 electoral votes to Clay's 105. The "dark horse" also became a minority president, with 49.3 percent of the popular vote.

The vexing Texas question continued after the election. Polk, a Southern landowner and slaveholder, favored annexation. Seven days before Polk's inauguration, lame-duck President Tyler preempted him. Tyler had previously sought congressional approval for a treaty annexing Texas as the 29th state, but the effort was badly defeated in Congress; all but one Whig voted against it in the Senate. Now he tried a different tack. He called on Congress for a joint resolution favoring annexation, spelling out terms under which the "Lone Star State" could become part of the United States. The resolution passed easily on February 26, six days before Polk was to be sworn in, and was on the new president's desk on inauguration day. Texas was officially admitted on December 29, 1845.

"FIFTY-FOUR FORTY OR FIGHT!"

With the Texas issue off his plate, Polk took office on March 4, 1845, with a clear-cut set of goals he expected to achieve during his four-year term. That agenda included acquiring "all or part" of the disputed Oregon country from Britain, and Alta California and Nueve Mexico from Mexico.

Oregon was a tricky question. The territory between the Pacific and the Rockies was jointly administered and controlled by the United States and Britain. Processions of American Conestoga wagons labeled "Oregon or Bust!" were bumping across the Oregon Trail. Clamor arose for the United States to claim the whole territory up to the 54°, 40' parallel. "Fifty-four Forty or Fight!" cried belligerent voices spoiling for military action to back up the claim.

Polk first wanted to divide the territory peaceably at the 49' parallel, with the United States taking the southern half, contiguous to the rest of the country. British ambassador Lord Richard Pakenham emphatically said no, primarily to protect Hudson's

Bay Company installations along the Columbia River, which runs through modern-day British Columbia, Washington State, and Oregon. Spurned, Polk angrily withdrew the offer. He cited the Monroe Doctrine (see chapter 3) against European colonization of the Western Hemisphere. In what became known as the *Polk Corollary* to the Monroe Doctrine, he read the riot act to Britain:

"We must ever maintain that the people of this continent alone have the right to decide their own destiny." And moreover, America would not back down from its claims to the entire territory; no, indeed. "The only way to treat with John Bull is to look him straight in the eye," Polk wrote in his diary.

Now it was England's turn to back down. Lord Pakenham woke a pajama-clad secretary of state James Buchanan on a Sunday night to sheepishly confess that he had rejected the earlier American offer strictly on his own initiative. He had been upbraided by London for his unilateral action, and told to accept the 49th parallel offer. He and Buchanan then developed the "Oregon Treaty," dividing the territory and giving the United States its first window on the Pacific. The United States received the territory now comprising the states of Washington and Oregon, with some of the easternmost portions becoming parts of present-day Idaho and Montana.

"IT IS AMERICA'S MANIFEST DESTINY TO OVERSPREAD THE CONTINENT"

In the spring of 1845, journalist John O'Sullivan wrote in the *Democratic Review* about the Texas annexation, "[It is America's] manifest destiny to overspread the continent allotted by Providence for the free development of our yearly multiplying millions." A few months later, in the New York *Morning News*, he extended the concept specifically to Oregon and then Mexico. The United States had the right to claim the whole of the territory, he wrote. "And that claim is . . . for the development of the great experiment of liberty and federated self-government entrusted to us." It was not a matter of territorial aggrandizement. America was "upholding a moral ideal."

Polk himself never used the term, but "Manifest Destiny" quickly became an expansionist catchphrase (to be revived in 1898 as a reason for annexing the Philippines as a colony, and obliquely during the Iraq War of 2003–2009 to uphold America's "mission" to spread the concepts of liberty and democracy to other parts of the globe). And certainly Polk favored "overspreading the continent" from shore to shore.

Now he turned his attention to Mexico. Fearful that some European country might seize the territory, he dispatched the diplomat John Slidell to Mexico City to offer $20 to $30 million for Alta California and Nueve Mexico. In fact, he told Slidell confidentially, he could bid up to $40 million for the two.

When Slidell arrived, however, Mexican leaders were furious to discover that his mission was to acquire more territory, not to pay compensation for the loss of Texas, and they refused to see him. As a fig leaf for the refusal, they claimed that his diplomatic papers were not in order, and sent him home. Polk took the rebuff as an insult, even grounds for war. He ordered General Zachary Taylor to occupy a strip of land along the Rio Grande that was claimed by both countries, stepping up the pressure. Mexico sent its own troops across the border, attacked a U.S. outpost, and killed sixteen U.S. soldiers. Polk called that a flagrant cause for war. He told Congress that Mexico had "invaded our territory and shed American blood upon American soil." He asked for a declaration of war and Congress obliged, voting overwhelmingly in favor on May 13, 1846.

By the end of summer 1846, troops under General Stephen Kearny had captured New Mexico. After the comic-opera Bear Flag Revolt in California in June, when thirty-three U.S. settlers attacked the sleeping Mexican garrison in Sonoma, proclaimed a republic, and ran up a homemade flag emblazoned with a grizzly bear, Captain John C. Fremont rounded up troops and claimed the territory for the United States. General Winfield Scott landed troops in Vera Cruz on the Gulf of Mexico and drove on to Mexico City, capturing the capital after a bitter battle at Chapultepec. At the same time, Taylor wiped out Mexican resistance in the northern part of the country after battles along the Rio Grande and near the site of present-day Brownsville.

Although much of its territory was in U.S. hands, Mexico still held out until September 1847, when the government finally surrendered. The Treaty of Guadalupe Hidalgo, signed on February 2, 1848, officially ended the hostilities. The United States received from Mexico 1.2 million square miles (3,107,985.7 km²) of territory, increasing the size of the nation by one-third. The so-called "Mexican Cession" comprised the present-day states of California, Nevada, Utah, and Arizona, as well as parts of New Mexico, Colorado, and Wyoming. In return, the United States paid the bankrupt Mexican government $15 million, less than Polk had budgeted in his instructions to Slidell.

The United States paid a dear price in lives and treasure, though. Some 20,000 American soldiers died (although an estimated 50,000 Mexicans were casualties) and the war cost the nation $100 million. It also severely damaged the reputation of Polk, who had followed the action, had spent long hours poring over maps, and had developed war strategy almost battle by battle, ruining his health, it was said. He was now portrayed in Congress as a warmonger. After the treaty was signed, the House voted to censure him for starting the war, claiming he was guilty of an immoral act of aggression and an abuse of presidential power. Opponents also blasted him for being hoodwinked into paying $15 million for worthless land that contained nothing more than desert and mountains. It was said that the war and the resulting accusations led to his death from cholera only three months after leaving office.

On December 5, 1848, the outgoing president, who had kept his pledge not to run for a second term, delivered his farewell address to Congress. In it, justifying his claim that the war and the treaty were actually a bargain, he made the electrifying announcement that gold had been discovered in newly acquired California. Two days later, he displayed gold nuggets that had been presented to him. The news touched off the mad stampede known as the *California gold rush* and truly made the United States a nation "overspreading the continent" on its way to becoming the world's wealthiest superpower.

CHAPTER 5

MILLARD FILLMORE OPENS JAPANESE PORTS TO TRADE, MAKING THE UNITED STATES A PACIFIC POWER

1853

I N I542 A STORM BLEW A PORTUGUESE SHIP OFF COURSE AND ONTO THE SHORES of Japan; the crew became the first Europeans ever to set foot in the Land of the Rising Sun. But less than a century later, in the 1630s, Shogun Tokugawa Iemitsu began to expel all Europeans from Japan, and ultimately closed the country's borders, keeping the Japanese almost completely isolated from the outside world.

For more than two hundred years, Japan restricted its trade relations to China and the Netherlands, although commerce with the Dutch was negligible because they were permitted to send only one trading vessel to Japan each year. By the mid-nineteenth century there was a widely held consensus that whatever Western nation secured a trade agreement with Japan would score a diplomatic and commercial coup. As it happened, it was an almost-forgotten U.S. president, Millard Fillmore, who ended Japan's era of isolation and opened the country up once again to the West.

Fillmore had several reasons for wishing to establish relations with Japan. The United States now stretched, as he put it in his letter to the emperor of Japan, "from ocean to ocean." American commercial and whaling ships sailed freely across the Pacific, and the new steamships could reach Japan from California in only eighteen days. Friendly relations between the two nations would permit American vessels en route to China to pull into Japanese harbors for fresh water, provisions, and coal to power their steamships, or to make necessary repairs.

Until now, American sailors shipwrecked on the shores of Japan had been imprisoned, some were shamefully mistreated, and a few had been killed. In 1801 the United States had gone to war against Algeria to liberate American sailors who had been captured and sold into slavery by the Bey of Algiers, but Fillmore desired a peaceful method for resolving tensions between the United States and Japan. American markets longed for the silks, porcelain, lacquerware, and tea of Japan. In return, the United States offered the bounty of California—gold, silver, quicksilver, and precious stones.

At a time when Britain and France were building overseas empires, many in the United States were eager to extend American influence into Asia, perhaps even carve out an American empire there. An overseas empire would enhance America's prestige, open up new markets to American goods, and give Americans an opportunity to indulge in feelings of racial superiority as they carried Western civilization and Christianity to a corner of the globe most regarded as backward and benighted.

"It is our Manifest Destiny to implant ourselves in Asia," *The New York Herald* assured its readers. "The apparition of the Caucasian race rising upon the Yellow race . . . must wake up and reanimate the torpid body of Asia," declaimed Senator Thomas Hart Benton of Missouri. "The 'Gate of the Sun,' as the islanders call their empire, must open voluntarily or perforce . . . The time has come for it in the providence of God," said the editors of *The Presbyterian Review*.

Fillmore did not include empire building among his list of reasons for sending an American delegation to Japan, but for the sake of winning the support of the press and members of Congress like Benton, he didn't openly reject it either.

THE MOST PRESSING ISSUE OF THE DAY

On July 9, 1850, President Zachary Taylor died after a severe five-day gastrointestinal illness. The presidency passed to Vice President Millard Fillmore. Taylor had been a Southern aristocrat and career army officer. Fillmore had been born in a log cabin in the Finger Lakes district of New York State; to escape poverty he studied law and entered politics.

Fillmore came to office at a moment when the country and Congress were at each other's throats once again over the issue of slavery. According to the Missouri Compromise of 1820, every state above the latitude of 36° 30′ would be free territory, and everything below it would be slave territory. But in the years that followed the Compromise, Missouri, Arkansas, Florida, and Texas had been admitted to the Union as slave states, while only two territories, Michigan and Iowa, had joined the Union as free states. Worse still, with the conclusion of the War with Mexico in 1848, the United States had acquired vast new territories, all of which were below the 36° 30′ line of demarcation. Northerners and antislavery advocates feared that Southerners and the pro-slavery forces would dominate Congress.

Senator Henry Clay of Kentucky, himself a slave owner, drafted new legislation that would come to be known as the *Compromise of 1850*. It gave something to everyone: California would enter the Union as a free state, but the people of New Mexico Territory could decide whether they would permit slavery; owning slaves would remain legal in the District of Columbia, but buying and selling slaves would be abolished there and the new Fugitive Slave Act would require all citizens of the United States, whether in the North or the South, to help capture and return runaway slaves to their masters.

With the most pressing issue of the day resolved, at least for the time being, Fillmore was free to pursue other goals, such as establishing trade with Japan.

"SOMETHING OF A MARTINET"

Commodore Matthew C. Perry was fifty-eight years old when President Fillmore chose him to lead the American mission to Japan. He was the younger brother of the dashing Commodore Oliver Hazard Perry, whose victory over the British fleet on Lake Erie during the War of 1812 saved the Ohio Valley from a possible invasion while leaving Canada vulnerable to an American attack.

Matthew Perry was aggressive, imperious, decisive, a strict disciplinarian, and a man who could be relied upon to fulfill any mission. A fellow officer described the commodore as "a bluff yet dignified man, heavy and not graceful, something of a martinet; a duty man all over, held something in awe by junior officers, and having little to do with them; seriously courteous to others." During the Mexican American War (1846–1848), aboard the USS *Mississippi*, Perry pacified the coastal cities of Mexico. In 1851 Perry took the *Mississippi* to Turkey on a politically sensitive assignment—to transport the Hungarian revolutionary Lajos Kossuth, along with his wife and children, from Turkey to safety in England.

In addition to being dependable, Perry was also farsighted—witness his side-wheel steamer, the *Mississippi*. Most of Perry's fellow naval officers hated the idea of replacing America's fleet of sailing ships with steamers because they were new, they were unfamiliar, and they were mechanical. Most common seamen were hostile to the steamships, too—they did not know how to operate such a vessel, and they did not want to learn. Many representatives in Congress backed up the navy's retrograde point of view but for a different reason—to mothball the sailing fleet and replace it entirely with steamships would cost the federal government a fortune.

Perry was impervious to these objections. Steamships were faster than sailing ships, held steady in all weather, and were not subject to the vagaries of wind and tide. From Perry's point of view, it made no sense to cling to something outmoded when something so much better was available. In essence, that would be the argument he would make to the dignitaries of Japan.

THE SHOGUN TAKES NO CHANCES

The Japanese term for the country's isolationist policy was *sakoku*, which means Japan was a locked or chained country: No foreigner could enter, and no Japanese could leave. The policy was adopted in the 1630s, at a time when the Japanese aristocracy believed its civilization and sovereignty were in peril.

In the sixteenth century, Spanish and Portuguese merchants found their Japanese colleagues eager to trade Japanese luxury items for European manufactured goods, particularly firearms. And European missionary priests found converts among the peasants, the samurai, and even the nobility. By 1580 there were large churches in Nagasaki and Kyoto, a seminary where Japanese men were trained for the priesthood, a Catholic hospital on the southern island of Kyushu, as well as small missions scattered throughout the country. By 1612, there may have been as many as 400,000 Japanese Catholics out of a total population of approximately 12 million. That same year the government outlawed Christianity in Japan and began a period of intense persecution during which tens of thousands of Japanese Catholics, including women and children, along with many missionary and native priests, were martyred.

COMMODORE MATTHEW PERRY IS SHOWN MEETING WITH THE JAPANESE TO DISCUSS TRADE IN THIS 1856 AMERICAN LITHOGRAPH. PERRY ARRIVED IN 1853 WITH FOUR STEAMSHIPS, ALL PAINTED BLACK, AND LINED THEM UP SIDE-BY-SIDE BLOCKING YEDO BAY. THOUGH IT WAS A DIPLOMATIC MISSION, HIS AGGRESSIVE POSTURE SENT THE MESSAGE HE WOULD NOT TOLERATE JAPANESE HOSTILITIES.

English and Dutch Protestant traders were the catalyst for the destruction of the Catholic Church in Japan and the adoption of the country's strict isolationist policy. In fairness, that had not been their intention. The Spanish and Portuguese merchants, who had arrived in Japan first, enjoyed trading concessions and privileges and access to influential noblemen and government officials. The English and the Dutch traders wanted their share, and so they worked to undermine Japanese confidence in their Spanish and Portuguese trading partners. They spread a rumor that the Catholics would establish the Inquisition in Japan and initiate a full-scale persecution of Japanese non-Catholics. They told members of Japan's upper classes of the conquest of Central and South America, laying particular emphasis on what happened to the royal and noble families of the Aztecs and the Incas after the Spanish conquered their empires.

But the English and Dutch were undone by their rumormongering. Fearful that a conquistador-style army might invade Japan, Shogun Tokugawa Iemitsu (1604–1651) banished all Europeans from Japan—Spanish, Portuguese, but also the Dutch and English. The shogun was not taking any chances. Finally, he decreed that any foreigner who entered the country would be executed. The Europeans evacuated; Japanese Christians were executed or went underground, and Japan went into a kind of cultural limbo where nothing ever was supposed to change.

THE FIRST ENCOUNTER

Early in July 1853, Commodore Perry with his squadron of four ships, all of them painted black, approached Cape Sagami on Honshu, the largest island of the Japanese archipelago and the location of the imperial capital, Kyoto. Japanese fishermen working the offshore waters stopped what they were doing to gape at the sight as the squadron, the two steamships *Mississippi* and *Susquehanna* in the lead, bore down on the forbidden coast of Japan.

As the American ships entered the narrow strait at the mouth of Yedo Bay, Japanese coast guard boats advanced, their officers shouting and gesturing at the intruders to turn back. Instead of retreating, Perry gave the order to drop anchor. His four ships lined up side by side, effectively blocking the entrance of the bay. Although this was fundamentally a diplomatic mission, by assuming an aggressive posture Perry was conveying to the Japanese that although he had come to establish a cordial commercial relationship with the United States, he would not tolerate any threatening behavior.

In Yedo (present-day Tokyo), rumors that the ships in the strait were about to launch an invasion sent panic through the city. "The whole city was in an uproar," wrote one Japanese chronicler. "In all directions were seen mothers flying with children in their arms, and men with mothers on their backs. Rumors of an immediate action, exaggerated each time they were communicated from mouth to mouth, added horror to the horror-stricken. The tramp of warhorses, the chatter of armed warriors, the noise of carts, the parade of firemen, the incessant tolling bells, the shrieks of women, the cries of children, dinning all the streets of a city of more than a million souls, made confusion worse."

Back at the straits, coast guard officers attempted to board Perry's ship, but his crew, brandishing their guns, kept them back. Perry had brought along two linguists, S. Wells Williams and H.A.L. Portman, who spoke Japanese and Dutch. These gentlemen explained to the coast guard that the commodore was a man of the highest rank in the U.S. Navy and would only speak with a Japanese of equal rank.

An officer of the coast guard stated that Saberosuke, the vice governor of the region, was present. Would the commodore parley with him? Speaking through his interpreters, Perry replied that he would have nothing to do with a vice governor; the coast guard must bring the governor to him. The coast guard explained that protocol forbade the governor from boarding ships. They were at an impasse, until a resourceful member of the coast guard thought of a solution: Would the commodore appoint one of his officers to speak with the vice governor? Having thoroughly impressed the Japanese with his dignity and superiority, Perry agreed to this compromise and sent a flag lieutenant named Marcus Contee to speak with Saberosuke.

It was Saberosuke's duty to collect as much intelligence about the interlopers as he could, and so he was direct with Lieutenant Contee, asking him the name of his ships, the number of his crew, and how many guns they had. "We are armed ships," Contee replied, "and our custom is never to answer such questions."

Then Contee went on the offensive. The commodore had a letter for the emperor from the president of the United States. What day would be convenient for the emperor to grant the commodore an audience? As a lowly vice governor, Saberosuke could not arrange audiences with the emperor, so he tried indirection: The Americans must sail to Nagasaki, the only port in the country where foreigners were permitted to conduct business. Contee assured Saberosuke that Perry would not sail to Nagasaki. The commodore's mission was peaceful and friendly, but he would not suffer the indignity of being barred from the capital and forbidden to fulfill his mission to the emperor. Then Contee added one thing more—the coast guard ships must withdraw, or the American ships would fire upon them. Saberosuke ordered the vessels to sail back up the harbor.

COMMODORE PERRY PRESENTED A GIFT OF A MINIATURE RAILROAD FROM PRESIDENT FILLMORE TO THE JAPANESE. SAMURAI WARRIORS AND NOBLEMEN LINE UP TO TAKE TURNS RIDING THE LOCOMOTIVE IN THIS NINETEENTH-CENTURY WOODBLOCK PRINT.

© The London Art Archive / Alamy

A SHORT CEREMONY

Days passed while the Japanese tried to find a way to receive the Fillmore letter without granting Perry access to the emperor. They explained that the emperor was a sacred personage who received almost no one, but princes of the imperial family could receive the letter on the emperor's behalf. Perry was amenable to this.

Then the Japanese said that it would take many months before Perry could expect a reply from the emperor. The commodore answered that he would take his squadron to China, spend fall and winter there, then return in the new year. Some of the American officers dropped hints to their Japanese counterparts that when the Americans came back they would probably have more warships with them.

At Kurihama, a little place outside Yedo, the Japanese erected a reception hall for the ceremonial presentation of President Fillmore's letter. Perry and all his officers in full dress uniforms, accompanied by marines, sailors, and two brass bands—three hundred men in all—came ashore in cutters and longboats. They were met by the two princes, who had brought an entourage of thousands of warriors. While the bands played American patriotic tunes, the American and Japanese dignitaries filed into the reception hall. Two African American sailors had been chosen to carry two rosewood boxes that contained the president's letter, along with Perry's credentials, to the dais where the princes sat. The sailors set down the boxes. The princes rose and bowed to Perry and his officers. Then everyone withdrew. The entire ceremony had taken only a few minutes.

In February 1854 Perry returned, now with a fleet of ten black warships. On March 8, 1854, he came ashore at Yokohama for another ceremony, this time to work out the terms of a treaty of friendship between the Empire of Japan and the United States. The chief of the high commissioners agreed that as a start two Japanese ports would be open to American traders, and that an American consul would be welcome in Japan to protect American citizens and look after American interests. While the treaty was being written, Japanese and Americans entertained each other at banquets and exchanged gifts. President Fillmore had sent to the emperor clocks, telescopes, an entire telegraph station, a complete set of John James Audubon's *Birds of America*, one hundred gallons (378.4 l) of Kentucky bourbon, and a miniature railroad—about the size of trains found today in a children's amusement park—complete with track, engine, and passenger car. Samurai warriors and noblemen lined up to take turns riding the locomotive.

A MILITARISTIC SPIRIT

Millard Fillmore's intent to open Japan to the West changed the country dramatically. The Japan Commodore Perry visited in 1853 was a feudal society, virtually unchanged since the Middle Ages, but within twenty years Japan would become a new nation. The Japanese imported American and European technology, introduced compulsory education, stripped the samurai and nobility of their feudal privileges, guaranteed certain human rights, including freedom of religion, ratified a constitution, and modernized the military, with the Prussian army and the British navy as their models.

By 1894 Japan was ready to flex its military muscles. It declared war on China and defeated her. In 1904 and 1905, Japan waged war against Russia, utterly defeating one of the greatest empires on earth. These conflicts were the beginnings of Japan's drive to establish its own Asian empire. A militaristic spirit dominated the government throughout the first decades of the twentieth century, culminating with World War II, which saw Japan aligned with Nazi Germany and Fascist Italy. It was Japan that dragged the United States into the war with its surprise attack Pearl Harbor. The war ended after the United States dropped two atomic bombs on Japan.

Today, more than one hundred and fifty years after Perry won a trade agreement from the Japanese, commerce between the United States and Japan is a mainstay of the economies of both nations. In 2009 the United States exported $65.1 billion in goods to Japan, while importing $139.3 billion in Japanese goods. President Fillmore saw Japan as a convenient refueling and reprovisioning station on the way to China, but by the twenty-first century Japan would rank as America's fourth largest trading partner.

CHAPTER 6

ABRAHAM LINCOLN SIGNS THE EMANCIPATION PROCLAMATION

1863

PRESIDENT ABRAHAM LINCOLN AND HIS WIFE MARY WENT TO BED BEFORE midnight on New Year's Eve 1862, but neither could sleep. Lincoln's restlessness kept the First Lady awake. Cross because she was tired and because she knew what was troubling her husband, she asked in a sharp tone, "Well, what do you intend doing?"

Mary Lincoln was referring to the Emancipation Proclamation, the document that would declare all the slaves in Confederate territory free. Everyone in both the North and the South knew about the proclamation—a draft of it had been in circulation for months as Lincoln canvassed his cabinet, Congress, the army, the press, and churchmen for their opinions. Now, after months of often acrimonious debate, Lincoln had resolved to sign the proclamation into law and liberate four million men, women, and children on New Year's Day 1863. Yet here he was, in the small hours of the morning, second-guessing himself.

It was a long-standing custom in Washington, D.C., for the president to hold an open house on New Year's Day. Anyone was welcome to enter the White House, shake the president's hand, and receive his best wishes for a happy new year. Noah Brooks, a reporter for the *Sacramento Union* and a friend of Lincoln's, described the scene. "[The] press was tremendous, and the jam most excessive; all persons, high or low, civil, uncivil, or otherwise . . . were all forcing their way along the stately portico of the White House to the main entrance."

All morning the president greeted his fellow Americans. Then he excused himself and went to his office. The final, formal version of the Emancipation Proclamation, prepared by the State Department, lay on his desk, but Lincoln couldn't sign it. After three hours of shaking hundreds of hands, his whole right arm trembled from the exertion. Describing the moment sometime later, Lincoln recalled, "I paused, and a superstitious feeling came over me which made me hesitate." But the feeling passed, and once he felt the strength return to his hand, he sat down before the proclamation, took a pen, and slowly signed his full name. Looking up at Secretary of State William Seward, Massachusetts Senator Charles Sumner, and the other distinguished gentlemen invited to witness the signing, Lincoln smiled and said, "That will do." Then turning to Seward and Seward's son, Frederick, the president said, "I never, in my life, felt more certain that I was doing right, than I do signing this paper."

FREEDOM IS COMING

White Americans debated from the Civil War's outset whether it was being fought to preserve the Union, maintain states' rights, or abolish slavery, but these arguments made no impact on the slaves themselves. They were convinced that a Union victory meant their freedom. Wherever Union troops appeared, crowds of jubilant slaves came out to greet them. A federal artilleryman recalled his experiences in rural Louisiana:

"Women dropped on their knees, seized with spasmodic religion, while men would pray and sing irrespective of what others were doing . . . crying excitedly, 'Glory Hallelujah! Massa Linkim's comin'.'"

Not all the slaves restricted themselves to celebrating the arrival of the bluecoats—some collected their children and belongings and ran off to the safety of Yankee encampments. One of the first was an unnamed young black man who shortly before midnight on March 11, 1861, appeared in a canoe beside the wharf of Fort Sumter, the Union outpost in the middle of the harbor of Charleston, South Carolina. The war had not started yet, but South Carolina and six other states had seceded from the Union. The young runaway had been told that the soldiers in the island fort wanted to free the slaves; he had come to claim his freedom and place himself under the garrison's protection.

The runaways became known as *contraband*, a legal term that, under the international laws of war, entitled an army to confiscate property the enemy was using to conduct war. Brigadier General Benjamin Franklin Butler of Massachusetts argued that because slaveholders insisted that their slaves were not people but property, and because slaveholders used their "property" to advance the Confederate war effort, then any runaways who reached Butler's camp would be welcome. From Butler's perspective, every slave who ran away struck a blow against the Confederacy and for the Union. It was a devilishly clever argument that made Southerners near apoplectic.

But it also presented the Union army with the problem of how to feed, house, and clothe the contraband who fled to the Union lines by the thousands (by the end of the war in 1865, more than 11,000 runaway slaves had passed through the contraband camps

"FIRST READING OF THE EMANCIPATION PROCLAMATION OF PRESIDENT LINCOLN," AN OIL PAINTING BY FRANCIS BICKNELL CARPENTER IN 1864, DEPICTS LINCOLN AND HIS CABINET ON THAT MOMENTOUS OCCASION. CARPENTER SET UP A STUDIO IN THE STATE DINING ROOM AT THE WHITE HOUSE AND TOOK SIX MONTHS TO COMPLETE THE 9 X 15 FOOT (2.7 X 4.6 M) PAINTING, WHICH NOW SITS IN THE SENATE WING OF THE U.S. CAPITOL.

U.S. Senate Collection

in Washington D.C.). Yet in spite of the uncertainties of how they would live away from their masters, the runaways kept coming. After 250 years of slavery in America, freedom was coming, and the slaves were certain the soldiers in blue were bringing it.

STUDYING HIS OPTIONS

The Republican-controlled Congress was also inching toward the notion that the war was as much about freeing the slaves as preserving the Union. In March 1862, Congress passed a bill that prohibited the army from returning runaway slaves to their masters in Missouri and the other border states of Delaware, Maryland, and Kentucky—states where slavery was legal but where the state legislatures had not voted to secede from the Union. A month later Congress abolished slavery in the District of Columbia. Two months after that, in June, Congress outlawed slavery in the western territories of the United States.

Writing in his diary of this flurry of antislavery legislation, New York socialite George Templeton Strong observed, "Only the damnedest of 'damned abolitionists' *dreamed* of such [things] a year ago. John Brown's soul is marching on, with the people after it."

While abolitionists cheered Congress's boldness, Lincoln appeared to be cool on the subject of emancipation. The influential New York newspaper editor Horace Greeley published an open letter pleading with the president to recognize that "slavery is everywhere the inciting cause and sustaining base of treason." Lincoln replied, "My paramount object in this struggle *is* to save the Union and is *not* either to save or to destroy slavery. If I could save the Union without freeing *any* slave, I would do it; if I could save it by freeing *all* the slaves, I would do it; and if I could save it by freeing some and leaving others alone, I would do that."

In the meantime, the president was also considering other options. For example, he floated the idea of compensating slave owners by paying them $500 for each slave. These freed slaves would then be shipped to colonies in Africa or Central America. During the summer of 1862, Lincoln invited a group of black leaders to the White House to discuss the possibility of colonization. The idea was not Lincoln's—it had originated in 1816 when a wealthy freedman named Paul Cuffee transported thirty-eight free African Americans to Sierra Leone in Africa to start a colony. Cuffee's work was continued by the American Colonization Society, a Protestant philanthropic organization that had the support of such prominent men as Bushrod Washington (George Washington's nephew), Henry Clay, Daniel Webster, Andrew Jackson, and Richard Bland Lee and Edmund Lee (both uncles of Robert E. Lee).

"Your race suffers very greatly, many of them, by living among us," Lincoln told the African American delegation. "There is an unwillingness on the part of our people, harsh as it may be, for you free people of color to remain among us." Then Lincoln revealed his plan to purchase territory in Honduras or Nicaragua as a new home for free blacks as well as the slaves who would be free once the Confederacy had been defeated. The delegates rejected Lincoln's resettlement plan. "This is our country as much as yours," one delegate said to the president, "and we will not leave it." When Frederick Douglass, the foremost spokesman of black Americans, heard of Lincoln's plan he charged the president with "contempt for negroes."

Along with compensating slaveholders and sending African Americans to colonies overseas, emancipation of all slaves in the Confederacy was also on the table. Lincoln believed such an act would win the United States support from abroad, especially Great Britain, which, in spite of being openly antislavery, was being courted by agents of the Confederacy to enter the war on the side of the South. In addition to winning international approval, Lincoln believed that emancipation would hamstring the Confederate economy—slaves were the primary labor force of the South, particularly in agriculture. If the slaves ran off, plantation families would scarcely be able to produce enough food to feed themselves, let alone the Confederate army.

In fact, months before Lincoln invited black leaders to the White House to discuss colonization, he worked on a draft of a presidential proclamation to free the slaves. On May 28, 1862, Secretary of War Edwin Stanton informed Senator Charles Sumner of

A GROUP OF SLAVES WAVE COPIES OF THE EMANCIPATION PROCLAMATION, ALSO PINNED TO THE SIDES OF THE COACH. SLAVERY, HOWEVER, DID NOT DISAPPEAR WITH THE PROCLAMATION. THIS ILLUSTRATION APPEARED IN THE FRENCH NEWSMAGAZINE *LE MONDE ILLUSTRÉ* IN 1863.

Getty Images

Massachusetts that the president was working on such a document, and that it would be published "within two months." Although word of the proclamation was leaked to the press and Congress, Lincoln delayed publishing it. Since the war began in April 1861, the South had scored victory after victory against the Union troops; Lincoln wanted to release the proclamation only after the army had won a significant battle against the Confederates.

"FOREVER FREE"

The moment the president had been waiting for came in September 1862 in the farm country outside the town of Sharpsburg, Maryland. Confederate General Robert E. Lee led approximately 55,000 men into Maryland, the first stage of a full-scale invasion that would bring the war into the North. He was met by approximately 90,000 Union troops under the command of General George McClellan. For twelve hours on September 17, 1862, the two armies hurled themselves against each other, fighting along Antietam Creek, beside the little white clapboard Dunkers Church, and up and down a sunken dirt track that became known afterward as Bloody Lane. At the battle's end, about 5:30 p.m., some 23,000 Americans were killed, wounded, captured, or missing. It was the bloodiest day of battle in American history. Never before or since had the nation lost so many fighting men in a single day.

McClellan had turned back Lee's invasion of the North. Although he had thousands of fresh troops, McClellan did not pursue and destroy Lee's retreating army, in spite of a telegram from the president ordering him to "destroy the rebel army if possible."

Although McClellan ignored the order and let Lee get away, Lincoln still had the victory he had been longing for. On September 22, five days after the Battle of Antietam, he published his Emancipation Proclamation and declared that on January 1, 1863, "all persons held as slaves within any State, or designated part of a State, the people whereof shall then be in rebellion against the United States shall be then, thenceforward, and forever free."

Yet Lincoln's proclamation did not apply to all slaves, only to those in the Confederacy. The slaves in the border states remained unemancipated—and there were two reasons for this. First, the sudden emancipation of their slaves would almost certainly cause the slave owners of Delaware, Maryland, Kentucky, and Missouri to rebel against the Union, and thereby strengthen and reinforce the Confederacy. Second, as historian Allen C. Guelzo has pointed out, because the border states had not "removed themselves from the civil jurisdiction of the United States," i.e., because they were not in rebellion, the president could not invoke his war powers to free the slaves in those states. If he attempted it, the Supreme Court would declare his actions illegal and unconstitutional.

Enemies of slavery were disappointed, nonetheless. The editor of the *Spectator* in London criticized Lincoln's argument, saying, "The principle asserted [in the Emancipation Proclamation] is not that a human being cannot justly own another, but that he cannot own him unless he is loyal to the United States."

MIXED REVIEWS

Although the Emancipation Proclamation did not abolish slavery completely in the United States, it did ring the death knell of the institution. Throughout the North there were public celebrations and rallies. Lincoln biographer David Herbert Donald writes of "bonfires, parades with torches and transparencies, and, inevitably, fountains of oratory." The president's office was flooded with letters of congratulations from ordinary citizens. One correspondent assured Lincoln, "All good men upon the earth will glorify you, and all the angels in Heaven will hold jubilee."

Ralph Waldo Emerson, who had thought Lincoln too cool on the subject of abolition, now praised him as the president who had "been permitted to do more for America than any other American man."

Senator Thaddeus Stevens, a fire-eating abolitionist from Pennsylvania, had excoriated Lincoln for his slowness to move against slavery. Now he expressed the

"CONTRABANDS," OR RUNAWAY SLAVES, ARE PICTURED AT FOLLER'S FARM IN CUMBERLAND LANDING, VIRGINIA, IN 1864. SLAVE OWNERS TOOK "VICIOUS REPRISALS," ACCORDING TO ONE HISTORIAN, AGAINST THE FAMILIES OF RUNAWAYS, ESPECIALLY RUNAWAYS WHO JOINED THE UNION ARMY.
The Art Archive

bitter hope that the proclamation would incite the slaves "to insurrection and give the rebels a taste of real civil war."

A friend encountered Horace Greeley on the streets of New York and was delighted to see the editor "beaming with exultation" over the news. Military governors representing a dozen states traveled en masse to Washington to congratulate Lincoln.

But the reaction in the North was not uniformly favorable. Some Union troops—officers and enlisted men—resented that the object of the war had shifted from restoring the Union to restoring the Union *and* emancipating the slaves. And of course the Democratic newspapers in the North savaged Lincoln for his proclamation. In Illinois—the president's home state—the *Macomb Eagle* sneered, "Hoop de-dooden-do! The niggers are free!"

Reaction to the proclamation in the South was predictable, with Confederate President Jefferson Davis summing up the feelings of his people when he denounced the document as "the most execrable measure recorded in the history of guilty man."

Thomas A.R. Nelson, one of the foremost opponents of secession in eastern Tennessee, denounced "the atrocity and barbarism of Mr. Lincoln's proclamation."

"MY WORD IS OUT TO THESE PEOPLE"

The congressional elections of 1862 came just a few short weeks later, giving Lincoln a clearer measure of the Northern public's reaction to the Emancipation Proclamation. The Democrats in the North used the proclamation to play upon one of the primary fears of the laboring class—that the four million newly freed slaves would compete with them for jobs. Since an African American at that time would work for less than a white man, woman, or child, employers might be tempted to dismiss their white employees and replace them with an all-black workforce. The editor of *The Crisis*, a Democratic newspaper in Columbus, Ohio, warned its readers that if the Republicans returned to Congress, then Ohio working people would "have to leave Ohio and labor where niggers could not come." (Wherever that might be.)

The *Cincinnati Enquirer*, another Democratic newspaper, warned that if the laboring class did "not desire to see their place occupied by negroes," they had better vote the Democratic ticket.

William Allen, a former governor of Ohio, delivered a speech in Chillicothe in which he imagined hundreds of thousands of emancipated slaves slaughtering their former masters and mistresses, then, "with their hands reeking with the blood of murdered women and children," crossing the Ohio River and swamping the North's

BY THE END OF THE CIVIL WAR, 185,000 BLACK MEN HAD ENLISTED IN THE UNION ARMY. THE 54TH REGIMENT OF MASSACHUSETTS VOLUNTEERS, WHICH LOST HALF OF ITS MEN AND TWO-THIRDS OF OF ITS OFFICERS WHILE FIGHTING MOST FAMOUSLY AT FORT WAGNER, SOUTH CAROLINA, IS DEPICTED IN THIS NINETEENTH CENTURY COLOR LITHOGRAPH.

American School/Getty Images

labor market. So there could be no confusion about where it stood, the Democratic Party adopted as its 1862 campaign slogan, "The Constitution as it is, the Union as it was, and the negroes where they are."

The newspapers of Lincoln's own Republican Party, such as Greeley's *New York Tribune*, lamented "that cruel and ungenerous prejudice against color which still remains to disgrace our civilization and to impeach our Christianity." But such protestations did no good. In Ohio the Democrats won fourteen seats in the House of Representatives; the Republicans won three. In Indiana, the Democrats took seven seats; the Republicans, four. In Pennsylvania, which had gone strongly for Lincoln in 1860, giving him a 60,000-vote majority, the Democrats captured thirteen seats; the Republicans, eleven.

In New York the Democrats took seventeen seats; the Republicans, fourteen. New Yorkers also voted in a new Democratic governor. Across the Hudson River, voters in New Jersey elected a Democratic governor and gave four of its five seats in the House to Democrats.

In total, the Republicans lost thirty-one congressional seats in the election of 1862. They still had a majority in the House (101–77), but after this electoral disaster, would the Republican members jeopardize their seats in the next election by supporting Lincoln's Emancipation Proclamation?

Republican Senator William P. Fessenden of Maine blamed the debacle on "the folly of the president." Supreme Court Justice David Davis, an old friend of Lincoln's from his days of riding the circuit in Illinois, conceded that the Emancipation Proclamation "[had] not worked the wonder that was anticipated."

Lincoln suspected, correctly, that the election was also a referendum on how he, Seward, and Stanton had conducted the war thus far. He confessed to Massachusetts Senator Henry Wilson, "This intelligence will go to Europe; it will be construed as a condemnation of the war; it will go into the land of the rebellion, and will encourage the leading rebels and nerve the arms of the rebel soldiers fighting our men in the field."

When some of the president's political advisors suggested that he withdraw the proclamation, Lincoln, referring to the slaves, replied, "My word is out to these people, and I can't take it back." And as January 1, 1863, drew closer, Lincoln was more firmly settled in his resolve to sign the Emancipation Proclamation, despite opposing public opinion. In mid-December a group of senators and representatives from the border states tried to persuade Lincoln not to sign the proclamation. He rejected their proposal, saying, according to the December 20, 1862 *New York Times*, that he "considered slavery to be the right arm of the rebellion, and . . . it must be lopped off."

"HIS PEOPLE ARE FREE"

During the final hours of December 31, 1862, hundreds of men and women, black and white, crowded into Boston's Music Hall to await the stroke of midnight. They had not come to ring in the New Year, but to celebrate together the end of slavery in America. When the moment came and clock towers across the city began to toll twelve, a great outpouring of emotion swept over the hall. On the stage the runaway slave Frederick Douglass burst into tears. The Reverend Charles Bennet Ray, a black minister, stood and sang the hymn,

> Sound the loud timbrel o'er Egypt's dark sea,
> Jehovah hath triumphed, His people are free!

Suddenly the crowd began calling for Harriet Beecher Stowe, author of the blockbuster novel *Uncle Tom's Cabin*. As she rose from her seat in the gallery, her eyes brimming with happy tears, the crowd roared with cheers and applause.

At Camp Saxton in South Carolina, a similar celebration was being held by the 1st South Carolina Volunteers, one of the Union's new all-black regiments. After the chaplain finished reading the Emancipation Proclamation aloud to the troops, corps commander Thomas Wentworth Higginson stepped forward, but before he could deliver his speech the troops burst into "My Country 'Tis of Thee."

Yet for all the euphoria in the first hours of New Year's Day 1863, slavery did not vanish the moment Lincoln signed the Emancipation Proclamation. Historian Barbara J. Fields cites heartrending examples of slave owners who, after the proclamation had been issued, took "vicious reprisals" against the families of runaways, especially runaways who joined the Union army. In the border states, where the proclamation did not apply, irate masters and mistresses demanded that Union soldiers turn slave catcher and hunt down runaways (in most instances, the troops and their officers ignored these demands). There was even a horrible episode when government officials in the border state of Kentucky rounded up runaways from two slave states, Tennessee and Alabama, and sold them back into slavery.

Lincoln's Emancipation Proclamation was an imperfect document, but ultimately it would lead to what no other American document ever had—the end of slavery in America. The slaves knew it, and so did the men and women who called themselves their masters.

THE PROCLAMATION AND THE AMENDMENTS

Formally, the end of slavery came on December 18, 1865, with the ratification of the Thirteenth Amendment that abolished slavery throughout the United States. This was followed by the Fourteenth Amendment, which guaranteed "the equal protection of the laws" to "all persons born or naturalized in the United States," and the Fifteenth Amendment, which declared, "The right of citizens of the United States to vote shall not be denied or abridged by the United States or by any State on account of race, color, or previous condition of servitude."

Of course, in some parts of the United States it required the civil rights movement of the 1950s and 1960s to overturn local statutes and institutions that denied equal protection and the right to vote to African Americans. Nonetheless, these three amendments were very radical—they extended all the rights and protections of American citizenship to four million individuals who only a few years earlier had not been considered fully human. The Emancipation Proclamation made those amendments possible.

The Emancipation Proclamation still has its critics, and probably always will. Yet Lincoln took a bold step when he issued it. His proclamation was the first mortal blow against slavery. Its natural outcome was to recognize African Americans as full citizens of the United States. And it led to an event Lincoln probably never imagined—the election of an African American as president of the United States in 2008.

CHAPTER 7

RUTHERFORD HAYES ENDS RECONSTRUCTION BY WITHDRAWING FEDERAL TROOPS FROM THE SOUTH

1877

O N DECEMBER 2, 1874, FIVE HUNDRED WHITE MEN ARMED WITH WINCHESTER rifles surrounded the county courthouse of Vicksburg, Mississippi. A delegation entered the building, forced Sheriff Peter Crosby—a black man and a Republican—out of his office, and ordered him to leave town. If he stayed, they promised to kill him. The frightened man fled, and the mob installed a white Democrat as sheriff.

Crosby appealed to the governor of Mississippi, Adelbert Ames, who assured him his resignation was void because it had been exacted at gunpoint. Ames authorized Crosby to collect armed men to escort him back to Vicksburg and return him to office; the governor also issued a declaration ordering the white mob in Vicksburg to disperse. Meanwhile, a handbill Crosby had printed was distributed among the black churches of Warren County on Sunday morning, December 6.

"Citizens," proclaimed the handbill, "shall we submit to violent and lawless infringements on our rights? No; let us with united strength oppose this common enemy, who, by all the base subterfuges known to political tricksters, and the audacious mendacity of heartless barbarians, are trying to ruin the prospects and tarnish the reputation of every republican, colored or white, who aspires to fill any office of prominence, and who are daily defying the constituted powers of the law, and insulting those charged with its administration. *Fiat justicia ruat coelum!* [Let justice be done 'though the heavens fall.]"

Preachers read out the handbill, then urged their congregations to arm themselves and march with Crosby to Vicksburg.

THE SHOOT-OUT

On Monday, December 7, 1874, a little after noon, the sentinel in the cupola of the Vicksburg courthouse gave the alarm that a party of armed black men was approaching the town. The mayor had declared martial law and placed the defense of Vicksburg in the hands of an ex-Confederate soldier, Colonel Horace Miller, who assembled one hundred armed white men and rode out to meet Crosby and his supporters. The account of what happened next is confused. The white Vicksburg version tells how Crosby had four hundred heavily armed black men with him, led by a white Union veteran, Andrew Owen, who had sworn that Vicksburg would be "given over to plunder and the flames, and the women become the prey of the infuriated passions of the invading Negroes."

The black version says that Crosby had about one hundred and twenty-five men with him whose sole intention was to protect him as he reclaimed his office. They had not come to Vicksburg to rape the white women and burn the city.

The two groups met at a bridge that spanned a deep ravine on the outskirts of town. Miller called for a parley with Owen, which concluded with Owen agreeing to disband his men. "Boys, go back peaceable and quiet," he is supposed to have told them. Suddenly, one of the white men from Vicksburg opened fire. As other white men began to fire on the black men, Owen dove into a ditch. He survived the gunfight, but seven of Sheriff Crosby's supporters were killed at the bridge.

About the same time a gunfight erupted in the streets of Vicksburg, as gangs of white men rode to black settlements and shot unarmed black men. Ultimately, two white men and twenty-nine blacks were killed in what has come to be known as the Vicksburg Riots. But the incident was not over yet: On January 19, 1875, surrounded by a company of Union troops, Peter Crosby returned to his office in the Vicksburg courthouse.

"WE DO NOT KNOW WHAT TO DO"

From its inception, Reconstruction had created dissension and resentment that often erupted into violence. In April 1866 both houses of Congress passed the Civil Rights Act, which guaranteed that all adult male citizens of the United States would enjoy the same rights "without distinction of race or color, or previous condition of slavery or involuntary servitude." President Andrew Johnson had vetoed the bill, but Congress voted to override it—the first time in U.S. history that the House and Senate overturned a presidential veto.

Within days, white mobs rampaged across the former Confederacy, attacking blacks and white Republicans. In Memphis, Tennessee, anti–civil rights riots took the lives of as many as forty-eight people and left hundreds of black homes, schools, and churches in ruins. In New Orleans, a white mob attacked a meeting of black and white Republicans, killing approximately forty.

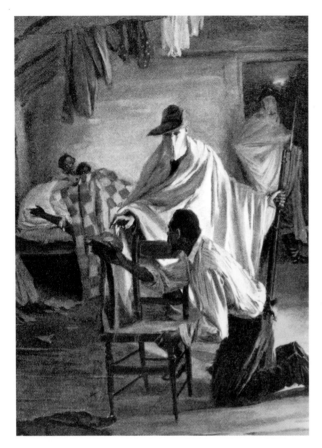

KU KLUX KLAN MEMBERS WRAPPED IN SHEETS RAID THE HOME OF A BLACK FAMILY IN THE 1800S IN THIS HAND-COLORED HALFTONE OF A NINETEENTH-CENTURY ILLUSTRATION. ONE NORTH CAROLINA JUDGE KEPT A TALLY SHEET OF THE ATTACKS ON BLACK CITIZENS AT THIS TIME: TWELVE MURDERS, NINE RAPES, FOURTEEN CASES OF ARSON, AND MORE THAN SEVEN HUNDRED BEATINGS—INCLUDING A 103-YEAR-OLD WOMAN.

© North Wind Picture Archives / Alamy

White supremacist organizations such as the Ku Klux Klan targeted "impudent negroes." They beat a former slave who had taken to court a white man who owed him money and would not pay the debt. In Florida, members of the Klan whipped an entire family of black farmers—including the children—for daring to farm their own land rather than sharecropping for a white landowner. In Georgia, Klansmen broke into the home of Abram Colby, a former slave who had been elected to the Georgia legislature. They dragged Colby into the woods, where they stripped him naked, beat him with sticks and leather belts, and then left him there to die.

Such outrages were commonplace across the South. A judge in the Piedmont region of North Carolina kept a tally sheet of attacks on black citizens: twelve murders, nine rapes, fourteen cases of arson, and more than seven hundred beatings—among those beaten was a woman 103 years old.

In 1868 W.A. Patterson, a freedman, wrote to North Carolina Governor William W. Holden, "The ku kluks klan [sic] is shooting our familys [sic] and beating them notoriously. We do not know what to do." Governors like Holden did not know what to do either. He had no local militia he could send out to arrest the malefactors because no white Southerner would fight for a Republican state governor, let alone the federal government. Black men would enlist, but there was the double fear that they would fare badly going up against the battle-hardened Confederate veterans who comprised the Klan, or that an all-black militia attempting to arrest white men would set off an all-out race war.

Race hatred was not the sole motivation of Southerners who attacked the former slaves. By the end of the Civil War in April 1865, the economy of the former Confederacy was in free fall. Historian John Hope Franklin described what Confederate veterans found when they returned home: "Fields were laid waste, cities burned, bridges and roads destroyed. Even most of the woefully inadequate factories were leveled, as if to underscore the unchallenged industrial superiority of the North. And if Union forces did not loot quite as many smokehouses and pantries as they were blamed for, what they did do emphasized the helplessness of the once proud Confederates."

For families that had known nothing but comfort for generations it was intensely bitter to see their former slaves begin to take the first steps toward prosperity while many white Southerners were on the verge of starvation. The newly liberated African Americans became the scapegoat of the newly defeated Confederates.

THE BETRAYAL

By 1876 many Northerners were sick of Reconstruction; after eleven years they had come to regard the program as a debacle marked by martial law, political scheming and corruption, and a bloody race war. Republican leaders in the North, hoping to win back at least some Southerners to the party, urged their presidential candidate, Rutherford B. Hayes, to show kindness and consideration to the South, end political and military support for the despised carpetbaggers, and reduce the political power of the freedmen.

Such policies, they believed, would attract intelligent, well-to-do Southern gentry back to the Republican Party. In a conversation with a New Orleans newspaper editor Hayes declared, "I believe, and I have always believed, that the intelligence of any country ought to govern it." It was a bland enough statement, but within the context of Reconstruction it can be read as returning the government of the South to the wealthy, well-educated, white Southern upper class and abandoning the principle that African Americans have a constitutional right to vote that the federal government must defend.

In February 1877, just a few days before Hayes's inauguration (until 1937, presidents were inaugurated in March rather than January), four Democrats from the South met with five Republicans from Ohio, Hayes's home state, in a Washington hotel. The details of the discussion have not come down to us, but Hayes's political confidant Stanley Matthews reported that the Ohioans assured the Southerners that, as president, Hayes would let Southerners manage their own affairs, without interference from federal troops.

At this time there were still Union garrisons in South Carolina and Louisiana, most of them posted to the grounds of the state capitol buildings, where they protected black and white Republican government officials from angry white Democrats. True to the promises made in his name in that Washington hotel room, one of Hayes's first acts as president was to order these federal troops to vacate their posts around the state capitol buildings and remain in their barracks. Black men such as Henry Adams of Louisiana viewed Hayes's actions as betrayal.

ONE OF RUTHERFORD HAYES'S FIRST ACTS AS PRESIDENT WAS TO REMOVE FEDERAL TROOPS FROM THE CAPITOLS OF SOUTH CAROLINA AND LOUISIANA. MANY AFRICAN-AMERICANS AND ABOLITIONISTS VIEWED THIS ACTION AS A BETRAYAL. HAYES IS PICTURED HERE IN A NINETEENTH-CENTURY LITHOGRAPH.

Mary Evans Picture Library/Alamy

"The whole South, every state in the South," he lamented, "had got into the hands of the very men that held us as slaves." Meanwhile, *The Nation* magazine assured its readers, "The Negro will disappear from the field of national politics. Henceforth, the nation, as a nation, will have nothing more to do with him."

As long as Southern state and local governments were in the hands of Republicans—most of them from the North—and as long as federal troops were in place to enforce the Fourteenth and Fifteenth Amendments to the U.S. Constitution, the newly liberated blacks could exercise their civil rights. There were many incidents of white-on-black violence, of course, yet under the protection of the federal government African Americans could vote, be elected to office, own property, start businesses, get an education, and send their children to schools. If the federal government put a halt to Reconstruction, all those achievements and all those rights were likely to vanish.

At the same time that President Hayes was preparing to put an end to Reconstruction, a political movement known as the Redeemers sprang up in the South. Their members included Confederate veterans and plantation aristocrats, as well as a new generation of politicians, who advocated for modernizing the South by introducing more industry, more schools, and improved farming methods. Although their economic ideas were progressive, the Redeemers' political goals were predictable: White men were to take control of their states, the political power of black men was to be curtailed, and new laws were to be adopted to marginalize African Americans.

A SERVANT OF THE PEOPLE

Rutherford Birchard Hayes was born in Ohio in 1822. His father died ten weeks before he was born, so his mother's brother, Sardis Birchard, moved in and became the boy's guardian. They developed a close relationship, more like father and son than uncle and nephew.

After completing his studies at Kenyon College and Harvard Law School, Hayes opened a law practice, first in what is now Fremont, Ohio, and then in Cincinnati. In 1852 he married Lucy Ware Webb; together they had eight children, five of whom survived to adulthood. Lucy was fervently opposed to slavery and an early supporter of the new Republican Party; persuaded by his wife, Hayes left the Whigs and joined the Republicans.

With the start of the Civil War in 1861, Hayes volunteered and was commissioned as a major in the Twenty-Third Ohio Regiment. He was wounded four times during the war and by 1865 was brevetted a major general. During the final year of the war, while he was still in the army, Ohio Republicans urged Hayes to run for the House of Representatives. Hayes agreed, but refused to request leave to campaign. "An officer fit for duty who at this crisis would abandon his post to electioneer," he said, "ought to be scalped."

Hayes won and took his seat in the House in December 1865, but he stayed only one term, returning to Ohio where he served as governor from 1867 to 1876. During his years in office his fellow Ohioans respected Hayes as a dedicated, hardworking, honest servant of the people. He was also a strict teetotaler and devout Presbyterian who gathered his family together every morning for prayers; often the Hayes family spent the evening singing hymns.

After the scandal-ridden administration of Ulysses S. Grant, Hayes was just the candidate the Republicans wanted. The Democrats, who had not won a presidential race since 1857 when James Buchanan had been elected, were desperate to get back into the White House. They nominated Samuel Tilden of New York, a crime-busting district attorney who smashed the corrupt Tammany Hall political machine and sent its chief, Boss Tweed, to prison.

On Election Night, 1876, it appeared that Tilden had won. Then, before dawn, one of the most astonishing periods of political chicanery in American history began as Republicans and Democrats in the swing states of Florida, Louisiana, and South Carolina threw out each others' ballots to gain the winning number of votes in the Electoral College. The contest dragged on from November 8, 1876, until March 2, 1877. Ultimately, after numerous recounts of the electoral votes and endless charges and countercharges of corruption, Hayes "won," with 185 electoral votes to Tilden's 184.

SOLIDLY DEMOCRATIC

During the two years he served in Congress, Hayes had supported the Reconstruction policies of the Radical Republicans. But by the 1870s, like so many of his fellow Northerners, he was disillusioned with the process. Rather than try to enforce the law and defend the civil rights of black Southerners, Hayes was ready to make friendly overtures to Southern whites. He believed, or at least he said he believed, that he could be conciliatory without compromising the rights of Southern blacks.

Other Northerners were more candid, saying that their friends in the South were correct: The black man was not ready for full citizenship in the United States.

By 1877 there were not many troops left in the South—only 3,280, most of whom garrisoned coastal defenses or guarded revenue offices. A few were stationed on the

grounds of the state capitol buildings in South Carolina and Louisiana to safeguard the Republican carpetbagger governments there—these were the troops President Hayes ordered back to their barracks. In the months that followed, these troops were sent out West to fight the Indians.

By focusing on economic issues rather than such divisive issues as enforcing the civil rights of blacks and rehashing the old tensions between North and South, Hayes imagined he could build a coalition of Northern and Southern Republicans. The president was so convinced of his plan that he dreamed of Republican governors, elected in free and open elections, recapturing North Carolina, Maryland, Tennessee, Arkansas, and perhaps even Robert E. Lee's home state of Virginia. He even convinced himself that such dramatic changes in policy would not cost the Republican Party the support of black Southerners—although what good their support would do if they could not vote was a question Hayes apparently did not contemplate.

During a tour of the South, one Southern Democratic leader after another assured Hayes that he would respect the political and civil rights of African American citizens. And Hayes believed them. When black Southerners complained that Hayes was deserting them, leaving them at the mercy of people who once owned them, he was genuinely confused and wounded. Hayes was not a fool, but a well-intentioned man who could be naïve about men whose intentions were less than pure.

The election of 1878 crushed Hayes's hopes. The South did not elect any Republican governors and sent only three Republicans to Congress. In 1880, when James A. Garfield ran for president (Hayes had decided not to seek a second term), not a single state of the old Confederacy went to the Republicans.

Hayes's attempt to attract Southerners back to the Republican Party by ending Reconstruction came to nothing. The South remained solidly Democratic. The Republican presidents who followed him—James Garfield, Chester Arthur, Benjamin Harrison, Theodore Roosevelt, William Howard Taft, Herbert Hoover, and Dwight Eisenhower—all tried to resurrect the Republican Party in the former Confederacy, and they all failed.

A MAN OF GOODWILL

Rutherford B. Hayes's decision to end Reconstruction was well intentioned and even in some respects made good sense. The Republican carpetbag governments in the South were a scandal. It took the Union army to enforce the law and protect African Americans in the South, which raised the question, how long must the army occupy the former Confederacy? In addition to these dilemmas, Hayes felt the pressure of a Northern public that was tired of Reconstruction. Furthermore, with Indian wars erupting all across the West, the government needed its troops in the Dakota and Arizona territories, not in South Carolina or Louisiana. And so Hayes put an end to Reconstruction and put his faith in the Southern politicians.

When those same white Southern Democrats barred black men from the polls, Hayes was outraged. "By state legislation, by frauds, by intimidation, and by violence of the most atrocious character," he said, "colored citizens have been deprived of the right of suffrage—a right guaranteed by the Constitution, and to the protection of which the people of those states have been solemnly pledged." Hayes could scarcely believe that the Southern Democrats had lied to him.

Rutherford B. Hayes was a man who believed in harmony, in reconciliation. He abhorred military force, coercive legislation, and a heavy-handed federal government. Sadly, he lived in an era when antagonisms—sectional, racial, political—were bitter and often turned bloody, and when dispassionate reason was in short supply. Being a man of goodwill himself, he was disposed to trust in the goodwill of others. He must

have been disappointed many times during his life, but he found the treachery of the Southern Democrats especially bitter.

Agriculture had always dominated the Southern economy, and by 1880 it had revived, with a new plantation aristocracy. These planters no longer owned slaves, of course, but the new system of sharecropping kept the African American tenant farmers in debt and poverty, bound to the land. New industries opened in the post–Civil War South, but few would accept black workers. African Americans were consigned almost en masse to work as field hands or unskilled menial laborers. To escape such conditions, in 1879 and again in 1881, about 60,000 African Americans left the South and settled in Kansas and the Indian Territory (modern-day Oklahoma).

The first decades of the twentieth century witnessed the great migration, when thousands of blacks left the South to escape lynch mobs and a new wave of white-on-black violence that erupted after the revival of the Ku Klux Klan in 1915. In the great industrial cities of the North, such as Chicago and Detroit, they hoped to find better wages, better housing, and political freedom. By 1950 the African American community had changed from a population that was largely Southern and rural to one that was predominantly Northern and urban. In most places in the North, the migrants still encountered segregation and discrimination, but in most instances at least they could vote. Nonetheless, segregation, discrimination in public places, and laws that barred blacks from exercising their civil rights were not outlawed until 1964, when President Lyndon B. Johnson signed into law the Civil Rights Act of 1964—ninety-eight years after Congress passed the first Civil Rights Act (see chapter 26).

THE FATE THAT AWAITS THIS AFRICAN-AMERICAN MAN SHOULD THE U.S. GOVERNMENT REMOVE FEDERAL TROOPS FROM THE SOUTH IS EVIDENT IN THIS IMAGE FROM THE *BIRMINGHAM* (ALABAMA) *NEWS* IN 1875. WITHOUT THE PROTECTION OF FEDERAL TROOPS, MANY BLACKS FACED VIOLENCE AND THE LOSS OF THE RIGHT TO VOTE, OWN PROPERTY, AND GO TO SCHOOL.

Library of Congress

CHAPTER 8

CHESTER A. ARTHUR:
THE "SPOILSMAN" WHO REFORMED
THE GOVERNMENT

1883

CHESTER A. ARTHUR OWNED MORE THAN EIGHTY PAIRS OF TROUSERS AND sometimes fastidiously changed them six or seven times a day, setting off each pair with a carefully tailored frock coat. He cultivated glorious and much-admired mustaches and sideburns that swooped across his cheeks in rich parabolas from upper lip to earlobes. He stood an imposing six feet, two inches, and carried himself with great dignity and poise, speaking always in a measured, cultivated baritone.

Apart from his elegant appearance, however, in 1880 people found little to praise about Arthur. He was dismissed as a toadying tool of the arrogant Senator Roscoe Conkling and his powerful New York political machine; the cartoonist Thomas Nast caricatured him as Conkling's bootblack. He had been nominated for the vice presidency strictly as a sop to Conkling, in the hope that New York would thus vote Republican in the upcoming presidential election. Then an assassin's bullet cut short the life of President James A. Garfield and propelled Arthur into the presidency. And the man lampooned as a dressmaker's dummy turned his back on Conkling and engineered a governmental reform that struck machine politics at its very root. Instituting a merit system for often graft-riddled government jobs wrought lasting change that eventually transformed American government at every level.

"TO THE VICTOR BELONG THE SPOILS OF THE ENEMY"

That pithy slogan is attributed to Senator William Marcy of New York, who used it in a Senate speech defending President Andrew Jackson's personnel policies. Declaring that democracy flourished with regular turnover of government employees, Jackson in 1829 had dismissed jobholders left over from the outgoing Federalists and filled their places with loyal Jacksonian Democrats. The "we're in, they're out" system rewarding one's followers, relatives, and cronies quickly became a guiding principle in U.S. politics, known in deference to Marcy as the "spoils system."

Divvying up the spoils became the first order of business with each new face in the White House, and the system became entrenched in state and local government as well. By 1860, federal, state, and municipal governments employed 49,200 people, and by 1884, the number of federal employees alone had topped 131,000, chosen more for their political affiliation than any semblance of qualification or merit.

The spoils system put all those jobs up for grabs. Newly elected officials were besieged every four years by hordes lured by salaries and the possibilities for graft. Even Jackson, whose election set off the stampede, was dismayed afterward when 30,000–40,000 aspirants camped out on the White House lawn, clamoring for 21,000 job vacancies. President Lincoln eventually took to leaving the White House by a side door to avoid the crowd waiting in front. President James A. Garfield angrily compared the office seekers lurking day and night outside the White House to "hungry vultures watching a wounded bison."

Even when they were successful, job seekers soon learned there were strings attached. Politicians who had sponsored them for appointment expected a payback—in coin of the realm. Jobholder "donations" would both fatten leaders' pockets and keep the victors in power. "Voluntary contributions" were required from even the lowliest clerks. The new officeholders in turn compensated themselves by illegally adding unofficial "fees" to every transaction, tucking the "fees" into their own pockets. Under-the-table payments were condoned, almost encouraged. George Washington Plunkitt of New York City's notoriously corrupt Tammany Hall expressed the prevailing attitude best: "I seen my opportunities and took 'em."

Chester Alan Arthur—only relatives and intimate friends addressed the dignified Arthur as "Chet"—was himself scrupulously honest, people agreed. The son of a Baptist minister, he was also an elder and a prominent churchman. He earned a law degree and Phi Beta Kappa recognition at Union College in upstate New York. Like others of his generation, he was quickly caught up by the Civil War. Volunteering for the New York militia, he was spotted immediately for his organizing and administrative skills, and before long rose to become the state quartermaster general. In 1862 he was taken into federal service and became successively the Union army quartermaster general and then inspector general. When the war ended he wore the star of brigadier general.

Benefiting from the Lincoln legacy, New York Republicans postwar built a powerful political machine; Roscoe Conkling ruled it with an iron fist. "Boss"

Conkling was a trial lawyer, a magnetic curly haired redhead with a compelling voice and a wicked sense of humor that skewered courtroom opponents and political foes alike. A two-term congressman and chair of the Commerce Committee, Conkling was also a powerful figure in both New York and Washington. Setting up a law practice in Manhattan, Arthur aligned himself with the Republican Party and volunteered for organization duties. Conkling quickly saw the ambitious young lawyer as a hard worker with formidable organizing talent and a gift for persuading others. He soon became Conkling's chief lieutenant, known as "The Gentleman Boss" for his courtly manner and dress.

The year 1868 saw both the first presidential election after the Civil War and the impeachment of Lincoln's successor, Andrew Johnson. The Republicans nominated the war hero Ulysses S. Grant. Grant, a West Pointer who had fought in the Mexican War, had little experience in politics and less interest. He famously said of the election of 1856, in which he was recently discharged from the military and didn't cast a ballot, "I didn't vote for Buchanan [the eventual winner] because I didn't know him, and I didn't vote for Fremont [a fellow army officer] because I did." Grant easily won election, swamping the Democratic nominee, former New York governor Horatio Seymour, by 214 electoral votes to 80. Among Grant's most ardent supporters were Conkling and Arthur.

THE COUNTRY GROWS UP

The post-election years were termed "the Gilded Age," as the country industrialized rapidly; the completed transcontinental railroad connected East and West and opened vast areas of the West to new settlement; the defeated South tried to rebuild itself; and inventions like the telephone, transatlantic cable, and incandescent lightbulb revolutionized the country—and made entrepreneurs rich. Washington had a central role in all these innovations, along with the financial and currency markets in New York. Speculators, get-rich-quick types, and "robber barons" quickly lined up at the public trough to cash in. Scandals abounded, some reaching into the highest ranks of the Grant administration and even his family.

Grant's first vice president, Schuyler Colfax, was implicated in the multimillion-dollar Credit Mobilier scam. Credit Mobilier of America was selling shares in a dummy corporation supposedly to finance construction of the final 700 miles (1,126.5 km) of the transcontinental Union Pacific Railroad. When a congressional investigation into its tactics loomed, Colfax, then House Speaker, and other legislators were awarded stock to block it. Credit Mobilier was disclosed as a fraud, but not before Colfax and others had sold their shares and cashed in.

"Black Friday" struck even closer to the Grant household. Convinced that the government planned to buy back paper currency issued in the Civil War, exchanging it for gold, financiers Jay Gould and Jim Fisk sought to corner the gold market, driving the price up and enabling them to sell at a huge profit. They enlisted Grant's financier brother-in-law Abel Corbin to keep them posted on the administration's plans. Gold prices had nearly doubled when the Treasury recognized the danger and dumped $4 million in gold. The price dropped and the corner collapsed, wiping out gullible investors who had joined Gould and Fisk. The two, however, personally escaped.

Then there was the "Whisky Ring." The government had levied heavy taxes on spirits to repay war debts. A group of distillers bribed Treasury officials to issue tax stamps at a fraction of their value. The trail led to Orville Babcock, Grant's private secretary, who was indicted for bribery. Grant, who had previously pledged to fire anyone involved in scandal, protected Babcock, but one hundred others were eventually convicted.

The "Indian Ring" in the War Department extracted bribes from businessmen seeking permits to trade on Indian reservations. Secretary of War William Belknap was impeached by the House for his part in the scheme. The Senate acquitted him.

Grant personally was naïve, honest, staunchly loyal to his friends, and unable to suspect anyone of trickery or dishonesty. He was never accused, nor was he suspected of illegal

THIS IS NOT THE NEW YORK STOCK EXCHANGE, IT IS THE PATRONAGE EXCHANGE, CALLED U. S. SENATE.

THIS SATIRE, WHICH ORIGINALLY APPEARED IN *PUCK* IN 1881, DEPICTS THE PATRONAGE SYSTEM IN GOVERNMENT. PRESIDENT CHESTER ARTHUR INTRODUCED COMPETITIVE CIVIL SERVICE EXAMS AND OTHER REFORMS UNDER THE PENDLETON BILL. HE WAS DUBBED THE "FATHER OF CIVIL SERVICE" FOR HIS EFFORTS.

Library of Congress

behavior. But as corruption cascaded, infecting city and state governments, Grant and "Grantism" came to signify an atmosphere of governmental graft and political dishonesty.

THE WELL-PAID COLLECTOR

In 1871, as scandals proliferated, Conkling persuaded Grant to name his protégé Chester Arthur to the plum job of collector of customs of the Port of New York. The appointment made Arthur the third highest-paid official in the federal government. The collector's task was to levy fees, customs duties, and tariffs on all shipments into the nation's busiest port, which in 1872 totaled almost $149 million a year. He controlled a workforce of more than one thousand people, all chosen through the spoils system. Having all those jobs to hand out and all those wealthy importers doing business in the Customs House looked like a treasure trove for the Conkling machine. Such a job generator could cement the party in power for decades.

Like that of Grant, Arthur's personal conduct was considered above reproach. In politics he could be ruthless, but he was also a man to be trusted. Occasionally, the new collector would waive duties for friends and expedite their shipments. Republican contributors returning from Europe knew they could steer in expensive champagne duty-free. Arthur, however, fended off temptations to enrich himself illegally. But also like Grant, he was too trusting of his friends. He named three personal friends as deputy collectors. Two never reported for work but collected their salaries anyway. The third, Chief Deputy John Lydecker, ran the office while Arthur came in late and concerned himself with politics. Lydecker was subsequently charged with fraud and forced to resign.

And Arthur stuck resolutely to the spoils system, filling his staff with Conkling loyalists until they numbered twice as many as needed for the work performed. Under pressure he introduced written examinations for staff promotions. Employees considered them a joke. Asked to identify the three branches of the U.S. government, one Arthur-Conkling favorite aspiring for a higher job answered, "The army and the navy." The man received the promotion anyway. Arthur continued the practice of assessing employees 2 percent of their salaries (later raised to 4 percent) for political contributions. But he was popular with businessmen and importers and remained collector until forced out in 1878 by the new president, Rutherford B. Hayes.

Asked to identify the three branches of the U.S. government, one Arthur-Conkling favorite aspiring for a higher job answered, "The army and the navy." He was promoted anyway.

A backlash against "Grantism" began even before the president left office. Over vehement Republican opposition, Senator George Pendleton of Ohio introduced a bill establishing government-wide civil service—Conkling airily dismissed it as "snivel service"—and setting up a Civil Service Commission to conduct it. But Congress never funded the new agency, and it died in 1875. Reform was an issue in the 1876 presidential campaign but was largely overshadowed by Reconstruction.

In 1880, however, "Grantism" again came under attack. Grant had now been out of office for four years. Conkling and fellow "Stalwart" Republicans who resolutely followed the party line argued that the supposed taboo on three presidential terms applied to three *consecutive* terms. In their view, Grant had served eight years and could now start afresh. The "Half-Breed" Republicans supported the party but wanted new policies and new leaders. They backed Senator James G. Blaine; a third group supported Senator John Sherman. The three groups wrangled for thirty-five ballots

CHESTER ARTHUR ASCENDED TO THE OVAL OFFICE IN 1881 AFTER PRESIDENT JAMES GARFIELD WAS FELLED BY AN ASSASSIN'S BULLET. HIS CIVIL SERVICE REFORMS WERE EXPANDED TO ALL BUT A FEW GOVERNMENT POSITIONS, THOUGH HE DID NOT LIVE TO SEE THIS HAPPEN, DYING OF BRIGHT'S DISEASE A LITTLE MORE THAN THREE MONTHS AFTER LEAVING OFFICE. THE IMAGE WAS CREATED BY NEW YORK ARTIST DANIEL HUNTINGTON.

at the party convention before turning in exhaustion to the dark horse James A. Garfield, an Ohio congressman and former Civil War general.

Conkling was furious. He considered Garfield a weak candidate and a reformer. Besides, he foresaw certain defeat. The Democrats had chosen another victorious general, Winfield Scott Hancock. A difficult election loomed ahead. The country, like the party, was narrowly divided. Republican leaders knew that the powerful New York boss, whose state controlled the largest block of electoral votes, must be placated. They offered the vice-presidential nomination to another Stalwart favorite, Levi P. Morton. Morton dutifully trooped to Conkling for the Stalwarts' blessing. Conkling turned him down flat. The leaders then suggested Arthur as a second choice. He was not only a Stalwart but also Conkling's pet. They sent a delegation to call on him with the offer.

Arthur heard them out and went to Conkling, glowing. He had been in politics for twenty-five years and had never held elective office, nor had he even been considered for one. He told Conkling of the offer. "Well, sir, you should drop it as you would a red hot shoe from the forge," Conkling snorted.

"I sought you to consult, not . . ." Arthur began. Conkling, still smarting from the Grant defeat, cut him off. "What is there to consult about? That trickster from Mentor [Garfield] will be defeated before the country!"

Arthur began again. "There is something else to be said . . ."

"What, sir, you think of accepting?"

"The office of vice president is a greater honor than I have ever dreamed of attaining," Arthur responded.

"If you wish for my favor and respect, you will contemptuously decline it," Conkling shot back.

The longtime second banana defiantly drew himself up. "Senator Conkling," he said firmly, "I shall accept the nomination and I shall carry with me the majority of the delegation." Conkling glared at him and stalked off.

Conkling eventually calmed down and rallied support behind the Garfield-Arthur ticket, which squeaked to victory by only 8,355 votes. The two candidates never campaigned together, and Garfield kept a marked distance from his running mate, apparently fearing that association with a machine politician like Arthur would sully his Boy Scout reputation. (According to one historian, when Arthur called on Garfield after the convention, the presidential nominee refused to invite him into the house.) Conkling, not at all dismayed by the narrowness of the win, saw Arthur's vice presidency as an entrée to federal jobs for his supporters. He made repeated efforts to obtain appointments through Arthur's influence, only to be snubbed by President Garfield each time. The Conkling machine and Arthur, as its supposed representative, would have no say in Garfield's presidency.

"NOW ARTHUR WILL BE PRESIDENT!"

Then, on July 2, 1881, when the Garfield administration was less than four months old, the president was shot in the back twice as he boarded a New York train at Washington's Baltimore and Potomac railway station. Arrested on the spot by a railway policeman, a deranged little man named Charles Guiteau declared to the officer, "I am the Stalwart of Stalwarts! Now Arthur will be president!" He was to repeat that assertion again and again over the next ten weeks. Garfield lingered until September 19, the presidency on hold, until he succumbed to a systemic infection and poor medical care. Late that evening, New York Judge John R. Brady went to Arthur's Fifth Avenue apartment and swore him in as president. The oath was given again two days later in Washington by Chief Justice Morris Waite, just to make sure it was official.

Although no one seriously believed that Guiteau was linked to Arthur, the assassin's bullets added fresh fuel to the civil service controversy. Guiteau was well known in Washington as a relentless if quixotic job seeker who besieged not only the White House but also the State and Treasury Departments, pleading his credentials as a loyal Stalwart entitled to his reward. Newspapers and political leaders agreed, though, that his action had probably doomed the spoils system and made reform inevitable.

As the dying Garfield weakened it became evident that Arthur would succeed to the presidency, but the vice president refused to assume his elevation. He even remained in New York most days so that he would not be seen as hovering around the dying president's bedside in Washington waiting for news. He made no plans for his supposed new administration.

When Garfield died, Arthur urged all cabinet members to remain in their posts and continue government business already underway. In December 1881, he delivered his first address to Congress, perfunctorily reviewing international and hemispheric relations, then turning to financial matters, noting a budget surplus and discussing possible tax and tariff reductions. At last he brought up the subject foremost in most minds: reform. He recalled that in a campaign speech he had (mildly) endorsed the principle that government appointments should be based on the candidate's character, experience, and references. He opposed competitive examinations, he repeated, because they would favor book learning to the detriment of the applicant's personal attributes. And the longtime defender of the spoils system repeated that regular infusions of new blood into the government service were beneficial. It was hardly a forceful endorsement of reform.

Now that his onetime protégé was president, Conkling made repeated efforts to influence him, but Arthur held him at arm's length. He was politically shrewd enough to recognize that the public saw Conkling as the very symbol of what was wrong with government. He wanted to avoid the implication that Conkling might be the power behind the presidential throne. And Conkling was already losing his once-vaunted strength politically. His New York machine turned on him and refused to endorse him for another Senate term. Conkling was stunned and humiliated. Sympathetically, Arthur offered him a seat on the Supreme Court. A bitter Conkling declined and returned to his law practice.

Meanwhile, public demand for an end to governmental graft and corruption was reaching a frenzy. Cries for reform dominated the 1882 elections at both national and state levels. Republicans clung to control of Congress, but by a much reduced margin. Arthur, ever the realist, understood the voters' message clearly. Now even some of the most notorious spoilsmen clamored to climb onto the reform bandwagon, declaring that they had stood for clean, nonpolitical government service all the while.

In January 1883, the president spelled out his own heartfelt conversion. He signed the Pendleton Act, establishing competitive examinations as the cornerstone of a new civil service policy, with a new, nonpartisan Civil Service Commission to enforce the rules. Mandatory contributions of either time or money to political campaigns would be strictly forbidden. Every new job applicant would have to pass a written examination. The new rules would initially apply to only 10,000 government jobs, but the president could broaden coverage as he saw fit. He also pledged to throw the presidency's whole weight behind the new plan.

The president's epiphany was greeted with rave notices. "In his message President Arthur gives the order 'right about face' to the Stalwart army," editorialized the *Chicago*

Tribune. The Senate immediately passed the new Pendleton bill by a lopsided vote of 38–5 without a single Republican in opposition. Two days later the House voted 155–47 after only thirty minutes of debate. President Arthur signed the measure on January 16, 1883.

Arthur, though a latecomer to the table, received full credit and the title "The Father of Civil Service," plus a greatly enhanced reputation. Even an ever-cynical Mark Twain declared, "It would be hard indeed to better President Arthur's administration."

Arthur did not live long to enjoy the acclaim or see civil service protection expanded to all but a few government positions, which in 2009 numbered two million. Seriously ill with the kidney disorder Bright's disease during his last weeks in office, he did not bid for reelection and died little more than three months after leaving the White House. Conkling, long estranged from the man whose political career he had launched, is said to have wept uncontrollably at the funeral of someone once better known for his wardrobe than his presidential leadership.

CHAPTER 9

WILLIAM MCKINLEY ANNEXES THE PHILIPPINES AND MAKES THE UNITED STATES AN IMPERIAL POWER

1899

THE SPANISH-AMERICAN WAR, A PETTY CONFLICT THAT WAS OVER IN A MATTER of months, was the catalyst for America's annexation of the Philippines. Spain in 1898 was a third-rate power; its once-vast empire teetered on the brink of extinction and its once-formidable navy was a worn-out antique. After the United States, regarded in 1898 as an emerging military power, defeated the Spanish and seized their former colonies—Cuba, Puerto Rico, Guam, the Philippines—America came to be seen by the international community as a world power.

The war began with a big bang. At 9:40 p.m. on February 15, 1898, the USS *Maine* exploded at its moorings in Havana harbor and sank. The blast occurred at the ship's forward, where five tons (4,536 kg) of gunpowder was stored and where most of the enlisted men were sleeping. The *Maine*'s captain, Charles D. Sigsbee, was in his cabin in the aft portion of the ship, finishing a letter.

"I was enclosing my letter in its envelope when the explosion came," he recorded later. "It was a bursting, rending, and crashing roar of immense volume, largely metallic in character. It was followed by heavy, ominous metallic sounds. There was a trembling and lurching motion of the vessel, a list to port. The electric lights went out. Then there was intense blackness and smoke."

Sigsbee hurried topside, where he found the deck slanting downward sharply in the direction of the obliterated bow. By the light of his burning ship he could see lifeboats coming from neighboring vessels to rescue survivors. "Chief among them," Sigsbee wrote, "were the boats from the *Alfonso XII*. The Spanish officers and crews did all that humanity and gallantry could compass." The explosion tore to bits the front third of the battleship. Sources vary, but approximately two hundred and sixty men died in the disaster.

The U.S. Navy sent a commission of inquiry to investigate the explosion of the *Maine*; after four weeks of study it concluded that a mine had been detonated beneath the battleship. The commissioners did not name the saboteurs because they had no evidence to identify them.

The American press was not so reticent. Two days after the sinking of the *Maine*, *The New York Journal*, owned and operated by newspaper tycoon William Randolph Hearst, proclaimed in a front-page banner headline, "Destruction of the War Ship *Maine* Was the Work of an Enemy." In a secondary headline, the newspaper offered a $50,000 reward "for the Detection of the Perpetrator of the *Maine* Outrage!" Other newspapers followed suit, publishing their own sensationalist stories until the national press was crying for war with the prime suspect, Spain. The Spanish government denied the allegations, but few people in America believed Spain's protestations of innocence.

President William McKinley, however, would not be pressured into war. He took his time and considered the matter carefully, but ultimately on April 11, 1898, he asked Congress to approve military action against Spain, beginning with a naval blockade of Cuba. Congress approved the president's proposal. In retaliation, on April 23 Spain declared war on the United States. Congress declared war on April 25, but backdated its statement to April 21 so it would appear that the United States had taken the initiative in the crisis.

ANYTHING BUT IMPULSIVE

Born in Ohio in 1843, William McKinley was a devout boy who dreamed of becoming a Methodist minister. When the Civil War began in 1861, he enlisted as a private on the Union side. By the war's end he had risen to the rank of brevet major and had been assigned to the staff of his fellow Ohioan, Colonel Rutherford B. Hayes. The friendship McKinley and Hayes formed during the war lasted all their lives; in fact, it was Hayes who used his connections in the Republican Party to help McKinley begin a career in politics. Following in his mentor's footsteps, McKinley served first in Congress, then as governor of Ohio.

In 1871 he married Ida Saxton, the belle of Canton, Ohio, a vivacious, intelligent, cultivated young woman who had studied in Europe and then returned home to work in her father's bank. Their first child, Katherine, was an enchanting little girl and the McKinleys were blissfully happy. Then, two years into their marriage, their luck turned. Ida's mother died. Soon thereafter she gave birth to another daughter, Ida, a sickly child who died at five months. The delivery had been hard and left Ida McKinley a physical

WHAT SUNK THE *MAINE*?

Thirteen years after its destruction in 1898, the wreckage of the USS *Maine* could still be seen in Havana harbor. In 1911 the U.S. Navy authorized a second, more thorough investigation of the sinking of the battleship. Army engineers built a *cofferdam*—a watertight wall—around the wreck, pumped out the water, and sent in explosives experts to examine the damage. Photographers recorded the event. Because the plates of the hull were bent inward, the navy's experts concluded that the damage was caused by a mine planted beneath the ship.

There are other theories, however. In his 1976 book, *How the Battleship* Maine *Was Destroyed,* Admiral Hyman Rickover argued that it was a spontaneous combustion fire in the coalbunkers, located next to the ship's gunpowder magazine, that caused the explosion. In 1898, the same year the *Maine* was destroyed, the crew of the USS *Oregon* discovered a spontaneous combustion fire in the

ship's coalbunker and were able to douse it before it reached the powder magazine. That same year a spontaneous combustion fire broke out in the coalbunker of the USS *Brooklyn*; thermometers installed in the bunker detected the fire and set off the ship's alarm in time for the *Brooklyn*'s crew to put out the fire. The *Maine* was equipped with the same temperature detector and alarm system as the *Brooklyn*, yet its alarm did not sound. Perhaps the *Maine*'s alarm system was defective.

In 1999 *National Geographic* magazine hired Advanced Marine Enterprises (AME) to revisit the *Maine* disaster. Using computer-modeling technology, AME concluded that "it appears more probable than was previously concluded that a mine caused the inward bent bottom structure and the detonation of the magazines."

AME's report did not please supporters of Admiral Rickover's theory, and so the debate regarding exactly how the *Maine* was destroyed still rages on.

wreck. Heartbroken at the double loss of her mother and her infant daughter, Ida lived in fear that something might happen to Katherine. Tragically, in 1875, Katherine contracted typhus and died, too. For the next twenty-six years Ida suffered from a host of unidentified, incurable maladies. Often she was bedridden, heavily sedated by her doctors, who could think of nothing else to alleviate her distress.

In his professional life, McKinley was a protectionist, one who believed that placing high tariffs on imports would protect American jobs and American industries from being undercut by cheap foreign goods. After the economic depression of 1893, McKinley took the national spotlight, arguing that his aggressive protectionist measures would end unemployment and revitalize American industries. By 1896 McKinley had become a nationally recognized figure; the Republicans nominated him for the presidency. Upright, sober, dependable McKinley inspired more confidence among voters than his opponent, William Jennings Bryant, whose high-flown oratory often seemed overwrought. McKinley won the White House by a margin of 271 Electoral College votes to Bryant's 176.

As president, McKinley was anything but impulsive. He took his time mulling over the various solutions to an issue before making a decision. Once he made up his mind, however, he was consistent. For example, America's victory in the Spanish-American War gave it the beginnings of an empire, and so McKinley became more assertive in world affairs. He urged Congress to annex the Hawaiian Islands to consolidate the growing U.S. presence in the Pacific. He sent U.S. troops to Nicaragua—twice—to safeguard American business interests there. He also sent 2,000 troops to China to help the European powers crush the Boxer Rebellion, which targeted American and European missionaries, businessmen, and diplomats.

On September 6, 1901, President McKinley was in Buffalo, New York, visiting the Pan-American Exposition. After delivering a speech he stood in the exposition's Temple of Music to greet well-wishers. An anarchist named Leon Czolgosz approached the president, drew a .32 revolver, and shot McKinley in the chest. As he collapsed, McKinley warned his private secretary, "My wife, be careful . . . how you tell her. Oh, be careful."

But Ida McKinley rose to the crisis. She sat calmly beside her husband's bed for six days as he succumbed to the gangrene that infected his wound. William McKinley died on September 14, 1901. Forty-five days later, having been found guilty of murder, Leon Czolgosz was executed in the electric chair.

ANTI-SPANISH SENTIMENT SIMMERS UNDER THE SURFACE OF THE *NEW YORK JOURNAL* HEADLINE AFTER THE SINKING OF THE *U.S.S. MAINE*. TO THIS DAY, NO ONE HAS AGREED ON WHAT CAUSED THE EXPLOSION ABOARD THE SHIP ON FEBRUARY 15, 1898, WHILE IT WAS MOORED AT HAVANA HARBOR IN CUBA.

AN OFFER FROM SPAIN

On July 3, 1892, in the district of Manila known as Tondo, a thirty-one-year-old Filipino author and political activist, José Rizal, founded La Liga Filipina, the Filipino League, to petition the Spanish colonial government of the islands for a series of reforms. La Liga wanted the Philippines to become a province of Spain with representation in the Spanish national assembly, the Cortes. It called for freedom of assembly, freedom of speech, and that Filipino defendants enjoy the same protections under the law as

Spanish defendants. The colonial government ignored La Liga's demands, then three days after its inaugural meeting, arrested Rizal, banishing him to a remote peninsula on the island of Mindanao.

The day after Rizal's arrest, twenty-nine-year-old Andres Bonifacio founded the Katipunan, a secretive revolutionary society that rejected Rizal's peaceful methods and limited ambitions to reform the colonial government; instead, Katipunan called upon all Filipinos to take up arms and drive the Spanish from the Philippines. In December 1896, the Spanish executed José Rizal for treason; by then, Filipino insurgents were already at war with their Spanish overlords.

The fight was led by Emilio Aguinaldo, a twenty-seven-year-old member of the Katipunan and Andres Bonifacio's main rival for supreme leadership of the Philippine Revolution (the struggle ended in 1897 when Aguinaldo's men arrested Bonifacio and convicted him on a trumped-up charge of treasonous activities against the revolutionary cause).

Late in 1897 the Spanish colonial government made Aguinaldo an unexpected offer: If he agreed to go into exile, they would guarantee in writing that in three years' time Spain would give the Philippines its freedom; furthermore, Aguinaldo would receive an indemnity of 400,000 pesos. Aguinaldo agreed and went into exile in Hong Kong. But when war broke out between Spain and the United States in 1898, Commodore George Dewey had Aguinaldo picked up in Hong Kong and carried him to Luzon, the large northern island of the Philippine archipelago, where he would rally Filipino insurgents to attack the Spanish. As Aguinaldo collected his guerrillas, Dewey steamed off to blockade Manila. Many historians, Filipino and American, have argued that representatives of the U.S. government promised Aguinaldo that the Philippines would be independent once the Spanish were defeated. It's possible, but that assertion has never been proven.

A BRIEF WAR

On May 1, the U.S. Navy's Asiatic Squadron of six ships, led by the USS *Olympia*, defeated the Spanish squadron in a brief battle that cost the United States only nine wounded. Dewey did not land U.S. troops in the Philippines but contented himself with blockading Manila. Meanwhile, Aguinaldo's army of insurgents captured virtually all of Luzon and was in a good position to attack Manila, but he refrained, believing that the Spanish were about to surrender to the Americans and he could proclaim an independent Philippines with the support of the United States.

Unbeknownst to Aguinaldo, Dewey planned to negotiate terms of Spain's surrender of the islands without Aguinaldo. On August 13, American troops led by Major General Wesley Merritt attacked Spanish positions in Manila. After putting up token resistance—a face-saving device that still cost seventeen American dead and one hundred and five wounded—the Spanish garrison surrendered. The next day a formal ceremony of surrender was held in Manila, and once again neither Aguinaldo nor any representative of the insurgents was invited to participate.

American troops now occupied Manila, and Merritt and Dewey refused to permit any of Aguinaldo's men to enter the capital. Nonetheless, Aguinaldo went forward with establishing an independent government for the Philippines. He called a congress at Malolos in the province of Bulacan, north of Manila, where the delegates ratified their country's independence and began to draft a constitution. On January 1, 1899, Emilio Aguinaldo was proclaimed president of the Philippine Republic. The United States made no statement that recognized Aguinaldo's office or the existence of an independent Philippines. Having evicted the Spanish, the American government had already decided to keep the Philippines as its own possession.

TAKING UP JOSÉ RIZAL'S MANTLE, EMILIO AGUINALDO, PICTURED, LED FILIPINO INSURGENTS AGAINST THE SPANISH COLONIAL GOVERNMENT AND LATER U.S. TROOPS. HE WAS PROCLAIMED PRESIDENT OF THE PHILIPPINE REPUBLIC IN 1899, BUT WAS CAPTURED IN 1901 BY FILIPINOS SUPPORTING THE UNITED STATES.

Library of Congress

"A RED-HOT IMPERIALIST"

The idea that America should annex the Philippines was an extension of the doctrine of Manifest Destiny, which declared that America's borders must span the continent from ocean to ocean. Once the Pacific shore had been reached, American expansionists asserted that the United States should advance across the ocean and acquire an overseas empire.

Influential men such as Theodore Roosevelt, assistant secretary of the navy; Captain Alfred Thayer Mahan, the naval historian and strategist; Senator Henry Cabot Lodge of Massachusetts; and newspaper publisher William Randolph Hearst called for an American empire in Asia. Now that the Philippines had fallen into America's lap, it seemed foolish to these men that the United States should hand it over to Aguinaldo. Proponents of annexation argued that the Philippines would give America easy access to the markets of China and Japan, and warned that if the United States did not acquire the islands, some other powerful nation—Japan or Germany were the two named most frequently—would move in and seize them.

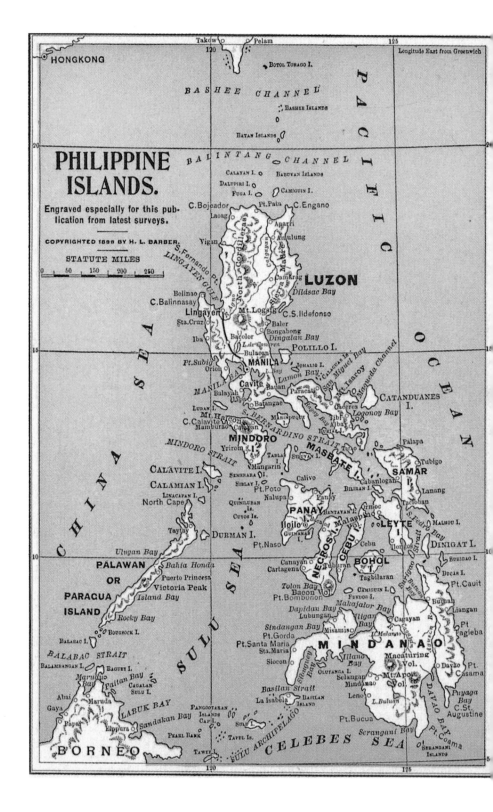

FILIPINOS, LED BY AUTHOR AND POLITICAL ACTIVIST JOSÉ RIZAL, BEGAN SEEKING REFORMS FROM THE SPANISH COLONIAL GOVERNMENT IN 1892. THE GOVERNMENT BANISHED RIZAL TO A REMOTE PENINSULA ON THE ISLAND OF MINDANAO, SHOWN ON THIS MAP OF THE PHILIPPINES IN 1899, BEFORE FINALLY EXECUTING HIM. THE MAP ORIGINALLY APPEARED IN MURAT HALSTEAD'S *FULL OFFICIAL HISTORY OF THE WAR WITH SPAIN* (1899).

Not everyone in the United States was enthusiastic about such a venture. Former President Grover Cleveland denounced "the dangerous perversions" of annexation. The industrialist and philanthropist Andrew Carnegie worried that empire building was too expensive, that America should concentrate on strengthening its domestic economy. Philosopher William James objected to the idea of subjugating the Filipinos. But none were as scathing as author Mark Twain.

Writing in *The New York Herald*, Mark Twain said, "I left these shores, at Vancouver, a red-hot imperialist. I wanted the American eagle to go screaming into the Pacific. It seemed tiresome and tame for it to content itself with the Rockies. Why not spread its wings over the Philippines, I asked myself? And I thought it would be a real good thing to do. . . . But I have thought some more, since then, and I have read carefully the Treaty of Paris [which ended the War with Spain], and I have seen that we do not intend to free, but to subjugate, the people of the Philippines. We have gone there to conquer, not to redeem."

"BENEVOLENT ASSIMILATION"

While the debate raged, President McKinley remained ambivalent. He had been reluctant to enter into war against Spain, even after the battleship *Maine* blew up in Havana harbor, putting off his decision until mid-April, two months after the disaster. Now that the war had been won and U.S. troops were stationed in the Philippines he could not decide whether the United States should keep the islands or turn them over to Aguinaldo's fledgling and unrecognized government. Finally, he prayed over the question. He described his experience on November 21, 1899, to a group of visitors who would understand—the General Missionary Committee of the Methodist Episcopal Church.

"I walked the floor of the White House night after night until midnight," the president said, "and I am not ashamed to tell you, gentlemen, that I went down on my knees and prayed to Almighty God for light and guidance more than one night. And one night late it came to me this way—I don't know how it was, but it came: that we could not give them back to Spain—that would be cowardly and dishonorable; that we could not turn them over to France and Germany—our commercial rivals in the Orient—that would be bad business and discreditable; that we could not leave them to themselves—they were unfit for self-government—and they would soon have anarchy and misrule over there worse than Spain's was; and that there was nothing left for us to do but to take them all, and to educate the Filipinos, and uplift and civilize and Christianize them, and by God's grace do the very best we could by them, as our fellow-men for whom Christ also died. And then I went to bed, and went to sleep, and slept soundly, and the next morning I sent for the chief engineer of the War Department (our map-maker), and I told him to put the Philippines on the map of the United States . . . and there they are, and there they will stay while I am president!"

Apparently, President McKinley was not very well informed on the subject of the demographics of the Philippines: The great majority of Filipinos were already Christians. Their ancestors had converted to the Catholic faith three hundred years earlier.

On December 21, 1898, Elwell S. Otis, military commander of American troops in the Philippines (Merritt had retired), received explicit instructions from McKinley: "The future control, disposition, and government of the Philippine islands are ceded to the United States." The army was to occupy the entire country, and show by its courtesy and gentleness of behavior that "the mission of the United States is one of benevolent assimilation." Filipino insurgents, however, were subject to the rule of law.

ATROCITIES ON BOTH SIDES

On the night of February 4, 1899, Privates William Grayson and Orville Miller of the 1st Nebraska Volunteers were on guard duty on Sociego Street in Manila's Santa Mesa district. Grayson and Miller heard whistling, which they suspected might be insurgent signals. When a Filipino appeared out of the darkness, Grayson twice ordered him to halt. "Then he shouted 'Halto!' to me. Well, I thought the best thing to do was to shoot him. He dropped. If I didn't kill him, I guess he died of fright," Grayson said twelve days later in a report to army officials. "I saw that another was left. Well, I think I got my second Filipino that time." The first man Grayson shot was Corporal Anastacio Felix. He was the first casualty of the Philippine-American War.

The United States never issued a formal declaration of war against Aguinaldo's government, but between 1899 and 1902 more than 125,000 American troops would serve in the Philippines. In 1900 McKinley sent William Howard Taft, a federal judge and former solicitor general of the United States, to set up a government in the islands. Taft replaced the archaic Spanish colonial legal code, established a new judiciary, created a civil service, and devised a system of local councilors and provisional governors to collect taxes and oversee public works projects.

As for Aguinaldo's army, it had resumed the tactics of guerrillas, ambushing American troops and raiding their bases. As their casualties climbed to five hundred, American troops retaliated by burning villages,

PRESIDENTIAL CANDIDATE WILLIAM JENNINGS BRYAN IS SHOWN BLOWING UP WILLIAM MCKINLEY, EMBLAZONED WITH THE WORD "IMPERIALISM." BRYAN, ALONG WITH MARK TWAIN, ANDREW CARNEGIE, AND OTHERS, STRONGLY OPPOSED THE ANNEXATION OF THE PHILIPPINES. THE SATIRICAL ILLUSTRATION WAS THE CENTERFOLD IN THE SEPTEMBER 19, 1900, ISSUE OF PUCK.

Library of Congress

herding suspected insurgents into concentration camps, and shooting any insurgents who fell into their hands, including those trying to surrender. Filipino insurgents struck back by burying American prisoners alive or slicing off their ears and noses.

By the war's end, more than 4,000 Americans had lost their lives, about 1,000 in battle, the remainder to disease; approximately 3,000 were wounded. Between 16,000 and 34,000 Filipino troops and guerrillas died in the war, as well as at least 200,000 Filipino civilians, although some sources claim that the actual civilian death toll was closer to 1.5 million.

A GROUP OF AMERICAN SOLDIERS STANDS AROUND THE BODIES OF TWO DEAD FILIPINOS. BY THE WAR'S END, MORE THAN 4,000 AMERICANS HAD LOST THEIR LIVES. BETWEEN 16,000 AND 34,000 FILIPINO TROOPS AND GUERRILLAS DIED IN THE WAR, AS WELL AS AT LEAST 200,000 FILIPINO CIVILIANS.

Library of Congress

The Philippine Revolution ended on March 23, 1901, when Philippine Scouts—Filipinos who fought with the United States—captured Emilio Aguinaldo. Unwilling to prolong a war he had come to regard as unwinnable, Aguinaldo swore allegiance to the United States and called upon all Filipino insurgents to lay down their arms.

The United States ruled the islands until 1916, when Filipinos were granted self-rule but remained an American territory. As a result, when Japan invaded the Philippines in 1941, both American and Filipino troops and civilians fought in defense of the islands, and after the surrender of the Philippines, endured the Bataan Death March together and suffered together in the same concentration camps. In 1946, the Philippines won its independence.

McKinley's ambition for an American empire came to nothing. The United States never expanded beyond the islands it acquired from defeated Spain. And as for Mark Twain, Andrew Carnegie, and other critics of American expansionism, they were out of tune with the times. France, Spain, Portugal, Russia, Germany, and even Belgium all wanted overseas empires.

Yet McKinley's decision to annex the Philippines did eventually create a "special relationship" between the islands and the United States, manifested economically, politically, and in terms of security such as the establishment of the Clark Air Force Base and the Subic Bay Naval Base (both closed in 1991). The United States remains the Philippines' largest trading and investment partner, with $17 billion in trade and $6.7 billion in investments as of 2008.

CHAPTER 10

THEODORE ROOSEVELT: GUESS WHO'S COMING TO DINNER

1901

AT FIRST GLANCE, THE TWO MEN AT OPPOSITE ENDS OF THE DINNER TABLE THAT evening in 1901 appeared quite similar. Both were dressed in black formal wear with starched white collar and cravat of the style prescribed by Washington custom for an evening dinner. Both spoke in measured, cultured tones and vocabulary, bespeaking advanced education and familiarity with complex issues. They exuded qualities of worldliness and leadership along with an air of responsibility. Between them sat the hostess, quietly but elegantly dressed, listening politely to the male conversation but seldom joining in.

But there was one marked difference between the two men. Theodore Roosevelt, the newly minted president of the United States, was white. His guest, Booker T. Washington, the president of the renowned and highly respected Tuskegee Institute in Alabama, was black. And that casual dinner—and Roosevelt's decision to invite a black man, a "Negro" in turn-of-the-century terminology, to the White House for the first time in U.S. history— was to ignite a firestorm of opprobrium and hatred across the country. But it was also to give America its first gentle nudge that the Civil War was over and that the time had come to reexamine the relationships between the races and how whites and blacks might live together—an issue with which the nation was still grappling as the new century dawned.

Initially that interracial dinner was scarcely noticed. There was no White House public-relations machine to provide daily lists of White House callers and guests, as was to become routine in subsequent years. Besides, the gregarious new president was apt to invite for dinner at the last minute—no doubt to the despair of the kitchen staff—whoever happened to be in his office or whose name came to mind, so journalists had long since given up trying to fully and regularly chronicle the busy White House schedule. Thus it was not until two days after the dinner that the *Atlanta Constitution* published a three-paragraph, bare-bones report under the headline, "Negro Guest Entertained by Roosevelt."

The response was immediate, vicious, and nationwide. In *Theodore Rex*, the second volume of his magisterial Roosevelt biography, Edmund Morris describes the outpouring of venom, especially from the old Confederacy, now once more a full member of the Union and flexing its muscles.

"The most damnable outrage which has ever been perpetrated by any citizen of the United States was committed yesterday by the president, when he invited a nigger to dine with him at the White House," fulminated the *Memphis Scimitar,* using a word that even then was seldom seen in print. And that was one of the milder outbursts from editorial writers and Southern politicians directed at an esteemed educator who had been until then regarded as an "accommodationist," preaching that former slaves should let bygones be bygones, move on, and work side by side with whites for the good of the nation.

Washington famously urged blacks to think of themselves and whites as resembling the fingers, operating independently but cooperating in the hand to build America and advance the nation's progress. That message normally brought standing ovations from both black and white audiences. It had just the right up-by-the-bootstraps, we're-all-Americans-together ring.

"UP FROM SLAVERY"

The two men had been born only a few antebellum years apart, Washington in 1856, Roosevelt in 1858. But they grew up under vastly different circumstances. Roosevelt, of course, was a New York blue blood, a member of one of the city's oldest and wealthiest families. He was taught by private tutors, traveled through Europe with his family at age ten, and went on to a Harvard education.

Washington was the child of a female slave, a cook in the household of a small farmer, James Burroughs, in the Tidewater area of Virginia. His unknown or at least unacknowledged father was a white man, probably from a neighboring farm. His mother, Jane, was illiterate but determined that her son should be more than a field hand. Educating slaves was illegal in Confederate Virginia, but the young boy at least saw the inside of a classroom by carrying the Burroughs daughters' books to school.

After the Confederate surrender, the Thirteenth Amendment abolished slavery, and the Fourteenth and Fifteenth Amendments gave former slaves full equality and citizenship, and the right to vote. As described in Washington's autobiography, *Up from Slavery*, newly freed Jane in 1865 took ten-year-old Booker, his sister and brother, and walked 200 miles (321.9 km) to Kanawha County, West Virginia, to join his stepfather, Ferguson Washington. There the young boy worked in a salt mine, starting at 4 a.m. so he could attend school later in the day. Then he became a houseboy in the home of General Lewis Ruffner. Viola Ruffner took a shine to the bright, engaging youth, helped him with reading, and entered him in a nearby school.

A *NEW YORK TIMES* HEADLINE REPORTS ON THE FALLOUT FROM PRESIDENT ROOSEVELT'S DINNER WITH BOOKER T. WASHINGTON, THE FIRST AFRICAN-AMERICAN WHO HAD DINED WITH A U.S. PRESIDENT.

The Granger Collection, New York

At fifteen, Washington heard that Hampton Institute, Virginia, one of the first black colleges, would accept students who would work to pay their tuition, so he walked back across the state and became a Hampton student. Rejected at first because of his ragged clothes and disheveled appearance, he won admission by demonstrating that he could make a bed and work to pay his way. Before long, he was a lecturer on the school faculty. At twenty-two, Hampton Institute president Samuel Armstrong recommended him to Tuskegee Institute, then being established in Alabama.

Washington became Tuskegee's president and only teacher, with an enrollment of fifty students. He built Tuskegee (now Tuskegee University) into the South's premier black college, noted for the innovative agricultural research program of George Washington Carver, whose work on growing and developing uses for other crops such as peanuts helped convert the South from a one-crop cotton economy to a more diverse one. Carver's path-breaking research enhanced Tuskegee's reputation and made Washington a national figure.

THE BIG TENT

Roosevelt had been in office only a little more than a month when the controversial dinner took place. The new president saw it as his presidential duty to reach out to all segments of the population, including blacks. The freed slaves were, after all, American citizens, enfranchised by the Fifteenth Amendment, although they were frequently prevented from casting ballots, especially in the South.

Roosevelt was hardly a crusader for minority rights. Like many of his contemporaries, he firmly believed that blacks were an inferior race, still in an adolescent stage of development. They were not yet ready for the full rights and privileges of citizenship, nor for the social status that went with them. Indeed, he had been raised amid such beliefs. His mother Martha Bulloch Roosevelt, known as "Mittie," was from Georgia and subscribed to all the beliefs and values of the slaveholding South. Roosevelt believed that only through dedication and hard work could blacks gain full equality.

Washington's bootstrap rise to prominence was coupled with his insistence that peaceful cooperation, not militant confrontation, was the route to racial success. That message struck a chord of admiration in Roosevelt. When he heard that Washington was coming to the national capital, he wanted to meet him, learn his views, and perhaps hold him up to the nation as a shining example of black aspirations fulfilled.

He had qualms, at first. He recognized that he would be the first U.S. president to host a black man as a White House guest. Then he felt guilty about having such feelings and went ahead with the invitation.

He had another motive, too. He was looking forward to November 1904, when he would be up for reelection. Other Republicans were looking forward, too, most notably Senator Marcus Hanna, a Roosevelt critic and the redoubtable Ohioan who had been the architect of the McKinley victories in 1896 and 1900.

A political fight was already brewing in South Carolina over the appointment of a collector of customs in Charleston. Two candidates were being mentioned, one of whom was black and had Roosevelt's tacit backing. Although whites had raised obstacles to black voting and virtually all Southern whites were Democrats, much of the Republican Party machinery included blacks. They may not have been able to muster winning votes, but they still had a strong voice in selecting party nominees and dictating platforms. Perhaps a presidential chat with Washington would give the aspiring candidate for reelection more insight into Southern politics.

"AN INSULT TO AMERICAN WOMANHOOD"

The only other dinner guest that evening was Philip B. Stewart, a family friend who also happened to be in town. The dinner table conversation was less than Roosevelt had hoped for. Washington was quiet and dignified, almost aloof, perhaps shy in the presence of the president and an all-white audience. Roosevelt's brimming ebullience was not enough to draw him out. His wife said little and paid little attention to Washington. She was not interested, Morris wrote, "in anyone—black or white—who was not 'de notre monde' [of our world]." There was some desultory talk about Southern politics, then Edith Roosevelt excused herself and the evening ended quietly, the president politely escorting his guest to the door.

The two men had tacitly agreed that neither would comment on the meeting nor on any discussion that had taken place. None of this made any difference to the angry voices that were raised afterward. The fact that the president's wife had also dined with a black man particularly outraged them. Conjuring up visions of the president's wife and a black man possibly brushing knees under the table, Southern newspapers declared that the president's dinner invitation to a "darky" was an egregious insult to American womanhood.

"No Southern woman with a proper self-respect would now accept an invitation to the White House," thundered the *Scimitar*. Southern Democrat politicians quickly jumped in and ratcheted up the shouting even further. Senator Benjamin Tillman

of South Carolina, a virulent racist demagogue known as "Pitchfork Ben," threatened racial genocide. "The action of President Roosevelt in inviting that nigger [to the White House] will necessitate our killing a thousand niggers in the South before they will learn their place again!" Tillman bellowed.

The uproar increased when it was learned that the two would meet again, when they participated in the Yale University bicentennial celebration, where both would receive honorary degrees. They would not dine together but merely march in the same academic procession, but that did nothing to quiet things down. Then a rumor circulated that the president would be accompanied by his pretty eighteen-year-old daughter, Alice. That touched off more acrimony of the how-could-he-subject-her-to-such-a-thing variety. The outpouring of hate mail hardly paused when the rumor turned out to be false. One letter writer sarcastically suggested that Washington send his daughter to the White House: "Maybe Roosevelt's son will fall in love with her and marry her."

A CALMING VOICE

Roosevelt was stunned by the uproar. He had anticipated some negative reaction, but not on the scale that now washed over him. He sent quiet word to Washington at Tuskegee Institute, emphasizing, in the forceful style that was to become famous, that he "didn't care what anybody thought or said about it," and that he would continue to meet with, and learn from, anybody he chose. He was gratified that many Northern newspapers and political leaders applauded the move, and he basked in the warm praise he received in letters and telegrams from blacks throughout the country.

As for his critics, he declared, "I regard their attacks with the most contemptuous indifference, but I am very melancholy that such a feeling should exist in such bitterly aggravated form." A reassuring word came from Washington himself. He told the president that the invitation was a true statesmanlike gesture, and "the wise course is to pursue exactly the policy which you have mapped out in the beginning." The whole controversy, Washington wrote, had been vastly overblown, partly enflamed by the upcoming elections in several Southern states. "I cannot help but feel that good is going to come out of it."

Roosevelt remained troubled about the outcry. Others, including Mark Twain, cautioned him to go slow with such gestures in the future. After the president declared, "I shall have him to dine just as often as I please," Twain discreetly advised him that a president was not as free as an ordinary citizen to entertain whomever he liked. At the Yale celebration, Roosevelt sat on stage, fiddling with his hat, and did not look at Washington, who sat in the audience, nor greet him. He looked nonplussed when Supreme Court Justice David Brewer, alluding to the first president, remarked, to cheers, "Thank God, there have always been in this country college men able to recognize a true Washington, even though his first name be not George."

The incident, however, elevated Washington's already iconic stature among his fellow blacks. The White House evening was praised as a great triumph and an endorsement of his ideas. He was now seen as the leading voice for black aspirations, and his moderate stance became the accepted policy. Although Washington was never invited back for a social evening or a one-on-one dinner, he continued to have Roosevelt's deep respect and was repeatedly consulted quietly and indirectly about policy matters and Southern politics in particular. With his guidance, black aspirants were steered into government jobs and positions, and several postmasters were now picked from the black community. Roosevelt was renominated for president in 1904 with overwhelming support from black delegates.

But as the years went by with blacks still sentenced to economic if not official slavery, especially in the South, and lynchings occurring at the rate of more than one hundred a year without interference from local authorities or the federal government, blacks began to question Washington's turn-the-other-cheek policies. In 1909, after Roosevelt had left office, a new black leader sprang up in the person of W.E.B. Du Bois, a Massachusetts-born sociologist who had been the first African American to earn a PhD from Harvard. Du Bois preached equality, not accommodation, as the goal for blacks. His new organization, the National Association for the Advancement of Colored People (NAACP), stressed militancy and confrontation as the route to get there.

THEODORE ROOSEVELT AND BOOKER T. WASHINGTON ARE PICTURED IN DISCUSSION DURING THE PRESIDENT'S 1905 VISIT TO TUSKEGEE INSTITUTE, OF WHICH WASHINGTON WAS PRESIDENT.

Gradually the White House dinner was forgotten along with the accommodationist policies it generated. The fingers-of-the-hand analogy was discredited and it was decades before it was heard again, even in the civil rights movement or in the controversies over affirmative action. Washington's leadership role waned, along with his reputation, and young blacks especially turned their backs on him. At his death in 1915 he was considered, among civil rights activists, a has-been, almost a figure of derision. It was not until late in the twentieth century that the dinner came to be seen as a milestone, a seminal event in the march for recognition and equality.

CHAPTER 11

THEODORE ROOSEVELT BACKS A NEW GOVERNMENT IN PANAMA AND DIGS THE PANAMA CANAL

1903

I N 1846 THE UNITED STATES ENTERED INTO A TREATY WITH NEW GRANADA (NOW Colombia and Panama). New Granada granted the United States the right-of-way across the Isthmus of Panama; in return, the United States recognized New Granada's sovereignty over the isthmus. The status quo remained undisturbed for more than fifty years; then, on November 2, 1903, the Navy Department in Washington, D.C., sent a secret cable to Commander John Hubbard aboard the USS *Nashville*, ordering him to the city of Colon in Panama to prevent the landing of any troops, "either government or insurgent."

The source of the trouble between the United States and what is now Colombia was access across the isthmus. As of 1903 there was no canal in Panama—just a mud-filled, overgrown trench that a French construction company had abandoned fifteen years earlier. But if France had given up the idea of a canal across Panama that linked the Atlantic and the Pacific oceans, President Theodore Roosevelt had not.

In June 1902, the U.S. Congress passed the Spooner Act, which appropriated $40 million to purchase from Colombia the right to dig a canal across Panama. Roosevelt sent his secretary of state, John Hay, to Colombia to negotiate a treaty that would grant the United States a hundred-year lease for territory six miles (9.7 km) wide from the Atlantic to the Pacific. That same year, when the Colombian Senate refused to ratify the treaty, Roosevelt denounced it for obstructing a "highway of civilization," and accused it of being in violation of the treaty of 1846 that granted the United States the right-of-way across the Isthmus of Panama.

A READY-MADE REVOLUTION

That might have been the end of the matter, but President Roosevelt knew there were elements in Panama that wanted to break free of Colombia and establish an independent nation. Roosevelt let it be known through his agents in Panama that if an independence movement sprang up, the United States would not oppose it.

With this encouragement, revolutionaries in Panama began to organize in the summer of 1903, and by October they were ready to seize power—up to a point. At most, they could furnish arms for 600 men, not nearly enough to defeat the Colombian army and navy. And so the United States intervened under the pretext of safeguarding its interests under the terms of the treaty of 1846. America was not interfering in Colombian-Panamanian politics; it was simply protecting its right-of-way in Panama, specifically the single railway line that crossed the isthmus.

On November 3, 1903, Commander Hubbard came ashore at Colon and took control of the railway line. According to Roosevelt, Colombia had threatened the railroad and was intent upon frustrating the construction of a canal in Panama. By these actions, the president said, Colombia was clearly violating America's right-of-way across the isthmus. Over the next few days, as nine American battleships arrived along Panama's eastern and western coasts, it became clear to the Colombian government that any hope it entertained of reclaiming Panama was futile. For all intents and purposes, the United States was in control of the province.

From the day Hubbard led American troops ashore, events moved quickly in Panama. A constitution was presented to the people for ratification (it had been written in the United States); a Panamanian flag was ready to be adopted (it had been designed and sewn in the United States); and the United States had its first minister, or ambassador, to independent Panama waiting in the wings—Philippe Bunau-Varilla, an ardent promoter of the canal project.

Two months later, in a speech before Congress, Roosevelt explained that when Commander Hubbard went ashore at Colon, he acted "with entire impartiality toward both sides, preventing any movement, whether by the Colombians or the Panamanians, which would tend to produce bloodshed."

As for the revolution, the people of Panama "rose literally as one man," the president explained.

"Yes," quipped Senator Edward Carmack of Tennessee, "and the one man was Roosevelt."

PLANTING THE FLAG OF LIBERTY

Theodore Roosevelt wanted a canal in Panama, even if he had to support a halfhearted revolutionary movement to get it. Like so many men in the U.S. military and

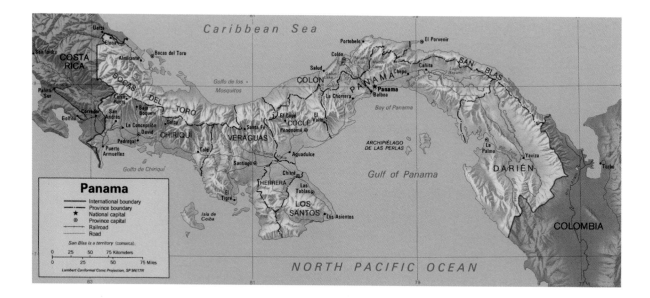

government—not to mention many ordinary American citizens—Roosevelt believed that a canal linking the Atlantic and Pacific oceans had become an economic and military necessity. The United States had territories in the Pacific now, such as Hawaii, and since the Spanish-American War of 1898, the United States had territories in Asia—the Philippines and Guam. It took two months for a ship to sail from New York around Cape Horn to California; a canal across the Isthmus of Panama would shave 8,000 miles and many weeks off that journey.

Furthermore, Roosevelt was among those who believed the United States had a moral obligation to "bring civilization into the waste places of the earth," as he put it in a speech delivered earlier in 1903. It was America's destiny to plant the flag of liberty in lands that had known only tyranny and oppression; that is why Roosevelt had supported the annexation of the Philippines in 1898, and why he dropped anything-but-subtle hints that he would support an anti-Colombian revolution in Panama.

AN AMERICAN SUCCESS STORY

Theodore Roosevelt was descended from one of the old Dutch families of New Amsterdam. He was born in 1858 in the Gramercy Park neighborhood of Manhattan, the second child and eldest son of a wealthy, influential, and rambunctious family. His father, Theodore Sr., was a beloved New York philanthropist. His mother, Martha Bulloch, was a gracious Southern belle, whom some literary historians believe was in part the inspiration for Scarlett O'Hara, the heroine of *Gone with the Wind*.

In 1880 Roosevelt married Alice Hathaway Lee, the daughter of a prominent Massachusetts banker. Roosevelt adored his wife. "She was beautiful in face and form," he recalled, "and lovelier still in spirit." In 1884 the couple was expecting its first child. On St. Valentine's Day, hours after giving birth to a daughter, Alice died—not of complications from childbirth but from kidney disease that had gone undiagnosed during her pregnancy. Earlier that same day, Roosevelt's mother died of typhoid fever.

To escape the pain of this double tragedy, Roosevelt left his infant daughter with his sister and departed New York for the Badlands in the Dakota Territory. He bought a cattle ranch outside Medora in what is now North Dakota. Roosevelt looked entirely out of place in the Badlands: His cowboy "outfits" had been custom-made in New York. He had bought his bowie knife at Tiffany's. He spoke in a high-pitched twang, with an Ivy League accent, and he never caught on to the lingo of the West; on one memorable occasion he urged his hired hands to ride faster, crying, "Hasten forward quickly there!" And he wore spectacles. He looked and sounded like a rich boy playing cowboy, but once, when a rough character insulted him in a saloon, Roosevelt knocked out the man with a single punch. From that day on, the folks in the Badlands realized that Roosevelt was a lot tougher than he looked.

After more than two years out West, Roosevelt returned to New York and married Edith Kermit Carow—an old childhood friend; together they had five children. Then Roosevelt entered politics. He served as police commissioner of New York City, then assistant secretary of the navy, then governor of New York. When Congress declared war against Spain, Roosevelt enlisted, and brought with him dozens of his friends from out West, forming them into a brigade he nicknamed the "Rough Riders." Roosevelt and his Rough Riders became legendary after storming a Spanish position atop San Juan Hill in Cuba.

His fame as a war hero brought him national attention; in 1898 the Republican Party selected him to be William McKinley's running mate. The McKinley-Roosevelt ticket won; three years later, when McKinley was assassinated, Roosevelt moved into the White House. He was forty-two years old, the youngest president in American history (John F. Kennedy was forty-four when he was inaugurated).

As a committed expansionist, Roosevelt looked for opportunities where America could demonstrate to the world its energy and ingenuity. It was this desire that motivated Roosevelt to take up France's failed Panama Canal project and make it an American success story.

BREAKING GROUND IN A CHAMPAGNE CRATE

As early as the sixteenth century there had been talk of digging a canal across Panama, but not until 1879 were such discussions taken seriously. That year in Paris an international assembly of engineers charted a route across the isthmus and named the man to direct the project—Count Ferdinand de Lesseps, the man who had dug the Suez Canal in Egypt, thereby giving Europe a short route to India and the Far East. De Lesseps was seventy-four years old in 1879, yet such was his standing among engineers that he was regarded as the only man capable of constructing a canal in Panama.

On January 1, 1880, a procession of horse-drawn carriages transported Ferdinand de Lesseps, his wife and children, and approximately a hundred Colombian and Panamanian dignitaries to the dock of Panama City, where a steam tug waited to carry the party three miles (4.8 km) up the Rio Grande to the site where excavation work would begin. The guests were in such a merry mood that they delayed casting off, and so missed the tide. De Lesseps was undaunted. Breaking ground for the canal was purely symbolic, he said, and the ceremony could be done anywhere, so he proposed acting it out on the boat. Someone filled a wooden champagne crate with sand, and someone else handed de Lesseps's ten-year-old daughter, Ferdinande, a brand-new pick. The little girl swung the pick, striking the sand, and everyone cheered. After other guests took turns "breaking ground" in the champagne crate, the bishop of Panama City, José Telesforo Paúl, blessed the project, and everyone returned to the dock.

De Lesseps believed the fifty-mile (80.5 km)-long canal could be dug in twelve years at a cost of about $132 million. Finding such a sum had not been difficult: Everyone who had invested in de Lesseps's Suez Canal project had become rich. And even the railroad that spanned the Isthmus of Panama was a moneymaker, generating $7 million of income in its first six years of operation. Consequently, de Lesseps had no trouble finding investors for his Compagnie Universelle du Canal Interocéanique.

FRAUD AND CORRUPTION

But Panama was not the Suez. This was not a flat desert, but a rugged, uneven terrain of jungle, swamps, and the Chagres River, which crossed the proposed path of the canal fourteen times. De Lesseps ignored these facts.

In addition to the near-impossible topography, there were poisonous snakes, incurable mosquito-borne diseases such as yellow fever and malaria, infernal, stifling humidity, and during the rainy season, torrential downpours. De Lesseps knew virtually nothing of all this—he had made a single visit to Panama during the dry season and leapt to the conclusion that digging in Central America would be no trickier than digging in Egypt had been.

He was tragically mistaken. During the dry season the work crews of local black and Indian laborers made slow but steady progress, but once the rainy season began the diggers found themselves sinking chest-deep into muck. The flooded Chagres River swept away men and heavy machinery. Frequent mudslides buried men and equipment, filling up in minutes trenches it had taken months to dig. And everywhere there were clouds of mosquitoes. They were a maddening annoyance, but no one at the time suspected the mosquitoes could be deadly.

As for construction of the canal, though the costs mounted, progress seemed to stall. By late 1888, after almost nine years of digging, only eleven miles (17.7 km) of trench had been cleared. The cost had skyrocketed to $287 million—more than twice de Lesseps's initial estimate. And at least 20,000 men had died, almost all of them of disease. In fact, the death toll was probably much higher because the company routinely laid off sick men, and company records do not report what became of these former workers. In December 1888, the Compagnie Universelle du Canal Interocéanique went bankrupt.

The investors were outraged. They accused de Lesseps of fraud and corruption, and the outcry against him was so great that the French government began an investigation into the company's finances. Not until October 1892 did the government assemble sufficient evidence to put de Lesseps and his son Charles on trial to assess damages they might owe to the canal company's investors. This would be a civil suit rather than a criminal trial because, as the public prosecutor explained, his goal was to recover some of the funds the shareholders had lost, not to impose "the sterile penalty of imprisonment upon an octogenarian in his dotage." At the time of the trial, Ferdinand de Lesseps was eighty-seven.

In spite of the prosecutor's desire for leniency, the court sentenced de Lesseps and his son to five years in prison. De Lesseps, who was suffering from dementia and kept at home, never learned of the convictions, nor did he do any jail time. A French court of appeals overturned the verdict on the grounds that Ferdinand and Charles had been tried after the statute of limitations for their crime had expired.

As for the canal, the Panamanian jungle reclaimed it.

COUNT FERDINAND DE LESSEPS, THE ARCHITECT OF THE SUEZ CANAL, BEGAN WORK ON THE PANAMA CANAL. HOWEVER, PANAMA WAS NOT SUEZ. AFTER ALMOST NINE YEARS OF DIGGING, ONLY 11 MILES (17.7 KM) OF TRENCH HAD BEEN CLEARED, MORE THAN 20,000 MEN HAD DIED, MOSTLY OF DISEASE, AND COSTS HAD SKYROCKETED.
Getty Images

THE CANAL IS UPSTAGED

During 1904, its first year of excavation in Panama, the United States repeated the disasters that had ruined Ferdinand de Lesseps. Disease and rotten food decimated the laborers as well as the American engineers and foremen, and $128 million was sunk into the project, with no discernible results. Then, in 1905, President Roosevelt sent John Frank Stevens to Panama as chief engineer. Stevens was a man much like the president—he was daring, a visionary, and tenacious, and he had a proven track record. Stevens was renowned for building the 1,700-mile (2,735.9 km)-long Great Northern Railway from St. Paul, Minnesota, through the Rocky Mountains, to Seattle, Washington.

Disgusted by the work crews' deplorable living conditions, Stevens began by cleaning up the camps. He hired Dr. William Gorgas, the man who had stamped out yellow fever in Havana, to direct sanitation crews. They drained swamps and sprayed pesticides, brought in fresh water, and installed a sewerage system. Then Stevens erected towns for his workers to live in, complete with paved roads.

Once he had gotten sanitation and living conditions under control, Stevens revealed his design for the canal. De Lesseps had tried to barrel through the jungle and mountains as if the entire isthmus were at sea level—that was one reason why he had failed. Stevens designed what he called "a lake and lock" canal. He would dam the Chagres River to create a giant, man-made lake in the center of Panama. A series of locks on the Atlantic side would lift ships gradually up to the lake; they would cruise across to the next set of locks, which would lower them down to the Pacific.

Stevens brought in gigantic American-made Bucyrus steam shovels to do the excavation work. He also built a railway that carried the tons of earth and rock to the site of the Chagres Dam. Just from the Culebra Cut, 100 million cubic yards (76,455,486 m³) of earth and rock were moved to the dam. The president was delighted with the progress Stevens was making. When he visited the canal site in 1906, he had himself photographed at the controls of a Bucyrus steam shovel.

A MUDSLIDE IN THE CANAL PREVENTS THIS BOAT FROM GOING ANY FARTHER. FREQUENT MUDSLIDES BURIED MEN AND EQUIPMENT, FILLING UP IN MINUTES THE TRENCHES IT HAD TAKEN MONTHS TO DIG.

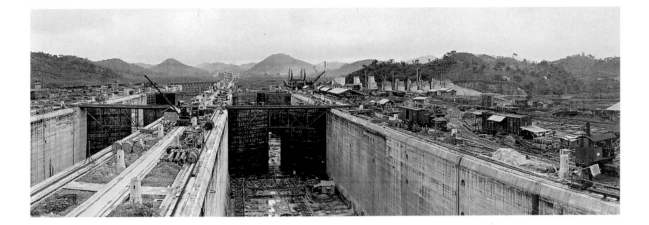

The Panama Canal opened officially on August 15, 1914, but the greatest engineering feat of its time did not get the attention it deserved: As the locks lifted the first ships up to man-made Lake Gatun, Germany was barreling across Belgium into France. The canal was upstaged by World War I.

PRESIDENT ROOSEVELT SENT JOHN FRANK STEVENS TO PANAMA AS CHIEF ENGINEER ON THE CANAL PROJECT. STEVENS USED A SERIES OF LOCKS, SHOWN HERE, TO MOVE SHIPS ALONG THE CANAL.

BRIDGING THE DIVIDE

From the beginning Theodore Roosevelt understood that the Panama Canal would play a central role in the global economy. Until World War I ended in 1918, traffic through the canal was spotty—about four ships a day—but after the Armistice the canal became very busy, processing on average five thousand ships a year. By 1939 annual canal traffic had risen to about seven thousand ships. And at a time when virtually all international trade goods were transported by sea, all the ships that transited the canal were commercial vessels.

The canal also became a boon to the people of Panama, thousands of whom found jobs in the Canal Zone, as the area along the canal came to be known. All along the fifty-one-mile (82 km) route other services sprang up—everything from ship repair bays, to bars for ships' crews, to restaurants and souvenir shops for tourists.

In his definitive account of the construction of the canal, *The Path Between the Seas*, David McCullough summed up the importance of the Panama Canal. "Primarily the canal is an expression of that old and noble desire to bridge the divide," he wrote, "to bring people together. It is a work of civilization."

And the driving force behind that civilizing endeavor was Theodore Roosevelt.

CHAPTER 12

THEODORE ROOSEVELT
PUTS THE ENVIRONMENT
ON THE NATIONAL AGENDA

EARLY 1900s

I N MAY 1901, FACTORY WORKER LEON CZOLGOSZ HAD LONG BEEN OUT OF WORK and living with his mother and father on the family's small farm in Warrensville, Ohio. He attended a speech that month given in Cleveland by the anarchist Emma Goldman, and, as he later told police, it was still "burning [him] up" on the afternoon of September 6, 1901, when he stood in line to shake hands with President William McKinley during a "President's Day" reception in the cavernous Temple of Music at the Pan-American Exposition in Buffalo, New York.

Czolgosz had swathed his right hand in a white handkerchief to hide the revolver he carried. At 4:07 p.m., it was finally his turn to shake the president's hand. William J. Gomph, the exposition's official organist, was playing in the background the sweet melancholy of Robert Schumann's *Träumerei*.

Czolgosz slowly extended what appeared to be his bandaged hand, President McKinley reached for it, and the wannabe anarchist squeezed off two rounds. One bullet was deflected almost harmlessly by a rib, but the other bore through the president's stomach, nicking his kidney and tearing his pancreas before it came to rest somewhere in the muscles of his back. "Go easy on him, boys," the victim called out as Secret Service agents and others pummeled the assassin.

Eight days later, the twenty-fifth president of the United States was dead. Hearing the news, Senator Marcus Hanna of Ohio cried out: "Now look! That damned cowboy is president of the United States."

PROGRESSIVE DYNAMO

Hanna's anguished exclamation was true, as far as it went. Theodore Roosevelt had not only owned, but also personally and quite successfully worked, a large ranch in the Dakota

Badlands. Not that he had been born to a cowboy's life. He grew up in a stately brownstone on East 20th Street, Manhattan, the son of old money and pampered privilege. As a young man, he served in the New York State Assembly, earning his stripes as a "Progressive," a zealous champion of political reform and an implacable foe of corruption. Gaining appointment to the U.S. Civil Service Commission, he set about reforming that body, and then, as president of the New York City Police Board, transformed the city's force from a brutal gang of casually bribed patronage appointees into a professional law enforcement agency that became the envy of municipalities across the country.

Appointed assistant secretary of the navy during President McKinley's first term, he was instrumental in preparing the Great White Fleet, pride of the powerful and modern U.S. Navy, for the Spanish-American War of 1898. Having done that, he left the cabinet to create the First U.S. Volunteer Cavalry, better known as the Rough Riders, to help fight that war in person.

Spain defeated, Cuba liberated, Theodore Roosevelt returned to the United States and got himself elected governor of New York before 1898 ended. He set about reforming the state's comfortably corrupt Republican machine, and then stepped down in 1900 to become McKinley's second-term running mate. *Stepped* down? He was pushed.

The very machine he had fought forced Roosevelt to accept the vice presidency (either that or get out of Republican politics entirely), an office that in 1900 was a dead-end repository for political hacks and has-beens. Senator Hanna, a principal cog in the machine, was delighted to have the young Progressive rabble-rouser safely entombed. No one dreamed that he would become president.

But that is just what happened. And President "Teddy" Roosevelt turned his brain and heart and hand to making plenty of trouble for everyone who lived and died by the status quo.

WILDERNESS APOSTLE

He took dead aim at the great "trusts," the monopolies that had a stranglehold on so much of American economic life, and compelled the breakup of some forty corporations to make room for competition. He gave to the working and middle classes what he called the "Square Deal," which included such reforms as the federal regulation of hitherto ruinous railroad freight rates and federal enforcement of standards for pure foods and safe and effective drugs. He consistently sided with labor unions against big business. And although he was both celebrated and notorious for advocating a pugnacious foreign policy he summed up by quoting a West African proverb—"Speak softly and carry a big stick"—he became in 1906 the first U.S. president to receive the

Nobel Peace Prize for his role in negotiating an end to the singularly bloody Russo-Japanese War of 1904–1905.

In later life, Roosevelt himself deemed his bold 1904 strong-arm negotiation of rights to construct and control the Panama Canal as the most important achievement of his presidency. The majority of historians disagree, and instead judge his decision to promote conservation of the nation's natural resources—today called environmental regulation or environmental protection—as his greatest legacy.

For all that Roosevelt accomplished before and during his presidency, the decision to use the presidency as a platform for environmental stewardship was rooted in that very "cowboy" identity Marcus Hanna so patronizingly bemoaned. Roosevelt had grown up in the genteel world of New York's upper crust a weak and sickly child. As a youth he discovered what he called "the strenuous life." He threw himself into a life of hard work and even harder play lived in the outdoors, in unspoiled nature, which he credited as a sovereign tonic that breathed new life into him, remolding a weakling into what he himself called a "Bull Moose." He had purchased his ranch in further quest of the strenuous life, and, working it, he learned both to love and to respect the natural environment.

What Henry David Thoreau had written years earlier of nature—"In wildness is the preservation of the world"—expressed Roosevelt's sentiments exactly, and his passion for the wild country drew him to both the writings and the persons of Thoreau's philosophical heirs, the great naturalists and conservationists of his own day. They included William T. Hornaday, instrumental in preventing the extinction of the American bison; nature writer John Burroughs; Sierra Club founder John Muir; and scientific forestry pioneer Gifford Pinchot, who served as chief of the U.S. Department of Agriculture's Division of Forestry from 1893 to 1898 in the McKinley administration and who would be chief adviser on conservation policy in the Roosevelt White House.

Back in 1872, during the administration of Ulysses S. Grant, Congress had created Yellowstone National Park, thereby establishing the precedent of setting aside certain tracts of land for ownership and protection in the name of the nation and for the enjoyment of the people. It was in a speech at the laying of the cornerstone of a new road and entrance to the country's first national park on April 24, 1903, that Theodore Roosevelt articulated his vision of the profound significance and value of a place like Yellowstone.

"Nowhere else in any civilized country is there to be found such a tract of veritable wonderland made accessible to all visitors, where at the same time not only the scenery of the wilderness but the wild creatures of the park are scrupulously preserved," he declared. "The only way that the people as a whole can secure to themselves and their children the enjoyment in perpetuity of what the Yellowstone Park has to give us is by assuming the ownership in the name of the nation and by jealously safeguarding and preserving the scenery, the forests, and the wild creatures."

As Roosevelt understood it, the concept of a national park was at the heart of the broader national stewardship of the natural environment. Speaking to the Conference on the Conservation of Natural Resources, which he convened at the White House in May 1908, the president explained that America had become "great because of the lavish use of our resources," but, he continued, "the time has come to inquire seriously what will happen when our forests are gone, when the coal, the iron, the oil, and the gas are exhausted, when the soils shall have been still further impoverished and washed into the streams, polluting the rivers, denuding the fields, and obstructing navigation."

Roosevelt went on to thoughtfully classify natural resources into those that "are or are not capable of renewal." Mineral and oil resources were not renewable, he explained, but soil, forest, lands, and waterways "cannot only be used in such manner as to leave them undiminished for our children, but can actually be improved by wise use." And it was the urgent duty of the government, he believed, to ensure that they *were* wisely used. "We are coming to recognize . . . the right of the nation to guard its own future in the essential matter of natural resources. In the past we have admitted the right of the individual to injure the future of the Republic for his own present profit. The time has come for a change."

President Roosevelt proclaimed it both a national right and a duty to "protect ourselves and our children against the wasteful development of our natural resources." He announced his belief that the nation "should earnestly desire and strive to leave to the next generation the national honor unstained and the national resources unexhausted."

A CAMPAIGN POSTER SHOWS WILLIAM MCKINLEY RUNNING FOR PRESIDENT WITH THEODORE ROOSEVELT AS HIS VICE-PRESIDENT. AFTER MCKINLEY'S ASSASSINATION, SENATOR MARCUS HANNA OF OHIO PROCLAIMED, "NOW LOOK! THAT DAMNED COWBOY IS PRESIDENT OF THE UNITED STATES."

Private Collection / Peter Newark American Pictures / The Bridgeman Art Library International

THE PASSION OF PRESIDENT ROOSEVELT, MIDDLE, FOR THE OUTDOORS DREW HIM TO THE NATURALISTS OF HIS DAY, INCLUDING CONSERVATIONIST AND SIERRA CLUB FOUNDER JOHN MUIR, FOURTH FROM RIGHT. THE GROUP IS STANDING IN YOSEMITE VALLEY IN 1903.

akg-images

Reading these words today, their truth seems obvious, even self-evident. Yet, at the dawn of the twentieth century and in the greatest capitalist democracy the world had ever known, what this American president proposed was nothing less than radical.

CREATING A NATION OF NATURE'S STEWARDS

As many saw it, his proposal leaped far beyond the precedent created by Yellowstone. When it was established in 1872, Yellowstone National Park occupied federal territory, which only later was divided into Wyoming, Montana, and Idaho, the three states over parts of which this national park today sprawls.

What Roosevelt wanted from Congress was to create many more Yellowstones and federally regulate natural resources within established "sovereign" states. Vast designated tracts, rich in minerals and timber, would be held by the nation, and would be protected from ownership, exploitation, or spoliation by any state, corporation, or individual. Roosevelt responded to the vehement objection that such an action was unconstitutional, an un-American usurpation and preemption of states' rights and private property rights, in a 1915 article written for *The Outlook* magazine: "We are fast learning that trees must not be cut down more rapidly than they are replaced; we have taken forward steps in learning that wild beasts and birds are by right not the property merely of the people alive to-day, but the property of the unborn generations, whose belongings we have no right to squander . . ."

American presidents have tended to come in two varieties: those who believe their primary role is to do nothing more than "faithfully execute" the laws Congress passes and those who believe the chief executive should take a leading role in proposing legislation for Congress to pass. Without question, senators and representatives enjoy in our system of government a direct relationship with the people, whereas presidents who aspired only to execute laws have rarely claimed such a relationship. In contrast, presidents who have wanted to make laws have invariably claimed precisely this. Theodore Roosevelt was such a president.

Roosevelt called the office of the chief executive a "bully pulpit," a platform from which a strong president could—and should—mold public opinion. This is what he did now. Bypassing Congress, which was heavily influenced by the legislators' home states as well as mining, forestry, oil, and agricultural interests opposed to national ownership and protection of large tracts of land, the president took his case directly to the American people. Through many speeches and public appearances, he transformed conservation into a popular national movement, very nearly a national religion.

It was this carefully cultivated public opinion that finally pressured a grudging Congress into passing the first game laws for what was then the territory of Alaska (1902 and 1908); appropriating funds for the preservation of bison (1902); creating the Wichita Game Preserves (1905); creating the Grand Canyon National Game Preserve (1906); passing the National Monuments Act (1906), which immediately created the Muir Woods and Pinnacles National Monument, both in California, and the Olympic National Park in Washington State, among many others over the years; and passing an act to establish the National Bison Range in Montana (1908).

Carried on the popular tide the president had raised, Congress also established five new national parks before his second term ended in 1909: Crater Lake, Oregon; Wind Cave, South Dakota; Sullys Hill, North Dakota (later redesignated a game preserve); Mesa Verde, Colorado; and Platt, Oklahoma (now part of Chickasaw National Recreation Area). The president also acted on his executive authority to set aside by executive order—which did not require an act of Congress—vast tracts as national forests.

THE PEOPLE'S TRIBUNE

But by 1908, the massed will of big farmers, grazers, and emerging water-power interests rolled over both the president *and* public opinion. Congress suddenly enacted legislation to transfer from the executive to itself the authority to establish national forests in a number of western states. This prompted Roosevelt to issue the so-called "midnight forests" proclamation, which protected by executive order 16 million acres (some 64,750 km²) of western forests just before the new legislation went into effect. By way of revenge, Congress killed, by refusing to fund, two key conservation commissions Roosevelt had created in 1908, the National Country Life Commission and the Inland Waterways Commission.

The president in his turn retaliated by becoming the first American chief executive to make extensive use of executive orders to advance every aspect of his domestic agenda, including his program of national forests and conservation, despite congressional opposition. In two terms, Roosevelt churned out 1,091 executive orders, nearly equaling the combined total of 1,259 issued by all twenty-five (counting Grover Cleveland's two nonconsecutive terms twice) presidents who had come before him.

Theodore Roosevelt's fight for the national parks, national forests, and federal stewardship of public lands forever changed American government. It pitted the president against Congress, elevating very nearly to the level of public law the executive order, a presidential power that had in the past been used sparingly and only for specifically defined issues of narrow scope and temporary duration, such as creating the occasional blue ribbon panel to propose programs to promote patriotism. As wielded by Roosevelt, the executive order was used to enact all that Congress refused to pass. The cause of national parks and environmental stewardship also moved him to develop the notion of the chief executive as what might be called the "people's tribune," a representative, protector, and champion of the people's rights—especially when this modern "tribune" judged that Congress was being more responsive to the special interests of big business and big agriculture than to the popular welfare.

The effect on government and the balance of power—between the legislative and executive branches as well as between federal and state government—of the president's decision to create national parks, national forests, and other federally protected lands was both profound and far-reaching. The issues of governance his decision raised are still felt today as presidents have made wars without congressional declaration or have attempted to shape and even create the legislative agenda of Congress.

Yet even more powerful and enduring is the mark Roosevelt's decision left on the American land and the American consciousness. Although Congress fought the president on the environment, especially after 1908, the genie was out of the bottle: A conservation movement born. Successive presidents and Congresses have sometimes tried to slow or even stop the movement, but it has consistently proved unstoppable.

Today there are three hundred and ninety-one national parks, forty national heritage areas, and 2,461 national historic landmarks. Some 84 million acres (about 340,000 km²) of the United States are managed by the National Park Service, and some 193 million acres (roughly 781,000 km²) by the U.S. Forest Service. As recently as March 30, 2009, President Barack Obama signed into law the Omnibus Public Lands Management Act of 2009, which added some two million acres (about 8,100 km²) to the National Wilderness Preservation System, established a unified National Landscape Conservation System, expanded the National Park System, and brought other lands under federal protection. The act traces its ancestry directly to the environmental activism of Theodore Roosevelt.

Beyond the physical legacy of many protected lands, Roosevelt's decision for environmental stewardship sowed the seeds of an ecological and environmental consciousness, not only among Americans but also throughout the world. People, presidents, and legislatures have not always acted in the best interests of the natural environment; although the consciousness of that environment, having been raised by the twenty-sixth American president, has sometimes dimmed, it has never been extinguished. The issues of value, use, ownership, legacy, conservation, and sustainability that Theodore Roosevelt articulated and acted upon have emerged today more urgently than ever.

BISON GRAZE AND DRINK IN YELLOWSTONE, THE NATION'S FIRST NATIONAL PARK, IN 1905. ROOSEVELT WANTED TO CREATE MORE SUCH PARKS, SETTING ASIDE LAND FOR CONSERVATION AND RECREATION.
Library of Congress

CHAPTER 13

THEODORE ROOSEVELT SENDS THE GREAT WHITE FLEET AROUND THE WORLD TO DRAMATIZE THE UNITED STATES' NEW ROLE AS A WORLD POWER

1907-1909

THE LINE OF SHIPS STEAMED MAJESTICALLY UP THE ROADSTEAD, THEIR white hulls gleaming brilliantly in the late February 1909 winter sun. Cheers erupted from both banks of the James River estuary in Virginia. Proceeding a precise four hundred yards (365.8 m) apart, America's sixteen largest battleships, one by one, dipped their colors as they passed the presidential yacht, the *Mayflower*. On the *Mayflower*'s weather deck, which was draped in bunting and flying the Stars and Stripes and the presidential banner, President Theodore Roosevelt flashed his trademark toothy grin, doffed his top hat (while shielding it against the wind), and heartily returned each salute.

"Isn't this bully!" he cried. It was indeed "bully." With bands and ceremony, America's "Great White Fleet" was home again from an unprecedented fourteen-month round-the-world cruise. The 43,000-mile (69,201.8 km) global circumnavigation carried a strong message: America was notifying the world that the young nation was now a major world sea power. It was a moment Theodore Roosevelt, now with less than two weeks remaining in his term of office, had championed for more than a decade.

A NAVAL POWER VISIONARY

In the early 1890s, Alfred Thayer Mahan, a historian and president of America's Naval War College, published two books that riveted the attention of governments worldwide. *The Influence of Sea Power Upon History, 1660–1783* and *The Influence of Sea*

Power Upon the French Revolution and Empire, 1793–1812 declared in emphatic terms that naval power was the key to success in global supremacy and empire building. The nation that controlled the seas, Mahan wrote, held the decisive factor in modern warfare. The great powers were already engaged in a fierce arms race and competition for empires. The Mahan doctrine intensified the competition.

No one studied the Mahan volumes more assiduously than that omnivorous reader, Theodore Roosevelt. "TR" saw that building a mighty fleet would enable the United States, with oceans on either flank, to protect itself and to spread its influence to all corners of the world. Named assistant secretary of the navy by President William McKinley in 1897, he aimed to carry out those ideas. His superior, Secretary John D. Long, aging and ill, allowed his youthful aide to order new vessels, recruit more men, buy new armaments and equipment, choose commanders, and move ships about.

In 1898, as tensions escalated between the United States and Spain over Spanish colonial possessions, Roosevelt—without notifying Long or President McKinley—directed Commodore George Dewey to station his Asiatic fleet in battle readiness near the Spanish-held Philippine Islands. When the Spanish-American War erupted, Dewey attacked and destroyed the antiquated Spanish fleet in the Battle of Manila Bay.

In 1900 he was nominated for vice president (some said to get the bumptious young man out of the way) and elected as McKinley won a second term. When Roosevelt became president, he resumed his effort to build the American navy into a force to be reckoned with. It wasn't until 1905, however, after he had been elected to a full term, that he saw his chance to dramatically bring international attention to America's new sea power.

JAPAN SURPRISES THE WORLD

On May 28, 1905, in the far-off Pacific, the world's leadership received an unexpected and unwelcome surprise. The supposedly invincible Russian fleet, after sailing 18,000 miles (28,968.2 km) around three continents, was totally destroyed by the upstart Japanese navy at the Tsushima Strait, off Manchuria. Thirty-seven Russian ships sank to the bottom within a few hours after the Japanese used a daring maneuvering tactic known as *crossing the T* backed up by high-explosive shells to bring overwhelming firepower onto the outgunned and poorly led Russian fleet with its undertrained crews.

In the postmortems after Japan's signal victory, naval experts assessed the strength and readiness of the world's fleets in terms of up-to-date firepower, leadership, training, speed, and maneuverability. Roosevelt bristled when told that the United States ranked

PRESIDENT ROOSEVELT, RIGHT,
IS SHOWN STROLLING ON THE
PRESIDENTIAL YACHT, THE
MAYFLOWER, WITH ADMIRAL ROBLEY
EVANS, WHOM HE SWORE TO
SECRECY ABOUT THE FLEET'S TRUE
MISSION: TO SAIL THE ATLANTIC TO
THE PACIFIC AND BACK AGAIN, IN AN
AROUND-THE-WORLD VOYAGE.
Library of Congress

near the bottom in virtually every category. Last place, were they? He'd show 'em, by George! He'd send his spanking new vessels to every hemisphere and set the other nations back on their heels.

"THE GIRL I LEFT BEHIND ME"

Two years passed before TR's brainchild could become a reality and the U.S. Atlantic Fleet embarked on its grand circle, pushing off from Hampton Roads, Virginia, as a navy band played "The Girl I Left Behind Me."

In the interim Roosevelt had to perform a lot of politicking, persuading, and preparation, plus pushing and shoving, not to mention beating back opposition within the navy itself. No grand fleet, ever, the admirals patiently explained, had completely circumnavigated the globe, so obviously it couldn't be done. Look at the obstacles: How would steam-powered, steel-hulled battleships obtain coal along the route of such a lengthy voyage? What ports would welcome such a huge number of visitors, probably dumping hundreds of rowdy sailors onto their docks and into their taverns?

And where would the money come from to finance such an extravagant idea? How would the homeland be defended if its naval shield were steaming halfway around the world? What excuse could there possibly be for undertaking such an adventure?

The one-sided battle of Tsushima Strait had supplied a partial answer. The Japanese Imperial Navy could obviously menace the American presence in the Pacific, especially its outposts in Hawaii and the Philippines. A domestic issue further inflamed feelings about Japan. Construction of the transcontinental railroad had brought hundreds of Chinese and Japanese workers to California, and they were still coming. Strident newspaper editorials and politicians began warning of a "Yellow Peril" threatening to engulf America. Cries arose for limiting the number of immigrants from Asia, or perhaps barring the door completely.

The Japanese denounced what they called discriminatory treatment. Congress passed immigration legislation setting strict quotas for Japan and China, and anti-American riots broke out in Tokyo and Shanghai, where demonstrators sacked the U.S. consulate. Chinese and Japanese immigrants in San Francisco demonstrated, too. The demonstrations were obviously engineered by the Japanese government, American demagogues cried out; Japan mustn't get away with such an insult. War in the Pacific was seen as a distinct possibility—the Imperial Navy might even attack the West Coast. But most of the U.S. Navy was based in the Atlantic.

Another Roosevelt brainchild, the Panama Canal, was just being started. It would take weeks, maybe months, to transfer battle strength around Cape Horn and into the Pacific. *Jane's Fighting Ships*—the bible of world sea power analysts that founder Fred T. Jane began publishing in 1898—declared that the U.S. Navy was far outclassed by the Japanese, noting that it was top-heavy with aging admirals, who averaged a good ten years older than those of other nations.

The navy also had to be made ready for such an audacious journey. American shipyards were already busily building new battleships, including the USS *Connecticut* and USS *Delaware*, which would carry powerful, long-range, eleven-inch guns and steam-powered turrets, but their launch was still months away. The voyage would have to wait for their completion, Roosevelt realized.

One of the lessons of Tsushima, like a lesson learned by the British in the Boer War, was that gaudy parade-

A POSTCARD COMMEMORATES THE VISIT BY THE GREAT WHITE FLEET TO AUSTRALIA, WHERE THEY WERE INVITED BY PRIME MINISTER ALFRED DEAKIN, WHO BELIEVED A VISIT BY AMERICAN WARSHIPS MIGHT CHECKMATE GROWING JAPANESE INFLUENCE IN THE REGION.

Naval Historical Foundation

ground uniforms or the bright hues of nineteenth-century vessels made them easy targets in war; the Japanese painted their fleet a concealing "battleship gray" to blend in with the sea, and other navies followed suit. Roosevelt would have none of that. He wanted his fleet to be seen, admired, and respected. That was the whole point.

As for the personnel, the U.S. crews and those of other nations were mostly hard-bitten, brawling, heavy-drinking men whose arrival in port caused business owners to shutter their shops and families to lock up their daughters. Roosevelt wanted his crews on liberty to be goodwill ambassadors. He wanted clean-cut American boys, he said, "like the one on the Cracker Jack box." A new recruiting campaign targeted young men on farms and small towns in the Midwest seeking adventure beyond the dull home horizon. "Join the Navy and See the World" became the new recruiting slogan.

A NAVAL RECRUITING POSTER FROM 1917 SEEKS APPLICANTS. THE GOVERNMENT HAD USED SIMILAR POSTERS YEARS BEFORE TO RECRUIT SAILORS FOR THE GREAT WHITE FLEET; ROOSEVELT WANTED CLEAN-CUT BOYS "LIKE THE ONE ON THE CRACKER JACK BOX," HE SAID, TO BE GOODWILL AMBASSADORS.

Library of Congress

As for the cost of the trip, which Roosevelt knew skeptics would question, he told confidants that he had set aside enough money to cover the first half of the trip. Thus, he chortled, he would send the fleet on its way and it would be up to Congress to appropriate enough money to bring the ships back.

JUST PRACTICE

Rumors about the real purpose of all this preparation and fitting-out raced across Washington and around the fleet. Roosevelt deftly sidestepped the questions, not even fully confiding in the officers who would command the operation if it occurred. Finally, without fully giving away his closely guarded secrets, he announced that the full Atlantic fleet would engage in a practice exercise in which it would leave its East Coast ports and sail completely around South America and up the Pacific until it docked in San Francisco. It would be just a drill, just an experiment to show that such a massive transfer could be performed if necessary, and to identify and work out any kinks or problems that it might encounter. Nothing more than practice.

Thus, as the armada of battleships and their auxiliary craft prepared to shove off from Hampton Roads on the surprisingly warm, cloudy morning of December 16, 1907, he called the navy's top admiral, Robley Evans, to the *Mayflower* and gave him orders he was not to confide to anyone until the vessels were safely in San Francisco. His true mission was to take the entire fleet from the Atlantic to the Pacific and back again, around the world—to demonstrate to skeptics that upstart America was now a naval powerhouse, to show the flag in all corners of the earth, to spread American goodwill everywhere, and with TR's ultimate aim, above all—to elevate America's prestige.

Then he shook hands with the admiral, clapped him on the shoulder (Evans, whose disabling gout had hobbled him in climbing the ship's ladder, winced with pain), and sent the great armada down the James estuary into the open sea.

HOT AND COLD RECEPTIONS

The fleet's first port of call was to be Trinidad, Britain's second-largest island colony in the Caribbean. Sailors, in starched dress whites, leaned over the rails to catch the first glimpse of palm trees and what they were sure would be a warm and boisterous tropical welcome with flowers, music, and nubile young maidens. But the docks were empty. There was not even an official welcoming party and Sir Henry Jackson, the colonial governor, was nowhere to be seen. A liberty party that went ashore found the streets deserted and the shops and bars closed.

True, their arrival was late. Admiral Evans, to keep the fleet together, had set top speed at only ten knots. Finally a uniformed officer in a launch appeared at Evans's flagship. The governor, he said, without apology, was ill. But if Evans were to take a hotel room in town, the governor would meet him there. There followed a stiff meeting in the hotel room. No, there would be no festivities or welcoming ceremony. The annual Governor's Ball, to which officers expected to be invited, had been canceled. Any plans for private welcoming parties had been called off.

It was a clear diplomatic snub. U.S. ambassador to London Whitelaw Reid protested to the colonial office, to no avail. It was soon learned that the snub was no oversight, but a deliberate affront. Britain was not about to offer a heroes' welcome to such a cheeky expedition, especially one by a former colony. Besides, Britain wanted to display its hostility to the world, particularly to its new ally Japan. Anyway, what right had America to parade its new battlewagons before the world's recognized queen of the seas? Such effrontery! The sailors returned to their vessels, where they spent a forlorn Christmas. After loading coal, the fleet departed, with the crews vowing never to visit Trinidad again.

Roosevelt had carefully picked to accompany the trip only sympathetic journalists whom he was sure would write flattering and "positive" stories, particularly his favorite, Franklin Mathews of the *New York Sun*. The correspondents responded with gushy stories about the fleet's "plucky deeds," "stout fellows," and handsome young officers who were sure to be idolized by young belles in every port. By some convoluted writing the cheerleaders managed to conceal the cool reception in Trinidad.

When the fleet reached the next stop, Rio de Janeiro, the city was dark.

Seamen could spot only dark spots on the city's famous beaches. Then lights strung across the hills abruptly illuminated the scene. The dark spots were people, hundreds of cheering people, many of whom had camped out for several days to greet the Americans. This was the kind of welcome the crews had been eagerly anticipating.

Evans had selected only two thousand carefully chosen men for shore liberty. The first night a few "carefully chosen" entered a bar near the beach and ordered drinks. Someone threw a bottle, a sailor threw one back, and soon a full-scale brawl broke out and spilled into the streets, where other sailors and locals joined in. Hastily called shore patrol and Brazilian police managed to quell the battle, but the next night the fighting resumed. The next day, Evans canceled all shore leave.

Brazilian president Alfonso Penna apologized profusely and persuaded Evans to let his crews "enjoy Rio." The next eight days were a seemingly endless round of receptions, dinners, dances, sightseeing tours, and toasts—toast after toast to America, President Roosevelt, and U.S.–Brazilian friendship—until the crews could barely stagger back to the ships. Correspondents filled their hometown papers with exultant stories about the glorious reception. The fleet considered the visit a triumph, the more so because Brazilian President Penna announced plans to enlarge his fleet and send it, too, around the world.

Roosevelt's sought-for prestige got further boosts in the hemisphere in ensuing days. Argentina and Brazil had long been rivals for leadership in the southern continent. Argentina had been omitted from the fleet's itinerary—the Rio Plata was said to be too shallow for the big battleships—but Argentina attempted to match Brazil by sending two squadrons to meet the Americans in the Atlantic and staged what Buenos Aires newspapers called "the greatest naval pageant ever to take place on the high seas."

Chile and the United States had had frosty relations since 1891, when "Fighting Bob" Evans earned his nickname by sailing into Valparaiso harbor and threatening to "blow the place to hell" after Chilean police shot and killed two American sailors and wounded seventeen others from the USS *Baltimore* after a barroom fight. This time Chilean warships met Evans's fleet and guided the ships one by one through the treacherous and fogbound waters of the Straits of Magellan, then delivered them to Punta Arenas, the southernmost and bleakest city in the hemisphere, where thirty thousand residents staged a lavish welcome. Then after the fleet wheeled about to pass in review before Valparaiso it was on to Callao, Peru, and the Peruvian capital, Lima, where the local populace also tried to outdo Brazil, with whom Peru was locked in a jungle border war. Then the fleet, weary of all this partying, nonetheless looked forward to an exuberant welcome home in San Francisco.

The correspondents now trotted out their most florid and overused purple prose to describe the fleet's return to an American harbor. It had been a "Roman triumph" proving "grandiose love from all nations," readers were told. While they were at sea Evans had told the fleet they would now continue on completely around the world. Roosevelt announced the new plan to the world. As a result he immediately received three more invitations from bypassed countries that had felt left out.

Australia was first. Prime Minister Alfred Deakin was alarmed about the "Yellow Peril" overwhelming the British dominion, and a visit by American warships might checkmate Japanese influence in the region. He wrote a secret letter of invitation to Roosevelt and London asking permission to host the American fleet. U.S. Secretary of State Elihu Root triumphantly released the letter to the press. Caught between pressure from Australia and America, London gave in and the fleet detoured to the Southern Hemisphere, visiting New Zealand as well.

Meanwhile, Britain dropped its sneers about those American showoffs and their pretension to world power, and began to praise the voyage as if it had viewed it favorably all the time. Ambassador Reid was invited to Buckingham Palace, where King Edward VII took him by the arm to talk about peace in the Pacific among Britain, the United States, and Japan. Two days later, the king wrote Roosevelt a personal letter: "We have watched with the greatest interest the cruise of your fine fleet in the Pacific and have admired the successful manner in which your admirals have so far carried out this great undertaking."

A few days later came another note from the Japanese embassy. A visit to Japan by the fleet, the note said, would produce a "reassuring effect . . . upon the traditional relations of good understanding and mutual sympathy . . . between the two nations." Roosevelt was clearly gaining the prestige he had so eagerly sought.

In San Francisco the pain-wracked Evans took his gout and departed, to be replaced by Rear Admiral Charles Sperry. Two newer vessels supplanted the *Maine* and the *New Jersey*, both of which had mechanical problems and were "coal hogs," which used up the fuel supply. The sailors were also joined in Australia by a group of wives, who had chartered a boat and followed their husbands' ships so as not to be left out of the celebrations. The wives and sailors agreed that Australia's welcome outdid all others; Admiral Sperry counted seventeen dinners, dances, and parties in one day.

They accepted the Japanese invitation, and then Roosevelt faced the dilemma of China, which had become convinced that the whole trip was to show American support for the Open Door Policy, which allowed all nations equal trading rights across China in return for recognition of China's borders so that the country would not be divided up by imperial-minded foreign powers. The fleet managed to visit both, to be welcomed in elaborate ceremonies in Yokohama and Shanghai, but China was miffed that the Japanese visit came first and that only half the fleet showed up, while the others were engaged in gunnery practice off the Philippines.

Kaiser Wilhelm of Germany insisted that the fleet visit German-held Samoa, but a typhoon forced cancellation, and a visit to Manila in the Philippines had to be dropped because of a cholera epidemic. Heading for home through the Suez Canal, the fleet accepted an invitation from France, which had previously jeered at the whole idea, and put in at the Riviera resort of Villefranche for more partying and celebrating. Then, under diplomatic pressure, Sperry divided the fleet into four sections, which made calls at Beirut, Algiers, Port Said, Athens, Malta, Tripoli, and Marseilles before Sperry decided enough was enough. They set out for Hampton Roads with one last pause, to give the battleships a fresh coat of white paint and polish up the scrollwork, just in time for Roosevelt's review and exclamations of "Bully!" on Washington's birthday, February 22, 1909.

MARCHING ON THE WORLD STAGE

Roosevelt sulked a little, if only briefly. He wanted to take up New York's offer of a final triumphant return by sailing up New York harbor, akin to a ticker-tape parade up Broadway, but this time the admirals put their collective foot down on the lame-duck president. He had to console himself with America's new but unmistakable prestige.

Foreign newspapers continued to praise the cruise. "The World's Greatest Success Story," one English paper declared. American newspapers crowed even more loudly. Roosevelt declared that the cruise had "immeasurably raised the prestige, not only of our fleet but of our nation. That was too modest, editorials said. America's prestige abroad had been doubled, no, tripled, and one calculated that the United States was now ten times more respected all over the world. "Never again will they laugh at Uncle

Sam," "The biggest event in American history, with twice the importance of Dewey's victory at Manila Bay," "The United States has marched on to the world stage and joined the ranks of the great powers" were only a few of the accolades.

Jane's Fighting Ships reserved judgment. It moved the United States up in its rankings, but still no better than third, behind Great Britain and Germany, with France moving up fast. *Jane's* concluded that the cruise had been a waste of time and effort. "The best professional opinion is that fourteen months have been lost for the drilling of the fleet."

After he read the clippings and the fan mail, no one could convince Roosevelt of that. "That is the answer to my critics," the outgoing president said, as the bands played and the cannons blasted away in salute at the welcome-home ceremonies at Hampton Roads. "I could not ask a finer concluding scene for my administration."

CHAPTER 14

WOODROW WILSON CLAIMS AN AMERICAN PLACE AT THE TABLE OF WORLD POWER

1917

I T STARTED IN 1914 WITH A WRONG TURN UP A DEAD-END STREET IN A TOWN whose name most Americans couldn't pronounce and in a country of whose existence even fewer were aware. The chauffeur driving Archduke Franz Ferdinand, the Austro-Hungarian heir-apparent, and his wife, the Grand Duchess Sophie, had been rattled first by a bomb hurled at the limousine and second by the archduke's peremptory order, following an understandably tense formal reception at the town hall of Sarajevo (the capital of Austria-Hungary's unhappy Balkan province of Bosnia and Herzegovina), to make an unscheduled visit to a military hospital so that he could visit those wounded by the blast that had been meant for him.

"What's this?" the archduke's military aide snapped at the driver. "We've taken the wrong way!"

The beleaguered chauffeur pulled the brake and spun the wheel in an effort to turn around. Hemmed in by crowds milling behind the open-top limousine, he had to slow to a crawl, and finally stop—as it so happened, directly in front of a café-delicatessen, where, sitting glumly at an outdoor table perhaps five feet (1.5 m) from the archduke and grand duchess, was Gavrilo Princip, yet another would-be assassin.

It was 11:15 a.m. on June 28, 1914, when Princip reached into the pocket of the shabby greatcoat that swallowed up his tubercular frame and withdrew the Browning revolver a Serbian nationalist had given him. He fired a bullet point-blank into the archduke and another into the grand duchess. A third drilled into the car door. The stricken couple exchanged a few words before dying, and thanks to the unreasonable demands of a vengeful Austrian government and the bewildering tangle of alliances and enmities that bound all Europe fatally and inextricably together, war rapidly engulfed the continent and its far-flung empires.

"HE KEPT US OUT OF WAR"

But not the United States, whose populace gazed from across the ocean at what they called the "European War" with a mixture of horror, fascination, self-satisfaction, and no little relief. They were remote from the fighting, they had no stake in the fighting, and, what is more, they were citizens not of some benighted autocracy hobbled by history but of an enlightened democracy that in 1912 had sent to the White House a college professor, former Princeton president, and New Jersey governor named Woodrow Wilson, who brought with him a host of sweeping Progressive reforms, including the introduction of a federal income tax, the creation of a central banking system, and the passage of labor laws, which included the curtailment of children's working hours. Now he studiously pursued a course of strict neutrality, and, in 1916, when he ran for a second term, he was conveyed to a narrow victory in large part aboard his memorable campaign slogan: *He Kept Us Out of War.*

Effective though it had been, the slogan wasn't quite accurate. As a neutral, the United States had the right—and under international law, the legal responsibility—to trade with both sides impartially. That was just fine with America's industrialists and bankers, who well knew that very good money was to be made supplying combatants with the stuff of war, including finance. So, in truth, America was very much in the war—and had been since the fateful, fatal summer of 1914.

But there was a difference between 1914 and 1916. At first, U.S. banks and businesses did deal evenhandedly with the belligerents. Whoever wanted to borrow and buy was welcome. More and more, however, the flow of U.S. trade and finance turned away from the Central Powers (Austria-Hungary, Germany, and their allies) and toward the Allies (France, Britain, Italy, and Russia). In part, the shift was the product of moral revulsion. The policies and actions of the Central Powers, especially Germany, were repugnant. Germany's declarations of war on France and Russia in 1914 had been naked acts of aggression, seemingly impossible to justify, and its invasion of France that year via neutral Belgium had been undeniably brutal.

The flow of atrocity stories issuing from "the rape of Belgium" was capped by the saga of Edith Cavell. An Englishwoman working as a Red Cross nurse in that German-occupied country, she secretly collaborated with an underground group formed to help British, French, and Belgian prisoners of war escape into the neutral Netherlands. In August 1915, Cavell was arrested by German authorities, who, on October 9, sentenced her to death. Despite appeals from American diplomats and those of other countries, she was shot by firing squad on October 12, an act interpreted as yet another example of German "barbarism."

THE OCTOBER 12, 1915 FIRING-SQUAD
EXECUTION OF BRITISH EXPATRIATE
NURSE EDITH CAVELL IN BELGIUM
ON CHARGES OF AIDING ALLIED
SOLDIERS TO ESCAPE CAPTURE
BY GERMAN OCCUPATION FORCES
HELPED TURN U.S. PUBLIC OPINION
AGAINST THE CENTRAL POWERS
AND MOVED THE NEUTRAL NATION
CLOSER TO ENTRY INTO THE WAR.

Getty Images

SLOUCHING TOWARD WAR

Still, during the 1916 presidential campaign season, it remained clear that most of the American people wanted no part in the actual fighting. For one thing, except in the cases of the Spanish-American War (1898) and the Boxer Rebellion (1899–1901), Americans by and large relished their isolation. For another, the country was a nation of immigrants. Its large German-American community was pro-German, raised significant charitable funds for the Fatherland, and either wanted Wilson to stay out of the war altogether or, if anything, enter on the side of the Kaiser. As for the even larger Irish-American community, it also sought neutrality, but was willing to side with any nation that fought *against* the hated English. To the rest of the American people—those who didn't run a bank, steel mill, or munitions plant—it made little difference who won this "Great War," just as long as America stayed out of it.

Certainly, Germany had no wish to acquire another enemy in a struggle whose biggest theater, the Western Front, had become hopelessly stalemated. The front had congealed into a blood-drenched gash of trench lines running through Belgium and France from the English Channel in the north to the border of neutral Switzerland in the south.

The front had congealed into a blood-drenched gash of trench lines running through Belgium and France from the English Channel in the north to the border of neutral Switzerland in the south.

German war policies, however, were making absolute neutrality increasingly difficult for the Wilson administration. On May 7, 1915, without warning, a German U-boat torpedoed the British passenger liner *Lusitania,* drowning 1,201 persons, including more than 120 Americans. Never mind that the German embassy in Washington had published a clear warning in the American papers before the *Lusitania* left New York:

NOTICE!

TRAVELLERS intending to embark on the Atlantic voyage are reminded that a state of war exists between Germany and her allies and Great Britain and her allies; that the zone of war includes the waters adjacent to the British Isles; that, in accordance with formal notice given by the Imperial German Government, vessels flying the flag of Great Britain, or any of her allies, are liable to destruction in those waters and that travellers sailing in the war zone on the ships of Great Britain or her allies do so at their own risk.

IMPERIAL GERMAN EMBASSY,
Washington, D.C. 22nd April 1915

Also never mind that the *Lusitania*, a civilian luxury liner, was registered with the Royal Navy's admiralty as an "auxiliary cruiser" and was loaded with a cargo of American-made munitions, including ten and a half tons (9,525 kg) of rifle cartridges, fifty-one tons (46,267 kg) of shrapnel shells, and a large amount of highly explosive gun cotton (nitrocellulose). Also on board were sixty-seven Canadian soldiers of the 6th Winnipeg Rifles. Never mind all this.

Wilson responded by condemning the attack as "unlawful and inhuman" and sent a strongly worded diplomatic protest to the German government on May 9, 1915. When he sent a follow-up protest the next month, on June 9—even after the U.S. Customs Service had confirmed the presence of military contraband onboard the *Lusitania*—Wilson's secretary of state William Jennings Bryan resigned in protest, claiming that the president was acting in a deliberately provocative manner.

And the *Lusitania* was hardly the end of it. In August, Germany sank another British liner, *Arabic*, also causing the loss of American lives. After this, however, the German government, truly fearful that America would be provoked into joining the war, announced the suspension of "unrestricted submarine warfare." From now on, U-boats would surface before attacking unarmed vessels and give warning sufficient to allow passengers and crews to abandon ship. The suspension lasted less than two years. As it became apparent to the German military that the new policy was allowing too many British convoy vessels to get through with the munitions that were taking a terrible toll at the front, Kaiser Wilhelm II ordered the resumption of unrestricted submarine warfare effective February 1, 1917. Three days later, Wilson severed diplomatic relations with Germany and, later that very day, a U.S. warship, the *Housatonic*, came under attack.

LAST STRAWS

Woodrow Wilson had been reelected on the *He Kept Us Out of War* slogan, but now, scarcely three months later, the aggregate heft of American big business and high finance had come to outweigh popular isolationist sentiment. High demand, an ample supply of gold, favorable shipping, and the realities of geography made dealing with the Allies far more reliable and profitable than doing business with Germany and the other Central Powers. In addition, U.S. moguls and bankers had developed a collective gut feeling, hardly justified by events, that the Allies would ultimately prevail, which made them seem a better credit risk than the Central Powers. Winners paid their debts; losers either couldn't or wouldn't.

By the start of 1917, American firms had done some $2 billion in business with the Allies, and U.S. banks had made $2.5 billion in loans to them. In contrast, those same banks had loaned by this time a mere $45 million to Germany. Politically, the United States might still be neutral. Financially, it had already taken sides.

But much as he hated war and resented the mounting pressures on him to enter the "European War," Wilson began, after his 1916 reelection, to perceive other, positive reasons for going to war. He had come increasingly to believe that the United States could be a leading voice in shaping the course of the postwar world, a course toward a future without war and without the tyrants and autocrats who make war. Wilson also understood that the United States would be required to pay for that voice with American blood.

These thoughts notwithstanding, he continued to hold back. Safely reinstalled in office, the president made a fresh stab at mediation. On December 18, 1916, he invited the Allies and the Germans to state, clearly and once and for all, their "war aims." His hope was that, with the air cleared, peace talks would naturally follow, but nothing came of the invitation.

Next, on January 22, 1917, the president took a new tack, appealing for unbiased international conciliation based on the goal of achieving "peace without victory" on all sides. It is a measure of Britain's war weariness that it confidentially communicated willingness to accept Wilson's mediation on these grounds, as did Austria-Hungary,

The Lost Cunard Steamship Lusitania
X Where the First Torpedo Struck. XX Where the Second Torpedo Struck.

the nation most directly responsible for the war in the first place. Germany, however, rejected the American president as a mediator, claiming that the United States had effectively ceased to be neutral and unbiased. Then came the German announcement on January 31, 1917, of the resumption of unrestricted submarine warfare.

The combination of what Wilson saw as German intransigence on the question of mediation and deliberate provocation in the form of unrestricted U-boat aggression prompted him to take his first unambiguous steps toward war. On February 3, 1917, he severed diplomatic relations between the United States and Germany. Later in the month, on February 26, he issued an executive order authorizing U.S.-flagged merchant vessels to arm themselves. He invented an eerily paradoxical phrase for the new policy: "armed neutrality."

"Armed neutrality" was the first administration-sanctioned action in what had for some time been a high-profile but entirely unofficial military preparedness movement. Wilson never criticized these private preparedness activities, but until the resumption

ON MAY 7, 1915, WITHOUT WARNING, A GERMAN U-BOAT TORPEDOED THE BRITISH PASSENGER LINER *LUSITANIA*, KILLING 1,201 PEOPLE, INCLUDING MORE THAN 120 AMERICANS. THE INCIDENT FURTHER HEIGHTENED TENSIONS BETWEEN THE UNITED STATES AND GERMANY. PRESIDENT WOODROW WILSON WOULD SEVER DIPLOMATIC RELATIONS WITH GERMANY IN 1917.

Getty Images

WILSON FUMBLES FOR PEACE

President Woodrow Wilson was an idealist and, by inclination, a pacifist. As a child in the South during the American Civil War, he had seen the awful ruin of war close up, and he had learned to hate war.

Early in 1916, he sought to avoid any possibility of America's entry into the war by bringing the conflict itself to a quick end. He sent his closest adviser, Edward M. House, to London and Paris to sound out Allied leaders on the idea of the American government's acting as mediator among the belligerents. It was a good faith offer that resulted in a tragically ambiguous agreement drawn up with the British foreign secretary Sir Edward Grey on February 22, 1916. The document warned that the United States might enter the war if Germany rejected Wilson's efforts at mediation, and it further stipulated that the right to initiate U.S. mediation rested not with the American president but with the government of Great Britain.

Thus, on the one hand, the House-Grey document was a sincere effort to bring about binding mediation, but, on the other hand, it was an American threat of war against Germany and a virtual announcement of impending alliance with Britain. In the end, the agreement was sufficiently disturbing to Wilson himself that, as the 1916 elections neared, he decided to suspend his peace initiative precisely because it might be perceived as a threat to enter the war or might even inadvertently lead to entry. Unfortunately, the German government had already seen the memorandum, which made Wilson look like anything but a disinterested broker.

of unrestricted submarine warfare, he had consistently met each call for an official policy with the response that the United States would remain the "champion of peace." Even after he severed diplomatic relations with Germany, he declared, incredibly enough, that he was "not now preparing or contemplating war or any steps that need lead to it."

Throughout late 1916 and early 1917, German attacks on British and American merchant ships continued; no fewer than three U.S. ships plying the North Atlantic commercial sea-lanes were sunk on March 18, 1917, alone. These outrages came hard on the heels of one other, which proved to be of even greater consequence.

THE ZIMMERMANN TELEGRAM

On February 23, 1917, Walter Hines Page, U.S. ambassador to the Court of St. James's—official title of America's chief diplomat in London—reported to Wilson the contents of a telegram British intelligence had intercepted and decrypted, from Germany's foreign minister, Arthur Zimmermann, to Germany's ambassador to Mexico:

On the first of February, we intend to begin unrestricted submarine warfare. In spite of this, it is our intention to endeavor to keep the United States of America neutral. In the event of this not succeeding, we propose an alliance on the following basis with Mexico: That we shall make war together and make peace together. We shall give generous financial support, and an understanding on our part that Mexico is to reconquer the . . . territory [lost as a result of the 1846–1848 U.S.-Mexican War] in New Mexico, Texas, and Arizona. The details of settlement are left to you. You are instructed to inform the president [of Mexico] of the above in the greatest confidence as soon as it is certain that there will be an outbreak of war with the United States and suggest that the president, on his own initiative, invite Japan to immediate adherence with this plan; at the same time, offer to mediate between Japan and ourselves. Please call to the attention of the president that the ruthless employment of our submarines now offers the prospect of compelling England to make peace in a few months.

It was a harebrained proposal, and, even though U.S.-Mexican relations were at a low point in 1917, Mexican president Venustiano Carranza had the abundant good sense to reject it. But when Wilson revealed the "Zimmermann Telegram" to Congress and the American people on March 1, it was more than enough to stir patriotic outrage.

Yet even now, it was the president's secretary of the Interior, not the president himself, who issued the most bellicose official response to the telegram. "We can stand Germany's arrogance no longer," Franklin K. Lane exploded on March 31.

If we are to believe the report of Wilson's longtime friend Frank Cobb of the New York *World* (some recent historians have accused Cobb of gross invention), the next day, April 1, Wilson confided to him that entering the war would erode America's soul: "The spirit of ruthless brutality will enter the very fiber of our national life, infecting Congress, the courts, the policeman on the beat, the man in the street. Conformity will be the only virtue. And every man who refuses to conform must pay the penalty."

Cobb later reported that he had never seen the president "so worn down" as he had appeared on April 1. No wonder. On April 2, when he mounted the rostrum before a special joint session of Congress to request a declaration of war, Wilson would famously proclaim that the "world must be made safe for democracy," and yet, if Cobb's report is truthful, the president seemed to recognize that fighting the war would risk nothing less than *destroying* democracy in the United States itself. Navigating the pretzel logic of it all must have been wearing indeed, and we are left wondering: On the very eve of his decision to go to war, was the president in a state of denial?

Certainly, he had avoided major preparations for war, though he winked at the ongoing unofficial preparations. Recent historians have gone so far as to conclude that, even as he delivered his thirty-two-minute war message to Congress beginning at 8:40 p.m. on April 2, 1917, he wistfully clung to the hope that America would not actually have to send troops to Europe. Given the war weariness on both sides, these historians suggest that he seriously believed that the mere threat of U.S. entry would be sufficient to end the war right then and there. Yet if the recollections of Wilson's personal secretary, Joseph Tumulty, are to be trusted (and, as with Cobb's report, some historians do not trust them), Wilson was not really so naïve. At some emotional and intellectual level, he squarely faced the reality that intimidation alone would not bring peace.

Tumulty recalled that, at about 10 p.m., having returned to the White House after delivering his war message, Wilson slumped in a chair at the table in the empty cabinet room. Tumulty entered, and Wilson locked eyes on him. Reflecting on the thunderous applause that had greeted his speech, the president said, "Think what it was they were applauding. My message today was a message of death for our young men. How strange it seems to applaud that." Wilson then put his head in his hands and wept uncontrollably, according to Tumulty.

Whether he really did cry in the minutes and hours after he delivered his war message, no trace of doubt had crept into the speech itself. He had spoken of fighting "for the ultimate peace of the world and the liberation of its people" and, of course, of making the "world . . . safe for democracy."

BLIND IDEALISM

There were economic and political pressures on the president to enter World War I, but it was the intensely idealistic motive of reforming the world, of making it safe for democracy and ending the very possibility of future wars, that finally overcame Woodrow Wilson's strong aversion to plunging into the Old World's bloodbath. So powerful was Wilson's idealism that it seems to have blinded him (as well as a majority of Congress) to the vast gulf separating the decision to declare war from America's utter inability, as of April 1917, to actually fight that war. Whereas the Central Powers fielded millions of men, the strength of the regular U.S. Army in April 1917 stood at about 200,000, barely on a par with the very smallest of European states.

That the American nation managed to summon the will and wherewithal to raise, train, and equip an army of 4.5 million by November 11, 1918, the day the war ended, having sent more than two million of these men to Europe, is an achievement beyond remarkable—and yet it does not diminish the recklessness of *declaring* war from a place of such profound unpreparedness.

Although Wilson had intended it as the "war to end all wars," we know that a defeated Germany, seething under the humiliating and economically ruinous terms of the Treaty of Versailles, became fertile ground for the rise of Adolf Hitler, so that the "Great War" had to be renamed World War *I* after a second, even deadlier world war erupted in September 1939. The lives of more than eight million soldiers and some 6.6 million civilians were violently ended by World War I, among them some 110,000 Americans.

A WORLD WAR I CARTOON SHOWS A HAND IN A GAUNTLET WITH THE IMPERIAL GERMAN EAGLE CARVING UP THE SOUTHWESTERN UNITED STATES. THE 1917 CARTOON BY ARTIST CLIFFORD KENNEDY BERRYMAN WAS IN RESPONSE TO THE ZIMMERMAN TELEGRAM, IN WHICH GERMANY URGED MEXICO TO DECLARE WAR ON THE UNITED STATES.

Library of Congress

By 1917, both the Allies and the Central Powers were all but "bled white" (to use a phrase common during the conflict), but it was the French and the British who were more certainly and rapidly losing both their will and their capacity to continue the fight. There can be no doubt that Wilson's decision to bring the United States into the war made the difference between Allied victory and defeat. Yet there is much to doubt about the wisdom of the decision. Not only did the expenditure of American lives obviously fail to bring an end to war, given the unthinking vindictiveness of the victors, but it also may well have ensured the outbreak of the war that followed less than two decades later—in which at least 22 million soldiers and more than 60 million civilians were wiped from the face of the planet.

In the longer term, Wilson's decision elevated the United States to a position of world power. Although the three isolationist Republican administrations that followed Wilson—those of Warren G. Harding, Calvin Coolidge, and Herbert Hoover—tried to retreat from this position, they could not do so permanently. For better or worse, the United States had become a major force in world affairs, whether in peace or in war. This role shaped the perceptions and policies of every president, beginning with Franklin D. Roosevelt, and, in the name of both defending and disseminating democracy worldwide, one commander in chief after another has committed American lives and treasure to wars in some of the world's most remote places, from Korea and Vietnam to Afghanistan and Iraq.

CHAPTER 15

FRANKLIN ROOSEVELT ESTABLISHES SOCIAL SECURITY, THE FIRST NATIONAL SAFETY NET FOR PEOPLE WITH DISABILITIES AND SENIORS

1935

BY THE MIDDLE OF 1934, PRESIDENT FRANKLIN DELANO ROOSEVELT, PATRICIAN son of patrician parents, had enacted numerous programs to help America's poor deal with the Great Depression. In the two years since he began his first term in office, Roosevelt had helped stabilize the banking system, propped up the stock market, rescued farmers through farm subsidies, and brought jobs to the jobless through such New Deal programs as the Works Progress Administration and the Civilian Conservation Corps.

Roosevelt had numerous fierce critics among Republicans, particularly the more conservative ones, who claimed that he was bringing socialism to America. Roosevelt dismissed this, saying that instead he was moving the country "forward to greater freedom, to greater security for the average man than he has ever known before in the history of America." And the American people were on his side. In the congressional elections that year, the GOP, already in the minority, would lose thirteen seats in the House and nine in the Senate. Of the nation's forty-eight governors, only seven would remain Republican.

One day in the late spring of 1934, Roosevelt summoned his secretary of labor, Frances Perkins, into the Oval Office. Perkins was the first female cabinet member in U.S. history, a small, slim, sedately dressed woman given to wearing tricornered hats. Her cool personality masked a fierce desire to help America's underprivileged. At the age of thirty-two in 1912, she witnessed the tragic Triangle Shirtwaist Factory fire, in which 146 garment workers died after a fire broke out in a sweatshop in lower Manhattan. The workers were unable to escape because the exit doors were locked.

Roosevelt and Perkins had agreed when she became his labor secretary that her focus would be on providing security for workers when they reached old age—for now there was none, unless workers happened to have a pension, which relatively few did. The Democratic Party, in its 1932 presidential platform, gave lip service to the idea of "social insurance," but, as usual, few politicians could agree on exactly how such a program should be enacted—who it might cover and who would pay for it. Most people felt that such a system could not possibly work if everyone was included, that anyone pushing the policy of social insurance needed to focus only on the very poor, the ill, or the very old.

But, that day in 1934, the president startled Perkins by telling her: "There is no reason why everyone in the United States should not be covered. From the cradle to the grave they ought to be in a social insurance system."

A PERILOUS OLD AGE

Up until the late eighteenth and early nineteenth centuries, the world's economy was mainly an agrarian one—extended families lived and died on the farms that were their source of security in old age. But with the coming of the Industrial Revolution, people broke their ties with the land, came to the cities, and worked for wages for others. Once they became too old or sick to work, they had nothing to fall back on and often no one to care for them. This trend was initially seen in Europe, which, in the late nineteenth century, began to develop early social security systems. Germany, under Chancellor Otto Bismarck, started the first state-sponsored old age retirement program in 1889. By the time of the Great Depression, thirty-four European and Latin American countries, including Italy, Spain, Switzerland, Portugal, Chile, and Uruguay, had some kind of social insurance program.

In the United States, progress had been slower, despite the fact that the great American firebrand Tom Paine had called for just such a social insurance system in *Agrarian Justice*, his last pamphlet, published in 1795 (his suggestion was that a fund be created—by taxing those with inherited property—that would pay out a fixed amount to everyone when they reached the age of fifty). During the nineteenth century, worker guilds provided some fallback for American workers, as did fraternal organizations like the Freemasons and the Elks, but Americans who had migrated to the big cities (and those left behind on dying farms during droughts or economic disturbances) had almost no support and perished in poorhouses or on the street.

Although progressive American thinkers had talked about social security for years, the unprecedented Great Depression brought the issue to a head. Now, 56 percent

A SOUP LINE FOR THE UNEMPLOYED
IN CHICAGO IN 1930. DURING THE
GREAT DEPRESSION, 2 MILLION
HOMELESS MEN WANDERED THE
COUNTRY, AND THE ELDERLY FOUND
THEMSELVES QUEUED UP IN SOUP
KITCHEN LINES OR DEPENDENT ON
VARIOUS CHARITIES.

Library of Congress

of the American population lived in big cities (double the number from forty years before) and, in the early 1930s, a quarter of such Americans were without jobs. Two million homeless men wandered the country, and the elderly found themselves queued up in soup kitchen lines or dependant on various charities. This was the situation Franklin Roosevelt was determined to remedy when he called Frances Perkins into his office.

"WE HAVE TO GET IT STARTED"

When Perkins heard how all-encompassing Roosevelt wanted to make his social security system, she was shocked. As she later related in her memoir, *The Roosevelt I Knew*: "I felt sure that the political climate was not ready for such a universal approach." Not only would the administration's political enemies raise a hue and cry, but so would many ordinary Americans, who, she felt, prided themselves on being independent and self-sufficient. Then there was the simple matter of paying for such a massive system at a time when the United States was only just beginning to get back on its feet again.

Roosevelt pushed aside her concerns. "We can't help that," he told her. "We have to get it started or it will never start." He was daily the recipient of letters like the one from a South Carolina woman who wrote: "Dear Mr. President, I'm seventy-two years old and have no one to take care of me." Or the one from a sixty-year-old widow in Virginia, who said, "I'm . . . greatly in need of medical aid, food and fuel, I pray that you would have pity on me."

He told Perkins he was creating a Committee on Economic Security (CES) and that she would be its chairperson. The other members would include high-powered cabinet officers: Attorney General Homer Cummings, Secretary of Treasury Henry Morgenthau Jr., and Secretary of Agriculture Henry Wallace. He also told her he had few resources to give the CES. "Be economical," Roosevelt told her. "Borrow people around the government from different bureaus. Don't go outside any more than you have to."

On June 8, 1934, Roosevelt announced to Congress that he had ordered the CES formed and tried to dispel the Republican protests that he knew were sure to follow:

Security was attained in the earlier days through the interdependence of members of families upon each other and of the families within a small community upon each other. The complexities of great communities and of organized industry make less real these simple means of security. Therefore, we are compelled to employ the active interest of the Nation as a whole through government in order to encourage a greater security for each individual who composes it . . . This seeking for a greater measure of welfare and happiness does not indicate a change in values. It is rather a return to values lost in the course of our economic development and expansion. . . .

In the meantime, the members of CES were hard at work trying to find a workable model for social security. They looked at foreign countries that had similar social programs as they tried to decide whether social security should be a federal program or a shared federal-state program, and how it should be funded. Through taxes on businesses? But businessmen whose testimony the CES heard claimed such taxes would prolong the Depression. Or through general taxes? But how much would taxes need to be raised to afford the inclusive, sweeping program Roosevelt imagined?

Also, what should the broad concept of social security include? Simple payments after a certain time in life? Disability and health insurance? Unemployment insurance? (At the time, only Wisconsin had an unemployment insurance program.) Roosevelt wanted to make sure all voices were heard in this debate and instructed Perkins to convene the first-ever national town hall forum on social security. The National Conference on Economic Security met at the Mayflower Hotel in Washington, D.C., in November 1934. One hundred and thirty-four guests from around the nation arrived—heads of business, labor union members, economists, and scholars. Roosevelt had allowed the CES to deliberate without his hands-on interference, but he did invite a group of attendees to the White House, where he gave a short speech addressing the issues he considered important.

"Unemployment insurance will be in the program," he told them, stressing that "it is not charity," because it would be funded by worker contributions. Certain progressive committee members pressed Roosevelt on the issue of health insurance; he said that he knew that illness "was a very serious matter for many families both with and without incomes," but he felt that health insurance might be too much for a fledging social security program to bear, although it might be added "later on."

"WE CAN'T SELL THE UNITED STATES SHORT"

By January 1935, the CES had concluded that social security should cover everyone— "from the cradle to the grave"—as Roosevelt had wanted. But there were two major problems that had to be overcome.

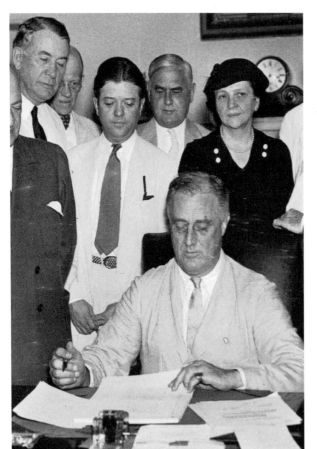

PRESIDENT FRANKLIN ROOSEVELT IS SHOWN SIGNING THE SOCIAL SECURITY BILL ON AUGUST 14, 1935. BEHIND HIM IN THE HAT IS SECRETARY OF LABOR FRANCES PERKINS, WHO SPEARHEADED THE CREATION OF THE SOCIAL SECURITY SYSTEM. HER COOL PERSONALITY MASKED A FIERCE DESIRE TO HELP AMERICA'S UNDERPRIVILEGED.

Associated Press

The first issue was whether a tax on employees and businesses to fund the social security program was constitutional. Frances Perkins worried about this until she happened to find herself at a reception with Supreme Court Justice Harlan Fiske Stone. Dispensing with small talk, she said to him that she was worried about social security.

"Your court tells us what the Constitution permits," she said to Stone.

And carefully choosing his words, Stone replied: "The taxing power of the federal government, my dear—the taxing power is sufficient for everything you want and need."

And he was right. Although there would be two major constitutional challenges to social security in the coming five years, the Supreme Court would strike them both down.

The other issue was that, until worker contributions built up enough to create a large social security fund, those who retired in the next few years would receive a woefully small amount of money. Therefore, the CES recommended that the social security program be initially funded with money taken from general tax revenues.

Roosevelt was resistant to using general taxes to fund his social insurance program. "Ah, but this is the same old dole under another name," he retorted to Perkins, meaning that social security would merely become another government welfare program, when what he wanted was a program in which each individual would fund his share, and which would ultimately be self-sustaining. When the CES then said it could pay for the program with deferred taxes—essentially letting future generations pay for it—Roosevelt replied: "It is almost dishonest to build up an accumulated deficit . . . We can't do that. We can't sell the United States short in 1980 any more than we can in 1935."

Eventually, Roosevelt agreed to temporary funding from general tax revenues and the CES finished its work and delivered its recommendations in a report to the president on January 17, 1935. Roosevelt introduced the report to both the House and the Senate at the same time, and then sat back, as was his wont, to pull strings from behind the scenes.

"THE HAZARDS AND VICISSITUDES OF LIFE"

Congress introduced four different social security bills in early 1935. Many onlookers wondered why the president allowed this many bills to head into committee rather than one single bill pushed by his supporters, but here Roosevelt's political savvy was supreme—he felt that numerous political targets for his enemies would make it harder for them to concentrate their focus than if they could target just one piece of legislation.

There was still a great deal of outcry, however. The National Association of Manufacturers called social security a path toward "ultimate socialistic control of life and industry." Many Republicans felt strongly that the vast bureaucracy created by social security "invites the entrance into the political field," as one Republican congressman grandiosely put it, "of a power so vast, so powerful as to threaten the integrity of our institutions and to pull the pillars of the temple down upon the heads of our descendants."

Roosevelt's enemies put forth rival social security proposals. Huey Long, governor of Louisiana, proposed a "Share Our Wealth" plan in which the federal government would guarantee every family in the nation an annual income of $5,000. Everyone over sixty would get an old age pension. The "Share Our Wealth" movement he launched had more than 7.7 million members.

Another powerful social insurance movement was started by Francis E. Townsend, a doctor from Long Beach, California, who in 1933 found himself unemployed and insolvent at the age of sixty-six. He therefore launched what became known as the Townsend Plan, in which every American citizen aged sixty or older would receive a pension of $200 a month provided that "their past life is free from criminality." The Townsend Plan had two million vocal adherents.

But neither of these plans (fortunately for the country's fiscal health) coalesced into a viable bill, mainly because they lacked the backing of the mainstream Democratic Party. The multiple bills that were introduced were combined after the usual political horse-trading; the result passed the House 371–33 and the Senate 76–6. And on August 14, 1935, President Roosevelt signed the Social Security Act into law, saying: "We can never insure 100

THIS DECEMBER 1939 IMAGE SHOWS A GOVERNMENT WORKER FEEDING SOCIAL SECURITY CHECKS INTO AN AUTOMATIC SIGNING MACHINE, WHICH COULD PROCESS 7,000 CHECKS PER HOUR. THE CHECKS, MADE AT THE U.S. TREASURY DEPARTMENT'S DISBURSING DIVISION, WERE MAILED OUT THE FOLLOWING MONTH.

Library of Congress

percent of the population against 100 percent of the hazards and vicissitudes of life, but we have tried to frame a law which will give some measure of protection to the average citizen and to his family against the loss of a job and against poverty-ridden old age."

"THE CORNERSTONE"

When he first met with Frances Perkins on social security, Roosevelt had sketched out for her an expansive, egalitarian vision of implementing the program. "The system should be implemented through the post office," he told her. "Just simple and natural—nothing elaborate or alarming about it. The rural free delivery carrier ought to bring papers to the front door and pick them up after they are filled out. The rural free delivery carrier ought to give each child his social insurance number. . . ."

Although this somewhat idealistic view of the role postal workers could play in bringing social security to ordinary Americans did not take into account the massive government machinery it would take to actually run such a program, Roosevelt's dream of postal workers carrying the word on social security came true, at least at first.

Starting in November 1936, postmen in New York and then all over the country delivered millions of applications. These were then filled out and brought to the local post office, where Social Security numbers were assigned. Then all the paperwork was sent to Baltimore, Maryland, where Social Security numbers were registered. At the same time, employers were registered.

It was a massive effort, but, beginning January 1, 1937, those who were working began accumulating credits toward an old age pension. More than 30 million people were registered and received Social Security cards in the first year. The first recipient of Social Security was a Cleveland motorman named Ernest Ackerman, who participated in the program for only one day before retiring. He contributed a nickel—and received seventeen cents in benefits.

The government began to issue the first monthly benefits in 1940, but quickly recognized that although the benefits stayed the same, inflation ate away at them. In 1950, the Social Security Act was amended to include a *COLA*, or Cost of Living Increase (in 1972, such COLAs were made automatic). In 1954, disability insurance was added, and in 1965, Lyndon Johnson (see chapter 27) pushed through a health insurance program called *Medicare* that extended health coverage to almost every American over the age of sixty-five.

SPONSORED BY THE SOCIAL SECURITY BOARD, THIS 1935 POSTER EXPLAINS THE PROGRAM AND HOW TO OBTAIN ADDITIONAL INFORMATION ABOUT IT. PRIOR TO SOCIAL SECURITY, PROGRAMS TO HELP OLDER AMERICANS WERE SCARCE.

Library of Congress

A GLANCE AT SOCIAL SECURITY

1935

Congress passes the Social Security Bill. President Franklin Roosevelt signs it into law on August 14, 1935.

2003

The government has issued 420 million Social Security numbers since 1936.

1930　1940　1950　1960　1970　1980　1990　2000

1936-1937

The first calendar year of the program. The government issued 37,139 Social Security numbers, the largest number in the program's history. Approximately 30 million applications for Social Security were processed between November 1936 and June 1937.

Source: www.socialsecurity.gov

There are, of course, numerous issues with the Social Security program that Roosevelt and his planners could not have foreseen. The great inflationary spiral of the 1970s meant that during that decade Social Security was faced with short-term deficits. The program was stabilized when payroll taxes were raised slightly and benefits decreased slightly. However the larger problem Social Security now faces is the retirement of the massive baby boom generation, which officially begins in 2010, but which has been ongoing for the past few years. Because of the very nature of the Social Security system—in which current retirees receive funds paid by younger men and women who are still working—there is always concern that the system will go broke. From 1937, when the first benefits were paid out, until today, the Social Security program has paid out $8.9 trillion. However, at the end of 2008, the Social Security Administration reported a $1.4 trillion nest egg of Treasury securities stashed away to help cushion the baby boom retirement.

Roosevelt understood that Social Security would go through changes: "The law," he said, "represents the cornerstone of a structure which is being built, but is by no means complete." But it has now become an integral part of American life, just as he envisioned.

CHAPTER 16

FRANKLIN ROOSEVELT TAKES A STEP TOWARD WORLD WAR II WITH THE LEND-LEASE PROGRAM

1941

THE WHITE HOUSE REPORTERS CROWDED AROUND THE PRESIDENT'S DESK that chill December afternoon in 1940, pencils and notepads ready—an informal press conference vastly different from the twenty-first-century counterpart, with its presidential podium, auditorium seating, and batteries of tape recorders, microphones, and television cameras. A radiant Franklin Roosevelt, cigarette holder at a jaunty angle, greeted them with an amiable wave. He knew most by first name and enjoyed the easygoing atmosphere, the banter and byplay. Although confined to his wheelchair, he gave the impression of mingling with friends.

The president looked suntanned and relaxed. Having won an unprecedented third term the month before, he had gone off on a two-week Caribbean cruise on the battle cruiser *Tuscaloosa*—ostensibly to visit military installations but actually for "fishing, basking in the sun and spoofing with cronies," an aide said. He had returned, however, to a world situation grown increasingly dire.

The muscular armies in Nazi Germany had overwhelmed Europe, forcing the surrender of France and giving the Germans total command of the continent. Savage nightly bombardments by the German air force, the Luftwaffe, had devastated Great Britain, leaving the cities ash heaps of flaming rubble—scenes that the horrified American public witnessed in movie newsreels and through the riveting "This Is London" nightly newscasts of Edward R. Murrow. Britain now stood alone against the victorious German armies. The beleaguered British, through their defiant, bulldoggish prime minister Winston Churchill, were desperately appealing to America for help— planes, ships, ammunition, weapons. Most of all, the once opulent British empire needed cash or financing to buy more. The struggle had drained its treasury of gold reserves and dollar credits. The British ambassador, Lord Philip Lothian, returning to the United States from London, had put it simply to reporters: "Well, boys, Britain's broke. It's your money we want."

Waving the cigarette holder, the president airily declared that he really had no announcements for the press corps, none at all. He had been on vacation, after all. Then he said, well, he might have one item of interest. Offhandedly, as though he had just thought of the idea and was chatting with friends, he proceeded in a few carefully crafted sentences to reveal a decision that was to change history. He announced what Winston Churchill would later term "the most unsordid act by any nation in history." The United States would furnish Britain with whatever it needed to carry on the fight. Help would be given not in the form of greenbacks or credits but in equipment, which Britain could return later. "What I am trying to do is eliminate the dollar sign," the president said. "Get rid of the silly, foolish old dollar sign."

In the folksy way his "fireside chats" had reassured a desperate America during the depths of the Great Depression, the president outlined for reporters what he had in mind, in simple terms that could be understood by every household in America and would resonate around the world.

Suppose, the president said, my neighbor's house catches fire. I have 150 feet (45.7 m) of garden hose that would help him quench the blaze. It would be my duty, my neighborly obligation, to offer him that hose and help him douse the flames. But suppose that my hose was badly damaged in fighting the fire, maybe torn by dragging it across the property or trampled under firefighters' boots. Suppose when the fire was out, the hose was no longer useable. My neighbor could return the hose, but of course, I don't want a hose I can't use. I want a useful hose. My neighbor should then feel himself obliged to replace the hose or give me money to buy a replacement.

What he was "thinking about" would work just like that. The United States would furnish arms and equipment to the Allies, and after the war ended, presumably victoriously, the winners would be expected to replace or pay for a replacement. It would be a gentlemen's agreement, worked out between friends, no strings attached.

The multibillion-dollar idea would go into the books as "Lend-Lease."

"THE NEW WORLD MUST RESCUE THE OLD WORLD"

Despite the president's casual disclaimer, more had happened on that two-week cruise than fishing, sunning, and swapping jokes. On December 9, 1940, a week after the presidential party embarked, a British seaplane skimmed to a landing alongside the *Tuscaloosa* and handed over a package addressed to the president of the United States.

PRESIDENT ROOSEVELT, AT
THE WHEEL, SITS NEXT TO HIS
SECRETARY OF TREASURY,
CONFIDANT, AND NEIGHBOR,
BANKER HENRY MORGANTHAU JR.,
IN 1933. MORGANTHAU BECAME
THE POINT MAN FOR THE LEND-
LEASE PLAN, HELPING REVISE
DRAFTS OF THE BILL.
Library of Congress

The prime minister of embattled Britain had spent days drafting and redrafting a long letter eloquently describing the plight of the war-torn country—militarily, politically, and especially financially. Britain's needs were desperate if it were to continue the fight that Churchill insisted was America's battle, too. If Britain fell, the Western Hemisphere would surely be the next target. The New World, he stated in a refrain that was to ring again and again in the House of Commons, must come to the rescue of the Old World.

According to Roosevelt's longtime close adviser Harry Hopkins, the president retired to his stateroom and scarcely emerged for two days. When he did appear, he was subdued and solemn. He apparently had read and reread Churchill's letter, reviewing the options available. At that point, Hopkins said, the idea for Lend-Lease took shape in his mind, although he discussed it with no one, including Hopkins.

When he returned to Washington, he immediately consulted his Hyde Park neighbor, confidant, and secretary of the treasury, the banker Henry Morgenthau Jr. The basic problems, after all, were financial. Roosevelt hadn't thought out all the details, but he had decided on the fire hose analogy. "It was a typical Roosevelt brilliant flash," Morgenthau said later, giving FDR full credit for dreaming up the proposal. What did Morgenthau think of the lending and leasing idea? "If I followed my own heart, I would say, 'Let's give it to them,'" Morgenthau recalled, but he accepted Roosevelt's plan. Thereafter Morgenthau and the Treasury Department, to the annoyance of Secretary of State Cordell Hull and other cabinet members, became the point man for Lend-Lease.

"AID SHORT OF WAR"

The United States and Roosevelt had already felt threatened by the European war clouds. FDR had called for a policy of "preparedness," launching a boom in the manufacture of planes, tanks, ships, and munitions. In October 1940, the United States conducted the first peacetime military conscription in its history, with men aged twenty-one to thirty-five, chosen by lot, to begin a year of military training. Washington, although technically neutral, also made clear that its sympathies lay with Britain and its allies, on whose side America had fought in World War I twenty-five years before.

There was also limited precedent for Roosevelt's proposal. In September 1940, after Churchill's importuning, FDR had turned over to the British navy fifty "four-pipe" destroyers left over from World War I to assist the British against submarine attacks, which were torpedoing British shipping in the Atlantic and choking off war supplies. In return, the United States received bases in Newfoundland and Bermuda, plus ninety-nine-year leases on air and naval bases on five Caribbean islands. But that action had been a quid pro quo, not an outright loan or grant. Moreover, it had been taken by a simple executive order. Roosevelt had carefully timed the "Destroyers for Bases" announcement for the Labor Day weekend, when Congress was in recess and the holidaying public wasn't paying attention anyway. He couldn't expect such a quiet reception for Lend-Lease. His proposal would require a healthy appropriation and a long-term commitment, neither of which could be achieved without Congress's approval.

Public-opinion polls showed that nearly 70 percent of Americans favored providing aid to Britain, but always with the caveat "aid short of war." Roosevelt knew that Lend-Lease would be a tough sell to the Congress and public. The United States was still smarting about the "war debts" of World War I, when the Allies ran up large bills for arms, munitions, foodstuffs, fuel, and loans—all on the cuff—and then reneged after the war, refusing even to pay the interest on the loans. When Washington pressed for repayment, Uncle Sam was portrayed as "Uncle Shylock," demanding his pound of flesh. When Europe began rearming in the 1930s, the United States cried, "Never again!" and declared itself neutral, with a policy of "cash and carry" for weapons purchases. You want to buy weapons, Europe was told, come and get 'em and pay cash on the barrelhead. For Britain in 1940, of course, that was easier said than done. Nazi submarines were sinking British freighters almost faster than they could be built, and there was no money to build more.

On December 29, Roosevelt solemnly addressed the nation in a "fireside chat" from his library in Hyde Park, first in the reassuring tone that had carried them through the dark days of the Depression. Then he said, "This is not a fireside chat on war." He declared that the world situation was the gravest that America and the world had faced since the 1930s. He emphasized what he knew Americans had heard on radio broadcasts and seen in newsreels, and particularly the threat to Great Britain.

"If Great Britain goes down," he said solemnly, "the Axis powers will control the continents of Europe, Asia, Africa, Australasia, and the high seas, and they will be in a position to bring enormous military and naval resources against this hemisphere. It is no exaggeration to say that all of us, in all the Americas, would be living at the point of a gun."

Britain and its allies, he added, "do not ask us to do their fighting. They ask us for the implements of war. We must have more ships, more guns, more planes . . . We must become the great arsenal of democracy."

Meanwhile, working nonstop and prodded by FDR, Morgenthau's staff was drafting a bill based on Roosevelt's "brilliant flash." Two young assistants worked frantically through the holiday period, sending repeated drafts to Morgenthau and Roosevelt, both of whom were at their Hudson Valley estates. Roosevelt wanted a bill that would give him full and unhampered authority to order what he deemed necessary and send it where he thought it would do the most good. It should state that the United States could lend the equipment but leave vague how it was to be repaid. It should include an initial appropriation of $5 billion to $7 billion. Morgenthau at first hesitated at such a sweeping measure, but he finally approved what his staff called "a shoot-the-works bill."

Drafts were also circulated to cabinet members, military leaders, and the British. Ambassador Lord Philip Lothian asked what repayment would be stipulated. The president's only concern, he was told, was "to make sure that you win." Repayment could be discussed later. At 5:05 p.m. on January 7, 1941, Morgenthau went to the White House with the final draft. At 5:15 the president—"in a grand humor," Morgenthau wrote in his diary—scrawled in large letters on the draft, "OK. FDR." That evening, in his State of the Union address, Roosevelt announced he was sending the proposed bill to Congress. On January 10, the bill was introduced simultaneously into both houses of Congress. Technically it was called "the Joint Resolution to Promote the Defense of the United States," but it quickly became known as the *Lend-Lease Act*. With a nod to history, it was given the title "H.R. 1776."

"AMERICA FIRST!"

Opposition was immediate and vocal. Not surprisingly, the German-American Bund demonstrated against a measure that the organization saw as a supposed neutral country illegally favoring a belligerent one, Britain, against the other, Germany. So did the American Communist Party; Stalin had just signed a nonaggression pact with Hitler and the two dictators had dismembered Poland. The party denounced Lend-Lease as a capitalist alliance against the world's workers.

Many felt that the Allied cause was already lost and Lend-Lease represented throwing good money after bad. America would be better off withholding aid to Britain and building up its own strength. The renowned aviator Charles A. Lindbergh and fellow members of the isolationist America First! Committee preached withholding aid and compelling Britain to negotiate for peace. "Lindy" had already angered Roosevelt by accepting the Iron Cross from Air Marshal Hermann Goering, commander of the Luftwaffe. He had also warned Americans that the German fliers were superior to the British in the air, with more advanced aircraft, despite their setback in the Battle of Britain.

Some of Roosevelt's strongest supporters turned against him on Lend-Lease. William Allen White, editor of the Emporia, Kansas, *Gazette*, and a longtime voice of progressive Republicans, had helped found the Committee to Defend America by Aiding the Allies. Now he resigned from the committee he had founded. He opposed Lend-Lease as granting dictatorial powers to the president and bringing the nation to the brink of armed intervention. He said America's motto should be "The Yanks Are *Not* Coming." Others, including members of Roosevelt's own cabinet, saw Lend-Lease and the vision of the United States as an "arsenal of democracy" as sure steps toward war. "We cannot permanently be in the position of toolmakers for other nations which fight," said Secretary of War Henry Stimson, a Republican and former secretary of state who had been appointed to add a bipartisan and war-hawk presence to the cabinet.

One of the most strident opponents was Roosevelt's onetime ally, Democratic senator Burton Wheeler of Montana. In a fiery speech Wheeler alluded to Roosevelt's New Deal Agricultural Assistance Act, which had attempted to boost depressed farm

77TH CONGRESS
1ST SESSION

H. R. 1776

IN THE HOUSE OF REPRESENTATIVES

JANUARY 10, 1941

Mr. McCormack introduced the following bill; which was referred to the Committee on Foreign Affairs

A BILL

Further to promote the defense of the United States, and for other purposes.

1   *Be it enacted by the Senate and House of Representa-*
2   *tives of the United States of America in Congress assembled,*
3   That this Act may be cited as "An Act to Promote the
4   Defense of the United States".
5   SEC. 2. As used in this Act—
6   (a) The term "defense article" means—
7   (1) Any weapon, munition, aircraft, vessel, or
8   boat;
9   (2) Any machinery, facility, tool, material, or
10   supply necessary for the manufacture, production, proc-

WITH A NOD TO HISTORY, THE BILL OUTLINING THE LEND-LEASE ACT OF 1941 WAS GIVEN THE TITLE "H.R. 1776."

National Archives

A GROUP OF WOMEN MARCH IN FRONT OF THE WHITE HOUSE PROTESTING THE LEND-LEASE ACT DURING THE WINTER OF 1940–41. OPPOSITION TO THE BILL INCLUDED ISOLATIONISTS, THE FAMED AVIATOR CHARLES LINDBERGH, GERMAN-AMERICAN ORGANIZATIONS, AND SOME OF ROOSEVELT'S STRONGEST SUPPORTERS.

income by reducing crops and herds, like plowing under young corn shoots or killing piglets and thus diminishing the supply. He called Lend-Lease the New Deal's "triple-A foreign policy; it will plow under every fourth American boy."

"That really is the rottenest thing that has been said in public life in my generation," Roosevelt raged.

Some opposition was simply reflexively anti-Roosevelt. Some charged that Lend-Lease was just a "power grab" by the president. The Republican presidential candidates defeated by Roosevelt in 1932 and 1936, Herbert Hoover and Alf Landon, attacked the bill. Hoover called it dictatorial. But Roosevelt got a tremendous boost when Wendell Willkie, the losing Republican candidate in 1940, endorsed Lend-Lease. Roosevelt immediately dispatched him to London as a special adviser to Churchill. Willkie helped Churchill draft a ringing speech aimed at Americans, closing with: "Give us the tools and we will finish the job."

"AN UNCLEAN BILL"

On January 10, 1941, the Lend-Lease proposal was simultaneously introduced into the new Congress by the Democratic leaders, Alben Barkley in the Senate and John W. McCormack in the House; McCormack warily announced it as "a bill further to promote the defense of the United States and for other purposes." FDR set out to use all his political persuasion, newly reelected clout—and guile—to get the measure passed.

Hearings on the bill began on January 15, 1941. Roosevelt, Morgenthau, and Secretary of State Cordell Hull had carefully steered them to hospitable committees that

FDR thought would provide a warm and speedy acceptance, while ostensibly allowing opponents full voice to express their views. The sessions quickly became front-page news countrywide and the most coveted ticket in Washington, playing to packed houses and attracting the city's social leaders, dressed in their best finery. Lindbergh's appearance brought a huge crowd that spilled down the Capitol steps; asked by one questioner which side he hoped would win the war, he answered, "Neither." Much testimony reflected the standard anti-Roosevelt or anti-British sentiment. Representative Hamilton Fish of New York called Lend-Lease "a Fascist bill" to allow Roosevelt to take over the government; Senator Bennett Clark of Missouri called Lend-Lease "the King's royal tax for the support of the British Empire." As the hearings progressed, however, public opinion polls showed that two-thirds of Americans approved the measure even at the risk of war.

Passage of the bill was actually a foregone conclusion, considering public sympathy for Britain and Roosevelt's personal power. Roosevelt had hoped for a "clean" bill, granting him the power he sought, but in the end was forced to accept certain amendments, while fending off others. Most of the amendments were aimed at limiting Roosevelt's authority. He had declared that he had no intention of assigning U.S. warships to escort supply-laden British ships across the Atlantic—"escorting could lead to shooting," he said at a press conference, "and shooting comes awfully close to war, doesn't it? That's about the last thing we have in mind." Nevertheless, Congress inserted a clause forbidding convoying, which other officials insisted he already had the right to order under the Constitution and international law.

Another proposed amendment would have limited aid only to Britain, an effort to block potential assistance to the Soviet Union, should it join the Allies. The amendment was defeated partly because the limitation would exclude aid to China, whose uphill struggle against Japan was a popular cause in the United States. Still a third proposed amendment triggered two days of intense Senate debate. Originally it stated that Lend-Lease should not be construed to allow U.S. forces to serve anywhere outside the Western Hemisphere. On a close vote it was revised to eliminate the geographical reference. The final version also included a time limit on the president's Lend-Lease authority, and requirements that he provide regular reports to Congress on the Lend-Lease program.

In another jovial press conference during the debate, the president facetiously suggested that the final bill should bar him from standing on his head, because it was the only thing not prohibited to him. (When the bill finally reached his desk for signing, a reporter asked what would be his first act under the new legislation. He answered with a laugh, "Go out to the middle of Pennsylvania Avenue and stand on my head! I'm still allowed to do that!")

Lend-Lease passed the House on March 10 by a lopsided vote of 317–71, with the Senate approving by 60–31. The president signed the bill on March 19, along with an appropriation bill for $7 billion to get things started. Within two weeks, the first Lend-Lease shipment was on its way to Britain, the beginning of a flood of munitions, weapons, vehicles, planes, and foodstuffs that would eventually total $50.8 billion—$31.3 billion to Britain, $11.2 billion to the Soviet Union, $5 billion to China, and $3.3 billion to France. When the news reached London, a grateful Churchill cabled Roosevelt: "Our blessings from the whole of the British Empire go out to you and the American nation for this very present help in time of trouble." Appropriately, the first Lend-Lease shipment to Britain included 900,000 feet (274.3 km) of fire hose.

A SPECIAL RELATIONSHIP

Lend-Lease, of course, moved the United States closer to war. Within nine months after it was signed, the Japanese attack on Pearl Harbor plunged the United States into all-out war. The nation quickly transformed itself from the arsenal of democracy into a full war footing. Over the next four years, it not only armed its allies and itself, but it also sent men—11 million American troops by the war's end.

As specified in the original legislation, Lend-Lease stopped with the war's end. And it stopped abruptly, as America's allies learned to their surprise, and dismay, after the Japanese surrender on September 2, 1945. By that time both Roosevelt and Churchill were gone from the scene. Roosevelt had died of a massive stroke in April, even before the German capitulation in Europe, to be succeeded by Vice President Harry Truman. Churchill's conservative party had been voted out of office and he had been replaced as prime minister by Clement Attlee of the Labor Party. It was Attlee who received the news and protested that Britain was still devastated militarily and economically and required continued assistance. It came in the form of the Marshall Plan, which called for the economic rehabilitation of Europe via American financial assistance.

Yet Lend-Lease also ushered in what Churchill called a "special relationship" between the United States and Britain, which saw the two countries tightly allied throughout the cold war and the fighting in Korea, Vietnam, Iraq, and Afghanistan, and standing together in international relations.

AMERICAN TWIN ENGINE BOMBERS, PROVIDED UNDER THE LEND-LEASE ACT, ARE BEING HOISTED ABOVE A SHIP IN AN UNKNOWN AMERICAN PORT. PRESIDENT ROOSEVELT TOLD THE AMERICAN PUBLIC THAT THE UNITED STATES "MUST BECOME THE GREAT ARSENAL OF DEMOCRACY."

National Archives

CHAPTER 17

FRANKLIN ROOSEVELT SIGNS THE GI BILL OF RIGHTS AND TRANSFORMS THE COUNTRY ECONOMICALLY, EDUCATIONALLY, AND SOCIALLY

1944

LES FAULK PINCHED HIMSELF. NO, HE WAS WIDE-AWAKE. BUT ON THAT BRIGHT June morning in 1949 he was standing where he had never expected to be, even in his most extravagant dreams. Dressed in a long black academic robe, mortarboard perched squarely on his head, he and two thousand other young men were inching in a serpentine line across the University of Pittsburgh campus.

On a sunlit stage below the university's landmark building, the Cathedral of Learning, Chancellor Rufus H. Fitzgerald greeted each man, and a few women, with a handshake, a word of congratulations, and a blue-and-gold folder containing a bit of parchment stamped with the university seal—a hard-earned college diploma. And each recipient, like Les Faulk, twenty-three, shook his head in pleased bewilderment and gratitude for a path-breaking act of legislation known to history as the *GI Bill of Rights*.

The GI of Bill of Rights, technically the Servicemen's Readjustment Act of 1944, or Public Law 346, was one of the most transformational legislative acts in U.S. history. It sent more than two million young World War II veterans to college and turned them into doctors, lawyers, teachers, scientists, congressmen—at one point, half the representatives in Congress were GI Bill alumni—plus two presidents, two Supreme Court justices, and, in the case of Senators George McGovern and Bob Dole, presidential candidates.

For most of the young men a college degree was a family first: Les Faulk, whose surname was originally Falcocchio, came from an Italian-speaking household where neither parent had finished high school. In Les's high school in Turtle Creek,

Pennsylvania (population: 9,805 in 1940), in the Depression years preceding World War II, fewer than 5 percent of graduates went on to higher education, including barber training and secretarial school.

A LASTING LEGACY

The GI Bill of Rights (quickly shorthanded to the GI Bill) was also one of the most lasting achievements of Franklin D. Roosevelt's four presidential terms. To his credit, FDR never claimed authorship. However, the idea of providing benefits to returning veterans to smooth their reentry into civilian life had been in Roosevelt's mind for a long time. Indeed, the seed was first planted decades before, when Roosevelt was assistant secretary of the navy and then a vice-presidential candidate in 1920, and World War I veterans were sent home with no more than a rail ticket and sixty dollars in cash.

Moreover, FDR was very much aware that the dictatorial governments he was facing in 1944—Nazi Germany and Fascist Italy—had been swept into power by disgruntled jobless World War I veterans, one of them the wounded, decorated corporal Adolf Hitler. Like many other Germans, Hitler felt betrayed by the nation's surrender in 1918 and angry that men who had fought and bled for four years were left to fend for themselves.

Roosevelt's predecessor, Herbert Hoover, also had been the target of veterans' wrath. In 1924, following precedents set after the Civil War, Congress enacted a bonus payment for World War I vets based on length of service—but in the form of certificates that could not be redeemed for twenty years. In the depths of the Great Depression, one in four men was out of work, reduced to selling apples on street corners or standing in breadlines.

In 1932 impoverished veterans led by a former army sergeant agitated to make the certificates immediately redeemable, when the money was desperately needed to feed families. A so-called Bonus Expeditionary Force of 15,000 veterans, with their families and other supporters, marched on Washington hoping to pressure Congress. They set up a makeshift camp of tents and shacks in Washington's Anacostia Flats district, across from the Capitol, while the Senate debated redemption. Capital police were sent in to disperse the protesters; when they resisted, police fired and killed two protesters.

Hoover then ordered army chief of staff General Douglas MacArthur to evacuate the camp. MacArthur sent in the Third Cavalry Regiment, led by six tanks and backed by a regiment of infantry with fixed bayonets and armed with Adamsite gas, to charge the "Hooverville" camp. Four people were killed in the charge and more than

IN 1932 IMPOVERISHED VETERANS
AGITATED TO MAKE THE BONUS
CERTIFICATES IMMEDIATELY
REDEEMABLE, WHEN THE MONEY
WAS DESPERATELY NEEDED
TO FEED FAMILIES. A TOTAL OF
17,000 VETERANS MARCHED ON
WASHINGTON TO PRESSURE
CONGRESS. CAPITAL POLICE WERE
SENT IN TO DISPERSE THEM; WHEN
THEY RESISTED, POLICE FIRED AND
KILLED TWO PROTESTERS.

a thousand injured. Hoover instructed MacArthur to call off the attack, but the general refused; he declared the "Bonus Army" was communist-led and bent on overthrowing the government. The encampment was burned to the ground. That ended the protest, but also helped spell Hoover's doom at the polls in November.

Roosevelt got the message. When a new "Bonus Army" appeared in May 1933, two months after his inauguration, the new president deftly balanced the veterans' demands with budget constraints. He sent his wife Eleanor to meet with the vets, pour coffee for them, and listen to their grievances. With her husband's consent she persuaded many of them to sign up for jobs building the Overseas Highway to the Florida Keys. In 1936, with another election coming up, Congress finally passed legislation allowing redemption of the bonus certificates.

IN TIME OF WAR, PREPARE FOR PEACE

The United States had been at war only a few months in 1942 when Roosevelt began planning for postwar, especially the expected flood of demobilized victorious veterans. Millions of men were rapidly being swept into the military—the final total would be more than 14 million under arms—and in 1942 manpower experts were gloomily predicting as many as six to eight million jobless when the war ended. The president named a commission to prepare for the readjustment period. He suggested considering subsidized education. Such a policy would not only reward veterans for their service but also provide a pool of trained personnel to jumpstart the postwar economy. Plus, sending the boys to school would postpone the date of finding jobs for them.

There were already precedents for governments underwriting education for returning veterans. After World War I the state of Wisconsin had farsightedly initiated a program granting vets four years of paid tuition at any public high school or college in the state. New York State set up a similar though more modest program for World War I vets. In 1943 the U.S. neighbor and ally Canada was exploring an education-for-veterans plan, too. All three were models for the report to the commission by General Lewis Hines of the Veterans Administration, which proposed in a general way a guaranteed college education to qualified veterans along with housing subsidies and unemployment pay.

By the fall of 1943, however, similar ideas were bubbling up in the ranks of the American Legion, the nation's largest veterans' organization, with 900,000 members. The Legion had been a bit behind the curve on the bonus issue and was determined to lead a veterans' benefits campaign after World War II. Afterward, several local Midwestern Legion posts claimed to have been the birthplace of the GI Bill, and there is no question that it was much discussed among Legionnaires, but it really gained momentum when the Illinois Legion state leadership took up the cause. Illinois governor John Stelle, a former Legion national commander, swung the Legion's national organization, with its powerful political clout, behind the program and also lined up a drumfire of editorial support in the Hearst national newspaper chain.

One December night in 1943 Harry Colmery, the Legion's legislative representative (lobbyist), sat down in a suite in Washington's Mayflower Hotel and wrote out on hotel stationery the proposed legislation reflecting what the Legion had in mind. It would grant everyone who served ninety days of government-financed college education or on-the-job training, unemployment benefits to tide them over until they found work, and government-

THE PRESIDENT SENT FIRST LADY ELEANOR ROOSEVELT, SHOWN HERE IN 1933, TO MEET AND LISTEN TO THE GRIEVANCES OF "BONUS SEEKERS," VETERANS SEEKING EARLY COLLECTION ON BONUS PAYMENTS FOR SERVICE. IN 1924 CONGRESS ENACTED A BONUS PAYMENT FOR WORLD WAR I VETS BASED ON LENGTH OF SERVICE, BUT PAYMENTS WOULDN'T BE AVAILABLE FOR ANOTHER 20 YEARS.
Associated Press

backed housing loans. In January 1944 Colmery's text with minor modifications was introduced in Congress as the Servicemen's Readjustment Act of 1944. A Legion public relations man, Jack Cejnar, gave it the catchy title "The GI Bill of Rights." (Colmery's original hotel-stationery text is now on exhibit in the Smithsonian Institution.)

With the wars in Europe and the Pacific clearly winding down, victory seemingly just around the corner, and virtually every American household with a member or friend in uniform, no politician could oppose a bill labeled the "GI Bill of Rights," and few did. Roosevelt himself kept hands off, recognizing that his name might energize opponents who saw it as more liberal meddling in domestic policy. He left the heavy lifting to congressional New Deal Democrats, one of whom, Senator Elbert Thomas of Utah, introduced a rival bill with even more generous benefits that was merged with the Legion version. The bill sailed through the Senate without a single negative vote. The House of Representatives passed its own bill also by a lopsided margin.

"A HANDOUT FOR SHIRKERS"

But there was a crucial difference between the two bills. Few voices were raised against the education provisions, although the waspish Robert Maynard Hutchins, chancellor of the University of Chicago, complained that opening colleges to all veterans would turn campuses into "hobo jungles," and President James Bryant Conant of Harvard University declared that it would lower standards and few veterans would be "qualified" for a college education.

More opposition coalesced around the unemployment benefits proposal. Opponents argued that an automatic weekly check from the government would create a generation of loafers unwilling to look for jobs. The GI Bill was nothing but a handout that would encourage shirkers, they said.

The dispute also focused on which government agency would administer the bill. The Senate version nominated the Veterans Administration. The VA would handle paying out the tuition to colleges and issuing checks for living expenses and unemployment benefits. The House bill wanted the job done by the states, through the state employment services. A compromise committee of seven members of each house was appointed to negotiate and agree on a final bill.

Congressman John Rankin, chair of the House Veterans Committee, was a rabid racist and an ardent advocate for states' rights as a way to uphold Southern segregation. He saw the Senate version as a threat to Southern racial "traditions." The military services during World War II had been strictly segregated, and the state agencies could be counted on to see that the color lines were clearly drawn for veterans, too. Certainly there should be no requirement that whites-only state colleges be required to admit black veterans as students. Moreover, paying out an automatic twenty to twenty-five dollars a week to all veterans would undercut the South's low-wage economy. Who would stoop over to pick cotton or labor in the clanking, high-pressure textile mills when they could receive as much or more for staying idle? Anyway, they would probably just spend all the newfound money on bootleg alcohol.

Some stiff rules were set for the committee's negotiations. A majority of each House or Senate delegation must vote for any compromise bill for it to be approved and sent to the full house for final passage. The seven Senate delegates drafted an amended bill based on the VA version, and persuaded three of the House delegates to side with them, while three others remained adamantly opposed.

The seventh representative, holding the crucial deciding vote, was the Georgia Democrat John Gibson. Gibson was in Georgia campaigning, but no one knew precisely where. After a speech in Valdosta he was believed headed to his home in Douglas, but he could not be reached. Gibson had left a proxy with Rankin to be cast in favor of the bill. Rankin refused to honor it, ruling that a member must be present and cast the vote in person. He further ruled that the final vote must take place at 10 a.m. on June 10, or the bill would be defeated. He was confident that Gibson could not return before that deadline.

A DRAMATIC RESCUE

The Legion set out to prove him wrong. They enlisted the aid of the state police and the *Atlanta Constitution*. The newspaper's switchboard operators phoned his home every fifteen minutes; state police roadblocked highways and stopped motorists ("I wasn't speeding, Officer," "Are you John Gibson? Okay, go on."). Eddie Rickenbacker, World War I aviation ace and Eastern Airlines president and a Legionnaire, was contacted; he authorized the airline to hold a Washington flight in Jacksonville, Florida, until Gibson arrived.

Just after 11 p.m. Gibson answered his home phone and found a state police car in his driveway. The state police escort took him to an Air Force base at Waycross, Georgia, and a military car traveling at ninety miles per hour at times propelled him through a slashing rainstorm to the waiting plane. At 6:37 a.m. the plane touched down in Washington. Just before 10 a.m., Gibson presented himself at the committee room to a crestfallen Rankin, and cast the deciding vote that saved the GI Bill.

The final, amended bill gave each veteran a year's tuition plus fees and the cost of books up to five hundred dollars. In addition to the year, veterans received an additional month for each month served, along with a fifty-dollar-a-month living allowance for single vets and seventy-five dollars for married vets. The bill also included government-backed housing loans and a twenty-dollar weekly unemployment stipend for a full year or until the veteran found work (which rapidly became known as *The 52–20 Club*.

The House approved the bill the next day, the Senate the following day. On June 22, Roosevelt signed it in the presence of legislators and Legion leaders. For the first time he took some public credit for a role in the landmark bill, noting in a signing message that he had sent several messages to Congress in earlier months advocating veterans readjustment measures, including education, housing aid, and unemployment payments.

At first, few people noticed. The nation was preoccupied with the Allied invasion of Normandy, and newspapers relegated the story to the inside pages. One who did notice was Don Balfour of Washington. Balfour had received a medical discharge and was paying his own way at George Washington University, while editing the student newspaper. A day after the signing ceremony, he was interviewing a VA official about the bill. "Suddenly I realized that I might be eligible," he recalled. "'Could I sign up for benefits?' I asked him. He said, 'Certainly.' The forms hadn't even been printed but by August I was officially on the GI Bill." By the end of the year Balfour had been joined by 88,000 fellow veterans. A year later, there were a million vets on campuses across the country. A year after that, their ranks had increased to more than two million.

The astonishing thing about this human cascade is that practically no one saw it coming. Manpower experts forecast that at most 8–12 percent of vets would opt for college; the bulk would return to farms and factories as quickly as they could. Earl McGrath, later U.S. commissioner of education, predicted only 125,000 to 150,000 vets would head for college each year; the final total for all years would be just under 600,000. Most colleges expected that only those whose schooling had been interrupted would take advantage of the GI Bill to complete their degrees, plus a normal-sized freshman class.

BETTER THAN BRICKLAYING

Les Faulk read about the GI Bill's college benefits in *Stars and Stripes*, as he was pushing across France into Germany as a combat infantryman with General Patch's Seventh Army. He didn't give the matter much thought. He and his buddies used to talk about what they would do after discharge, but a lot of it was just daydreaming and wishful thinking. Faulk had been a star athlete but an indifferent student in high school. College seemed beyond reach. "College was for the preachers' kids and the teachers' kids," he recalled later. But, he added, "You matured awfully fast in a foxhole."

When he came home to Turtle Creek, his father proudly announced that he had found his son what the town considered a good job—as a bricklayer's apprentice in a steel mill. The first day, Faulk discovered that the apprentice's assignment was to crawl into a cooling blast furnace to check which fire brick should be replaced. He quit that day and told his boss, "I'm going to college." "I read that only one vet in 20 who enters college will finish," the boss said. "I'm going to be that one," Faulk declared. At the 1949 commencement, he received his bachelor's degree in education, went on for a master's, and earned credits toward a doctorate—all on the GI Bill. He spent the next thirty-six years working as an elementary school teacher and principal.

All over the United States, similar stories were being told, of ambitious young men—and not so young men—crowding classrooms where they never had expected to be, even in their wildest dreams. The University of Pittsburgh enrolled more engineering students in Les's first year than in the five Depression years combined. Eleven thousand ex-GIs arrived at the University of Wisconsin in 1946, doubling the enrollment from 9,000 to 18,000 overnight. Rutgers University enrollment went from a prewar 7,000 to 16,000 in 1948. Stanford University swelled from 3,000 students to 7,000 within a year. Among the GI Bill students were 60,000 women and 70,000 African Americans.

WAR VETERANS ATTEND CLASSES AT THE UNIVERSITY OF WISCONSIN IN 1945. IN THE FIRST YEAR OF THE BILL, 88,000 VETERANS SIGNED UP; TWO YEARS LATER, 2 MILLION VETERANS WERE COLLEGE-BOUND COURTESY OF THE GI BILL. FEW WERE PREPARED FOR SUCH NUMBERS; COLLEGES SCRAMBLED TO PROVIDE ENOUGH STAFF AND CLASSROOM SPACE.

The GI boom transformed colleges and campuses; the schools scrambled to provide enough faculty, classrooms, laboratories, cafeterias, and study space for the vast student population. The schools also rushed to find housing, because many of the students came with wives and children. Quonsets and recycled barracks sprouted on once-pristine campus lawns. Single men arriving at Stanford from army barracks found themselves again sleeping in bunk beds in a converted army barracks. The State University of New York took over an old navy training base and turned it into freshman housing. Marietta College in Ohio obtained an old coast guard vessel and anchored it in the Muskingum River as a floating dormitory. And Wisconsin built a whole new town, Badger Village, with 699 apartments for student families, complete with its own post office, fire department, chapel, grocery, barbershop, and elementary school.

"If there is a baby," a Columbia University sociologist solemnly intoned in 1945, "college is almost out of the question for any reasonable man." Fathers turned out to be the most diligent and successful students; even the once-skeptical President Conant of Harvard marveled that they were the best students he had ever seen. Another demolished myth was that the "52-20 Club" would produce a generation of shirkers. In fact, less than one-fourth of the funds allotted to unemployment benefits were paid out.

The crowds began to thin out in 1951. Under law, the act itself expired in 1956, although a few veterans were allowed to complete their programs. The overstretched campuses returned to something resembling normal. In the twelve years of its life, the GI Bill had lifted a whole generation into one of the most educated and financially well-off in U.S. history. Of 14 million veterans eligible for benefits, 2.2 million jumped at the chance for a college education—all at a cost of $5.5 billion. (And, it was pointed out, the veterans paid that back, and then some, in higher taxes on their GI Bill–generated higher-education jobs.) The GI Bill placed a college degree within the reach of millions. And it changed the face of American higher education completely.

EXTENDING THE GI BILL

The GI Bill also left another lasting legacy. When the Korean War began, one of Congress's first acts was to revive the GI Bill and offer similar benefits to veterans who served in that fighting. It was extended again for veterans of the Vietnam War, then for "Operation Desert Storm" in Iraq, "Operation Iraqi Freedom," and to those who served during the Cold War. And now the Montgomery Act, named for the congressman who sponsored it, offers benefits to all who volunteer for military service.

Roosevelt never witnessed the impact of the first GI Bill adopted in his administration, nor the end of the war that generated it. He died of a massive stroke in April 1945. Some colleagues maintained that he was drafting a postwar "Freedom from Want" plan based on the GI Bill that would incorporate for anyone many GI Bill features, such as housing subsidies, unemployment payments, and guaranteed government-paid college education for all who wanted it.

In November 1994 Les Faulk assembled a group of his old schoolmates in the blue collar town to celebrate the fiftieth anniversary of their high school commencement. They included a federal circuit judge, a law professor, a psychologist, a microbiologist, an entomologist, two physicists, several entrepreneurs, a stockbroker, and a journalist— few of whom could have conceived of earning a college diploma half a century before. Les raised a glass in toast to his old mates.

"To the GI Bill!" he toasted. "To the GI Bill!" the others echoed.

CHAPTER 18

FRANKLIN ROOSEVELT, THE ATLANTIC CHARTER, AND THE FOUNDING OF THE UNITED NATIONS

1945

O N THE HOT AND STEAMY MORNING OF AUGUST 3, 1941—JUST FOUR months before the Japanese attacked Pearl Harbor—President Franklin D. Roosevelt's special train clanked out of Washington, D.C., on its way to New London, Connecticut. There the president and his cronies boarded the USS *Potomac*, for a fishing trip to Martha's Vineyard.

The handsome, gleaming *Potomac*—nicknamed "The Floating White House"—was a former Coast Guard cutter, 165 feet (50.3 m) long, capable of making thirteen knots (24.1 kph). Roosevelt, once assistant secretary of the navy under Woodrow Wilson, was passionate about the sea and spent as much time as he could fishing and sailing. During hot Washington summers, FDR was more at home cruising in his presidential yacht than he was in the White House. His sails were not solely for the purpose of recreation, however, since the vessel was the perfect place for top-secret strategy sessions with close advisors and meetings with congressmen over gin and tonics or whiskey.

That muggy August, however, as far as the White House press corps knew, Roosevelt had just hung out a "Gone Fishin'" sign. On August 4, he cruised to Martha's Vineyard, picked up his friend Princess Martha of Norway, along with her husband, Prince Karl, and spent a leisurely day fishing with them from the yacht's stern, in full view of starstruck vacationers. In fact—a nice touch—the president himself drove his guests back to their yacht club in a speedboat before returning to the *Potomac*. The next day, his silhouette with its uptilted cigarette holder instantly recognizable, Roosevelt sat in a deck chair aboard the vessel, chatting with friends and casually waving to other boaters.

Except that the person waving was not, in fact, FDR, but a smiling, cigarette-smoking body double, a Secret Service agent dressed as the president. Late the evening before, the *Potomac* had slipped away and sailed at top speed to a secret rendezvous with seven U.S. warships far off the coast of Martha's Vineyard. There, Roosevelt transferred to the heavy cruiser, *Augusta*, flagship of Admiral Earnest J. King, and by the time Roosevelt's body double was pleasing tourists, the president was in fact 250 miles (402.3 km) away, steaming fast through the U-boat-infested Atlantic waters, escorted by vigilant destroyers. Two days later, the *Augusta* arrived in the misty waters of Argentia Harbor, Newfoundland, a sheltered bay surrounded by low hills. There, on August 9, the HMS *Prince of Wales* arrived, still battered by seven high explosive shells that had struck it during its May encounter with the German pocket battleship, *Bismarck*. Aboard the *Prince of Wales* was British prime minister Winston Churchill.

In this tiny and remote harbor off the coast of Canada, the leaders of the world's only two still-functioning great democracies were about to have a momentous meeting that would sew the seeds for the founding of the United Nations.

"THE GREATEST CREED"

As World War I drew to a close, another U.S. president, Woodrow Wilson, had pushed tirelessly for a responsible body of world nations that might come together and be able to stop another bloody conflict such as the one that engulfed the world from 1914 to 1918. Wilson called his vision the "League of Nations." One of the most idealistic of American leaders, the former schoolteacher and Princeton University president preached that "there is no higher religion than human service. To work for the common good is the greatest creed."

During the peace negotiations at Versailles after the war, Wilson pushed for "a general association of nations" that would guarantee "political independence and territorial integrity to great and small nations alike." On June 28, 1919, forty-four nations signed the *Covenant of the League of Nations*. Shockingly, when Woodrow Wilson returned home, he was unable to get the U.S. Senate to ratify the League. Wilson campaigned for it, but he was hampered by strong isolationist sentiment in America and by the fact that he often came across as a pedantic academic attempting to scold the public into accepting the League. And in October of that year, he suffered a serious stroke that, while mainly hidden from the public, made it nearly impossible for him to campaign for the League.

The League of Nations, headquartered in Geneva, held its first General Assembly meeting in late 1920. It was to last for sixteen years and was for the most part ineffectual in influencing world affairs. There were numerous reasons for this. Most of the League's rulings against aggression depended on moral condemnation; there was little clout behind them, especially with America absent. Moral condemnation did little to stop the rise of Adolf Hitler or the spreading Japanese aggression in the Pacific

Rim. Too, the League Covenant called for unanimous decisions regarding sanctions against other nations, something that, in practice, was rarely achieved. Despite a few successes, the League was moribund by 1936.

Franklin Roosevelt, Wilson's assistant secretary of the navy, supported the League of Nations as a matter of Democratic Party loyalty. When he was drafted to run for vice president in 1920, on a ticket with James M. Cox, Roosevelt gave more than eight hundred stump speeches in favor of America joining the League. But Roosevelt had grown disenchanted with Wilson's idealism; he preferred to think of the League of Nations in terms of "practical necessity," as he told audiences. After Warren G. Harding defeated the Cox/Roosevelt ticket in a landslide, Roosevelt continued to think deeply about an approach to world peace, despite being stricken and partially paralyzed by polio in the summer of 1921. In 1923, he published a *Saturday Evening Post* article calling for the elimination of the onerous requirement for unanimity when the League of Nations wanted to use force to achieve its goals: "Common sense cannot defend a procedure by which one or two recalcitrant nations could block the will of the great majority."

Roosevelt became president in 1933; within six years the world was engulfed in war. And 1941 was a year of great crisis. Nazi Germany, whose armies had conquered Europe and were now driving deep into the Soviet Union, threatened Great Britain, whose existence Roosevelt considered crucial to America's well-being and survival. Roosevelt's Lend-Lease program (see chapter 16) had brought important American aid to England, but her future was precarious. In the Pacific, Japan's forces had swept through China and now invaded Southeast Asia, seeking oil. On August 1, only a few days before he arrived at Argentia Harbor, Roosevelt had frozen all Japanese assets in the United States and suspended trade with Japan, a step that would ultimately push Japan to attack Pearl Harbor in December.

"AT LAST WE'VE GOTTEN TOGETHER"

Late in the morning on August 9, Winston Churchill boarded the *Augusta*, wearing his navy blue peacoat and naval cap (Churchill had been first lord of the admiralty, the British equivalent of U.S. secretary of the navy), chewing on his ever-present cigar. Roosevelt, held steady by his son Elliot, stood to greet him as the national anthems of both nations played. The two men had met before briefly at the end of World War I, a meeting Churchill did not actually remember.

"At last," Roosevelt said to Churchill, gripping his hand, "we've gotten together."

In fact, Roosevelt had first requested the meeting in January 1941, sending his close advisor Harry Hopkins to Great Britain to meet with Churchill, who for his part expressed a nearly simultaneous desire to meet with Roosevelt. Over the ensuing months, the choice of meeting place was narrowed down to Bermuda and Newfoundland; at last Newfoundland was chosen as requiring a less dangerous journey for the prime minister, although Nazi submarine wolf packs also dogged sea approaches across the North Atlantic. The two men were accompanied by close advisors. Roosevelt had with him the cagey Harry Hopkins and Sumner Welles, his powerful under secretary of state, while Churchill's primary advisor was Sir Alexander Cadogan, under secretary of the foreign office.

Roosevelt and Churchill engaged in personal, one-on-one communication far more than many heads of state, believing that it was essential to avoid misunderstandings (they were to meet for a total of 113 days during World War II, and send hundreds of cables to each other). But on this occasion they came to Newfoundland with different expectations. Churchill, as he did so often during the war, played the suitor, attempting to woo the elusive Roosevelt. Specifically, he wanted Roosevelt to push

BRITISH PRIME MINISTER WINSTON CHURCHILL HANDS PRESIDENT FRANKLIN ROOSEVELT A LETTER FROM KING GEORGE VI ABOARD THE USS *AUGUSTA* IN AUGUST 1941. ASSISTING ROOSEVELT WAS HIS SON, CAPTAIN ELLIOT ROOSEVELT, RIGHT. THE SECRET MEETING WOULD PRODUCE THE LANGUAGE FOR THE ATLANTIC CHARTER.

© Topham / The Image Works

for an American declaration of war against Germany—or at least strong naval action against the German blockade of England—and a firm U.S. warning to Japan if it attacked British colonies in the Pacific.

Roosevelt, for his part, would not commit himself, although he personally felt that U.S. involvement in the war was an inevitability. Instead, he had asked for the meeting to receive assurances from Churchill that Britain would not attempt to make separate deals with Russia (now a U.S. and British ally) after Germany's defeat, deals that might undermine the preeminence of America's position in the world.

During most of the first day of negotiations, Churchill and Roosevelt felt each other out on their different views while Roosevelt doodled on a tablecloth with a burnt matchstick and Churchill, the more physically demonstrative of the two, hunched his shoulders and jabbed the air with his cigar. Dinner was served—broiled chicken, spinach omelet, and chocolate ice cream—and then Churchill returned to the *Prince of Wales*. The next day it was Roosevelt's turn to visit the British warship. It was a Sunday and a joint religious ceremony was held on the quarterdeck, conducted by both British and U.S. chaplains. Roosevelt nodded solemnly while Churchill tearfully sang along to "Onward Christian Soldiers," a hymn that would prove prescient. On December 10, 1941, nearly half the men present with Churchill and Roosevelt at the services that morning would die as the *Prince of Wales* was sunk by Japanese dive bombers and torpedo bombers.

Shortly after the service, while Roosevelt and Churchill talked, Alexander Cadogan handed Sumner Welles a document that would turn out to be far more important than the discussions the two leaders were currently having over breakfast.

"AN EFFECTIVE INTERNATIONAL ORGANIZATION"

In his State of the Union address in January 1941, Roosevelt had spoken eloquently of "a world founded upon four essential human freedoms," which were freedom of speech, freedom of religion, freedom from want, and freedom from fear. Franklin Roosevelt had entered the Argentia Harbor meeting with an idea in mind that he wanted Churchill and himself—leaders of the world's two major democracies— to issue some kind of joint statement, based on the four freedoms, "that would hold out hope to the world's enslaved peoples." This was an extraordinary idea at a time when the tide of totalitarianism was sweeping over the earth and the idea of a brighter future seemed all but impossible.

There had been some discussion of this between the staffs of the American president and the British prime minister prior to Newfoundland; on the voyage from England to North America, Churchill had taken the bull by the horns and drafted the document that Cadogan had handed Welles. The document, while focusing on a peaceful future for the world, had some thorny issues for Welles and Roosevelt, who pored over it that evening. In one of its five articles, Churchill's draft had demanded a British trade practice known as *imperial preferences*, whereby countries within the British empire could only trade where the British pound sterling was the recognized currency. This, Roosevelt and Welles felt, did not reflect a world that was rapidly changing,

A POSTER CREATED DURING 1936–41 PROMOTES ROOSEVELT'S FOUR FREEDOMS—FREEDOM OF EXPRESSION, OF RELIGION, FROM WANT, AND FROM FEAR EVERYWHERE IN THE WORLD— WHICH THE PRESIDENT DECLARED IN HIS 1941 STATE OF THE UNION ADDRESS. HE CALLED FOR ENSURING THE FOURTH FREEDOM THROUGH "A WORLD-WIDE REDUCTION OF ARMAMENTS."

Library of Congress

as nations emerged from the era of imperialism (there was the feeling, too, that such protectionist tariffs had added to the severity of the Depression).

Churchill was also more explicit than Roosevelt wanted to be in calling for "an effective international organization"—a new League of Nations—after the war. Although this was exactly what the American president wanted, he was sure the still-strong isolationist sentiment in Washington would strike it down.

On August 11, a hot, sunny day, Churchill and Roosevelt met in the admiral's quarters aboard the *Augusta* to discuss the final document. Roosevelt, his shirt open beneath his gray suit, told Churchill he must drop the "imperial preferences" issue; it would never be accepted in a new world order. Churchill protested, saying that while he was personally in favor of free trade, the British Commonwealth countries would never accept it. Finally, he was prevailed upon to take out the clause.

For his part, Churchill pushed Roosevelt to agree on the wording of "an effective international organization." To this, Roosevelt replied firmly that use of such a phrase would kill the entire document, because isolationists in Congress would not stand for it. Here, Roosevelt showed how different he was from Wilson—he intended to form a postwar League of Nations, but he was far more politically realistic, pragmatic enough not to destroy his goals by revealing them too soon. Once America was at war—and isolationism a discredited policy—he would be able to do far more.

THE ATLANTIC CHARTER

By the end of the day on August 11, the two leaders would come to agree on the final text of the document that would be dubbed (by a British newspaper, not by Roosevelt and Churchill) the *Atlantic Charter*.

The document began with a declaration of their joint decision "to make known certain common principles in the national policies [of Britain and America] on which they base their hopes for a better future for the world."

The charter enumerated eight points. First, that America and Britain "seek no aggrandizement, territorial or other." Second, that they wanted "no territorial changes that do not accord with the freely expressed wishes of the peoples concerned." Third, that these two major democratic powers "respect the right of all peoples to choose the form of government under which they will live."

The fourth article—the thorny one about free trade—spoke about all countries having "access, on equal terms, to the trade and raw materials of the world." The

HAS THE UNITED NATIONS LIVED UP TO ROOSEVELT'S EXPECTATIONS?

The United Nations has been in existence for sixty-five years and it's only fair to ask—is it as effective as Franklin Roosevelt and Winston Churchill had hoped it would be?

The answer is yes—and no. Certainly the UN has been far more effective than its predecessor, the League of Nations, for any number of reasons. For one thing, the United States actually joined the UN (it did not become a part of the League of Nations) and thus was able to throw its considerable weight behind the organization. For another, the UN has more resources than the League of Nations ever had, and considerably more enforcement power.

But the UN immediately ran into trouble because its major members—China, the United States, Russia, Great Britain—were at odds (usually implacable foes) during the cold war, thus making true consensus nearly impossible. More recently, the UN has mounted any number of peacekeeping missions to areas of conflict, including Bosnia, Rwanda, and Somalia, to name just a few, usually as part of a humanitarian truce between warring parties, or to patrol the peace after these parties reach agreement. These are dangerous missions where the UN is usually effective only when one of the major powers throws its support behind the peacekeeping force. Conversely, when one major power is determined to make an attack—as was the case with the United States' invasion of Iraq in 2003—there is little the UN can do to stop it.

Where the UN probably has lived up to Roosevelt's expectations is in the organization's humanitarian efforts, helping feed and shelter displaced people, bringing medicine to impoverished children, and the like. And the International Court of Justice at the Hague, the judicial arm of the UN, has been effective in addressing human rights violations all over the globe.

fifth article was written with an eye to improving world "labor standards, economic advancement, and social security."

It was in the sixth article that the document turned firmly to the future, speaking of a time after "the final destruction of Nazi tyranny" when there would be "a peace which will afford to all Nations the means of dwelling in safety within their own boundaries." The seventh article referred to the same safety in traversing the high seas.

And, finally, the eighth article. Here, the seeds for the future United Nations were sown. The article spoke of the future "establishment of a wider and permanent system of general security" in the world where the "disarmament of [aggressor] nations" would be possible. The United States and Great Britain would lead this system, helping to "lighten for peace-loving peoples the crushing burden of armaments."

TWENTY-SIX COUNTRIES SIGNED THE UNITED NATIONS DECLARATION OF 1942, PLEDGING TO THE PRINCIPLES OF THE ATLANTIC CHARTER, WHICH BOUND THEM TOGETHER OVER THE DEFEAT OF THE AXIS POWERS AND PROMOTED, AMONG OTHER PRINCIPLES, PEACEFUL SELF-GOVERNMENT AND TRADE RELATIONS.

Getty Images

On the evening of August 12, the *Prince of Wales* left Argentia Harbor. Roosevelt watched it go, standing on the quarterdeck of the *Augusta* while the band played "Auld Lang Syne." After a stop in Portland, Maine, the president returned to Washington and the text of the Atlantic Charter was released to the press, after first being cabled to Russian premier Joseph Stalin.

Stalin, who had not been informed of the Argentia Harbor meeting, predictably saw it as a plot between the British and Americans to exclude the Soviet Union from postwar spoils, but the American people reacted favorably—more than half of them approved Roosevelt's increased commitment to destroying Nazism and aggression explicit in the document. However, nothing, in immediate practical terms, happened following the issuance of the Atlantic Charter. It was not a formal treaty or agreement. Roosevelt later joked that the only signed copy he had seen contained both his and Churchill's signatures—but both in Churchill's handwriting!

"THE SCIENCE OF HUMAN RELATIONSHIPS"

The Atlantic Charter was only a beginning. After the surprise Japanese attack on Pearl Harbor on December 7, 1941, and Germany's subsequent declaration of war on the United States, America was finally, fully at war, and Roosevelt's hand was freed. On January 2, 1942, twenty-six countries signed, at Roosevelt's behest, the *Declaration by the United Nations*—the first time the phrase was used—which was not only an agreement to wage war against Germany and Japan but also a pledge to accept the principles laid down by the Atlantic Charter. The next year, four of the major signatories—the United States, Great Britain, the Soviet Union, and China—met outside Washington, D.C., and created a charter for the new organization, which they called the "United Nations."

There were still numerous disagreements as to the exact charter of the United Nations, but a major conference was planned for April 25, 1945, in San Francisco, where fifty countries would attend to create a UN charter. On April 11, in a statement issued on a day commemorating the birth of Thomas Jefferson, Roosevelt wrote that it was now the purpose of all people "to cultivate the science of human relationships—the ability of all peoples, of all kinds, to live together and work together, in the same world, at peace."

He issued the statement from Warm Springs, Arkansas, the location of his presidential retreat.

The next day, April 12, Roosevelt was sitting for a portrait while sorting through some correspondence when he suddenly reached his hand to his head and said, "I have a terrific headache," and collapsed. His personal physician was unable to revive him and Roosevelt was pronounced dead just before 4:00 p.m.

The country mourned a great loss. Among his many accomplishments, Roosevelt had successfully launched the United Nations. The San Francisco conference barely two weeks after his death resulted in a charter; the United Nations formally came into existence on October 24, 1945.

It had all begun with the Atlantic Charter, however, in a small harbor in a remote part of the world, when Roosevelt, practical yet visionary, had been able to look beyond the dark shape the world was in to something much brighter. As Supreme Court Chief Justice Felix Frankfurter wrote in a letter to Roosevelt: "We live by symbols and we can't too often recall them. And you two [Churchill and Roosevelt] in that ocean . . . gave meaning to the conflict between civilization and arrogant, brute challenge, and gave promise more powerful and binding than any formal treaty could, that civilization has brains and resources that tyranny will not be able to overcome."

CHAPTER 19

HARRY TRUMAN OPTS FOR ARMAGEDDON

1945

APRIL 1959, COLUMBIA UNIVERSITY, NEW YORK CITY. FORMER PRESIDENT Harry S. Truman, having just concluded one in a series of three informal lectures, opens the floor to questions. Before long comes the obligatory "What was the most difficult decision you had to make as president?"

It was one of those inevitable questions to which the anticipated answer must have seemed inevitable as well: The decision to drop the atomic bomb on Hiroshima and Nagasaki, of course. This, however, was not the answer Truman gave, not at Columbia in 1959, not anywhere at any time.

"The most difficult decision?" he'd answer without a moment's hesitation. "To go to war in Korea."

But the questioners almost never let him leave it at that. They were reluctant to believe that Korea could have been a harder decision than dropping the bomb. To his Columbia audience, Truman elaborated, explaining that, as a matter of fact, the "atom bomb was no 'great decision.' . . . It was merely another powerful weapon in the arsenal of righteousness. The dropping of the bombs stopped the war, saved millions of lives. It was a purely military decision."

That answer always left his questioners even more profoundly dissatisfied. Could Truman have really been so dull, so ignorant of the enormity of the power that had been placed at his command? Could he have been so profoundly unfeeling?

HISTORY AND PHYSICS

Although he had grown up poor in Missouri and had never gotten beyond the education purveyed in a small-town high school, Harry S. Truman was far from dull or ignorant. On the contrary, he possessed a nimble intelligence and, as circumstances revealed, was a phenomenally quick study.

President Franklin Roosevelt had tapped him in 1944 as his fourth-term running mate after his third-term vice president, Henry Wallace, had veered too far left for political comfort. Truman was not only safely dead center in the Democratic Party, but he had also made a name for himself as the straight-talking chairman of a high-profile Senate committee that successfully rooted out fraud, corruption, and inefficiency among war contractors. People liked that.

As for FDR, he had remarkably little interest in the man, and during the mere eighty-two days that Truman served as vice president, Roosevelt met with him only twice and exchanged little more than perfunctory pleasantries in the course of both meetings. Truman was sworn in as president at 7:09 p.m. on April 12, 1945, three hours and thirty-four minutes after Roosevelt's sudden death from a cerebral hemorrhage, and his candid plea to reporters the next day that they "pray" for him because he felt "like the moon, the stars, and all the planets" had fallen on him was no phony display of aw-shucks humility. The one thing he knew all too well was how very little he knew—because the dead president had told him almost nothing.

Among the many things of which Truman knew nothing was the Manhattan Project, the bold undertaking, as epic as it was super-secret, to transform theoretical atomic physics into an atomic weapon. Secretary of War Henry L. Stimson lingered for a moment after Truman met with the cabinet for the first time. He approached the president and spoke softly to him about the existence of a "new explosive of incredible power," but a full two weeks passed before Stimson delivered a comprehensive briefing on the atomic bomb. In the meantime, James F. Byrnes, the perennial FDR insider who was soon to become secretary of state, let slip to the new president that what they had was so powerful that it might be capable of wiping out entire cities, "killing people on an unprecedented scale," he marveled.

In his briefing, Stimson explained that the weapon was nearing completion and that it would soon be tested. Byrnes, a South Carolinian, both courtly and pugnacious, had rejoiced that the bomb would almost certainly end the war—the Germans were on the verge of collapse (and would in fact surrender on May 7–8), but the Japanese, though militarily defeated, showed no signs of quitting. Byrnes added that the bomb would surely put the United States in a position to dictate the political structure of the entire postwar world. Stimson was more subdued. The weapon would be one of unprecedented destructive power, and he shuddered to contemplate how it might alter the very future of humankind.

COLONEL PAUL TIBBETS, CENTER, AND THE CREW OF THE *ENOLA GAY*, WHICH DROPPED THE BOMB ON HIROSHIMA, ARE SHOWN IN THE NORTHERN MARIANA ISLANDS. HOURS LATER, TRUMAN TOLD THE AMERICAN PUBLIC VIA RADIO THAT THE BOMB "IS A HARNESSING OF THE BASIC POWER OF THE UNIVERSE. THE FORCE FROM WHICH THE SUN DRAWS ITS POWER HAS BEEN LOOSED AGAINST THOSE WHO BROUGHT WAR TO THE FAR EAST."

AFP/Getty Images

Truman listened to Byrnes and to Stimson, and then he pored over the briefing papers that had been given him. Later, years after he left the White House, he would comment that a modern president needed to get an education in two subjects above all others: history and physics.

"THE PRESIDENT . . . HAS TO DECIDE"

Truman was at the Berlin suburb of Potsdam, hammering out with Winston Churchill and Joseph Stalin both the shape of the war's closing act and the shape of the world that would follow it, when he received coded word that the atomic bomb had been successfully tested at 5:29 a.m. on July 16, 1945, on a desolate tract of New Mexico desert claimed by the Alamogordo Army Air Base. His initial reaction was smiling relief that a weapon that had burned up what was then the almost unimaginable sum of $2 billion and two years in its development had actually worked.

But there can be no doubt that Truman also fully appreciated the moral, even apocalyptic dimensions of the bomb. On July 25, 1945, he recorded in his diary, "We have discovered the most terrible bomb in the history of the world. It may be the fire of destruction prophesied in the Euphrates Valley Era, after Noah and his fabulous Ark." And there can be no doubt that he also appreciated the basic physics of the thing. On August 6, 1945, just hours after the B-29 flown by Colonel Paul Tibbets and named for his mother, *Enola Gay,* had dropped the first atomic bomb on Hiroshima, Truman made a radio broadcast to report and explain: "It is an atomic bomb," he said. "It is a harnessing of the basic power of the universe. The force from which the sun draws its power has been loosed against those who brought war to the Far East."

Truman understood. Modern physics had created an Old Testament apocalypse, and because neither physics nor apocalypse distinguishes soldiers from civilians, warlords from mothers and children, all would be consumed indiscriminately.

Truman understood, and although the power of the new weapon was terrible to contemplate, he also understood that a president's job came down to just one thing— making decisions. "The papers may circulate around the government for a while," he once remarked, "but they finally reach his desk. And then, there's no place else for them to go. The president—whoever he is—has to decide. He can't pass the buck to anybody. No one else can do the deciding for him. That's his job."

"THINK OF THE KIDS WHO WON'T BE KILLED!"

During the run-up to the July 16 test, the president was himself bombarded by the opinions, urgings, pleas, and protests of the small circle of military men, political leaders, and scientists who were privy to the bomb. On June 11, 1945, Nobel laureate Professor James Franck sent up through government channels the confidential report of a committee of seven of the nation's most distinguished scientists, who pleaded that the bomb not be used against a Japanese city before it was "revealed to the world by a demonstration in an appropriately selected uninhabited area."

Five days later, another panel of scientists, this one including Manhattan Project scientific director J. Robert Oppenheimer and Enrico Fermi, who had led the team that created the world's first sustained nuclear chain reaction, issued its own report, concluding that there was "no acceptable alternative to military use" of the bomb. Just eleven days after this, on June 27, Undersecretary of the Navy Ralph A. Bard composed a memorandum warning that using the bomb without prior warning would destroy "the position of the United States as a great humanitarian nation."

SECRET

July 3, 1945

A PETITION TO THE PRESIDENT OF THE UNITED STATES

Discoveries of which the people of the United States are not aware may affect the welfare of this nation in the near future. The liberation of atomic power which has been achieved places atomic bombs in the hands of the Army. It places in your hands, as Commander-in-Chief, the fateful decision whether or not to sanction the use of such bombs in the present phase of the war against Japan.

We, the undersigned scientists, have been working in the field of atomic power for a number of years. Until recently we have had to reckon with the possibility that the United States might be attacked by atomic bombs during this war and that her only defense might lie in a counterattack by the same means. Today with this danger averted we feel impelled to say what follows:

The war has to be brought speedily to a successful conclusion and the destruction of Japanese cities by means of atomic bombs may very well be an effective method of warfare. We feel, however, that such an attack on Japan could not be justified in the present circumstances. We believe that the United States ought not to resort to the use of atomic bombs in the present phase of the war, at least not unless the terms which will be imposed upon Japan after the war are publicly announced and subsequently Japan is given an opportunity to surrender.

If such public announcement gave assurance to the Japanese that they could look forward to a life devoted to peaceful pursuits in their homeland and if Japan still refused to surrender, our nation would then be faced with a situation which might require a re-examination of her position with respect to the use of atomic bombs in the war.

Atomic bombs are primarily a means for the ruthless annihilation of cities. Once they were introduced as an instrument of war it would be difficult to resist for long the temptation of putting them to such use.

The last few years show a marked tendency toward increasing ruthlessness. At present our Air Forces, striking at the Japanese cities, are using the same methods of warfare which were condemned by American public opinion only a few years ago when applied by the Germans to the cities of England. Our use of atomic bombs in this war would carry the world a long way further on this path of ruthlessness.

Atomic power will provide the nations with new means of destruction. The atomic bombs at our disposal represent only the first step in this direction and there is almost no limit to the destructive power which will become available in the course of this development. Thus a nation which sets the precedent of using these newly liberated forces of nature for purposes of destruction may have to bear the responsibility of opening the door to an era of devastation on an unimaginable scale.

In view of the foregoing, we, the undersigned, respectfully petition that you exercise your power as Commander-in-Chief to rule that the United States shall not, in the present phase of the war, resort to the use of atomic bombs.

AMONG THE SIGNATURES OF SIXTY-NINE MANHATTAN PROJECT SCIENTISTS ON THIS LETTER TO TRUMAN OPPOSING THE USE OF THE BOMB WAS THAT OF LEO SZILARD. THE HUNGARIAN REFUGEE PHYSICIST HAD, IN 1939, TALKED ALBERT EINSTEIN INTO WRITING A LETTER TO PRESIDENT ROOSEVELT, URGING HIM TO INITIATE ATOMIC WEAPONS RESEARCH TO BEAT NAZI SCIENTISTS TO THE BOMB.

Harry S. Truman Library and Museum

One of the seven scientists who had signed the June 11 report arguing for a demonstration of the bomb was Leo Szilard, the Hungarian refugee physicist who had, in 1939, talked America's most famous scientist, Albert Einstein, into writing a letter to President Roosevelt, urging him to initiate atomic weapons research to beat Nazi scientists to the bomb. Now, with that weapon an accomplished fact, Szilard drew up and circulated a petition on July 3, 1945, calling the atomic bomb "a means for the ruthless annihilation of cities" and appealing to the president simply to forbid its use—ever. Szilard persuaded no fewer than fifty-nine Manhattan Project scientists to sign the petition, which he withheld because, on July 17, he secured sixty-nine signatures on a new, even more strongly worded document.

This petition came just four days after eighteen scientists at the Oak Ridge, Tennessee, laboratory signed their own petition demanding a ban on the bomb. Days later, no fewer than sixty additional Oak Ridge scientists signed an appeal calling for a demonstration of the bomb. Impressive as these numbers were, a poll conducted at about this time of 150 Manhattan Project scientists working at the University of Chicago yielded 131 calls for the immediate military use of the atomic bomb without any prior warning.

Most of the Manhattan Project scientists who objected to the bomb or called for its harmless demonstration were left-leaning liberals who had worked on the Manhattan Project for the same reason that Szillard had: out of fear that Adolf Hitler would beat the United States to it. Now that Hitler was dead, there seemed to them no moral justification for using the weapon.

President Truman might have ascribed the reports and petitions to a combination of liberal idealism and feelings of guilt about what the scientists themselves had wrought, but there was no easy way to dismiss the opinion of General Dwight David Eisenhower, supreme Allied commander in Europe, who voiced his opposition to the bomb directly to Stimson during a July 20 meeting, arguing that the United States must not be the first nation to use such a horrific weapon.

Learning of this, the president was clearly taken aback—though not for long. He knew that, absent the atomic bomb, only two courses of action were available to end the war with Japan and thereby end World War II. Either the U.S. Army Air Forces would continue bombing Japan with conventional weapons while the U.S. Navy imposed a starvation blockade around the Japanese home islands or the bombing and blockade would have to be accompanied by a full-scale invasion of Japan.

The fact was that air raids had already flattened most of Japan's major cities, and the recent incendiary bombing of Tokyo had killed some 120,000 people in a single nightmarish raid. There was no question that Japan had been defeated militarily. All of its Pacific conquests had been lost, along with most of those in Asia. Day after day, the B-29s dropped their bombs with virtual impunity, as Japan no longer possessed an air force to speak of. Yet there was not a murmur of surrender, and while millions of Japanese soldiers had died and were still dying, there were still more than a million fresh troops available in the homeland itself.

The leaders of the U.S. Army Air Forces were alone in their opinion that continued bombing and blockade would be sufficient to beat Japan into surrender. The strategists in the other services argued that the Japanese leadership was all too willing to allow every one of their cities to be destroyed and all of their people to burn or starve rather than surrender. Some theorized that the concept of surrender did not even exist in the Japanese mind, which was, they argued, the product of a long history in which the nation had never surrendered. The Japanese died, but they fought until the very instant of their death, and so the army generals and navy admirals warned the president that this dying enemy would continue to take a terrible toll of American lives.

Experience proved this out. Through the entire war, in battle after battle, not a single Japanese officer had ever surrendered. Each Japanese-held Pacific island had fallen only after virtually every defender had been killed. A garrison of 21,000 had defended Iwo Jima through four bloody weeks. By the end of the battle, just 212 prisoners were captured. The rest of the garrison was dead. The price to the U.S. Marines who had invaded the island: 24,733 killed or wounded. And this was typical, not exceptional. It was a most bitter foretaste of what an invasion force could expect from the Japanese as they defended their home islands.

Yet if air and naval power alone would not end the war, the only alternative was invasion. The most optimistic of Allied estimates put the end of the war a year away, in June 1946, and the cost of the invasion at 250,000 American lives, with another 250,000 wounded. General Douglas MacArthur, who would lead the operation, predicted no fewer than a million casualties. A million American lives shattered in at least another full year of war. Against this flesh-and-blood reality, Truman weighed the ethical, diplomatic, moral, and general human cost of using atomic weapons. Against this urgently present fact he weighed the possibility of future hazards, future consequences. In a letter to his wife, Bess, the president wrote of his belief that the atomic bomb would "end the war a year sooner . . . and think of the kids who won't be killed! That's the important thing."

And so the decision was made. The bomb would be dropped.

REACHING CERTAINTY

Truman bolstered his decision with two additional considerations. First, at Potsdam, both Truman and Churchill had pressed an evasive Stalin to declare war against Japan. Truman proceeded on the assumption that the atomic bomb would not work, or would not prove as destructive as predicted, or would simply fail to end the war, and, therefore, the invasion would have to be carried out as planned. Its chances for success would be greatly multiplied by a simultaneous Soviet attack from the north, via Japanese-held Manchuria. There was a downside, of course. Both Truman and Churchill were well aware that once the Red Army invaded any part of Japan, that nation—or at least the northern end of it—would almost certainly become a Soviet satellite after the war.

Maybe that was the price of victory. At least, that is the way the situation appeared before the successful test in New Mexico. A *working* bomb changed the equation radically. It was apparent to Truman that if he could end the war with an atomic bomb *before* the Soviets began to invade, he might well keep Japan out of Stalin's hands.

During the three months between April 12, 1945, when Truman took office, and the successful test of the atomic bomb on July 16, Japan inflicted casualties on the soldiers, marines, sailors, and airmen of the United States amounting to nearly half the total of those from the preceding *three full years* of the Pacific war.

The second consideration was starker and more personal. Truman reasoned that if he decided to withhold a powerful weapon, a potentially war-winning weapon, he would be duly indicted and tried for treason—and quite properly convicted of it, too.

Even after he had made up his mind, the president continued to be assailed by those who insisted that Japan was actually at the very brink of surrender, so that there was no need to use the bomb or even to invade. The nation was in collapse, they said.

And it was true. Even the Japanese knew it. As it turned out, the Japanese high command had commissioned a study and, as early as January 1944, had concluded that the war was lost. Yet this was not the bottom line. Even though the militarists who dominated Japan's government were convinced that they no longer possessed the means to achieve victory, they resolutely clung to their refusal to surrender. It was a choice that cost lives, Japanese as well as American. During the three months between April 12, when Truman took office, and the successful test of the atomic bomb on July 16, Japan inflicted casualties on the soldiers, marines, sailors, and airmen of the United States amounting to nearly half the total of those from the preceding *three full years* of the Pacific war. As Truman saw it, the conclusion was inescapable. Military defeat was insufficient to prompt Japan's surrender.

"YOU GET ALL THE FACTS AND YOU MAKE UP YOUR MIND"

Yet this conclusion left open the issue of just what constituted "surrender." Truman knew very well what it meant to him and to the other Allies. It meant Japan's unconditional capitulation. As early as the Casablanca Conference of 1943, the Allied leaders had agreed that they would accept nothing short of unconditional surrender, and this was reiterated in the Allies' joint Potsdam Declaration of July 26, 1945.

Here was the problem: If unconditional surrender was alien to Japanese history and culture, literally unknown, perhaps it was also literally unthinkable. Some around the president counseled the outright abandonment of the Potsdam Declaration and advised instead negotiating a favorable peace. Stimson took a different tack, suggesting that "unconditional surrender" be redefined as the end of resistance, period.

Should peace feelers be sent out? Should the Stimson definition of surrender be conveyed to the Japanese? Were these acceptable alternatives to the atomic bomb?

If the intention of Stimson and the others was that one of these options be tried *before* the bomb was dropped, Truman rejected it. He believed that anything short of unconditional surrender—defined, quite simply, as surrender without condition— would betray the great sacrifices made by the Allies. If it took an atomic bomb to force unconditional surrender, to get Japan to think about the unthinkable, so be it.

For now, President Harry Truman was confident that he had followed his own straightforward formula for making a decision: "You get all the facts and you make up your mind." He made up his mind.

ARMAGEDDON

The United States dropped the first atomic bomb on Hiroshima on August 6, 1945. The blast killed perhaps 80,000, and another 50,000 to 60,000 died of injuries or radiation poisoning over the next several months.

The use of the second bomb, on August 9, against Nagasaki, required no presidential decision. The previous month, on July 25, President Truman had issued a military directive specifying that additional bombs were to be "delivered on [specified] targets as soon as made ready by the [Manhattan] project staff." In accordance with this directive, the second bomb was used as soon as it was available. Forty-five to seventy-five thousand were killed in the raid on Nagasaki, and untold numbers died later of injuries, burns, and radiation poisoning. As he had on the evening of August 6, after Hiroshima, Truman took to the airwaves following Nagasaki.

"I realize the tragic significance of the atomic bomb," he broadcast. "But we knew that our enemies were on the search for it. . . . We won the race of discovery against the Germans. . . . We have used it against those who attacked us without warning at Pearl Harbor, against those who have starved and beaten and executed American prisoners of war, against those who have abandoned all pretense of obeying international laws of warfare. We have used it to shorten the agony of war, in order to save the lives of thousands and thousands of young Americans." Then came the part of the broadcast intended less for American ears than for

THE ATOM BOMB WAS DROPPED ON NAGASAKI, THREE DAYS AFTER THE BOMBING OF HIROSHIMA. BETWEEN FOURTY-FIVE AND SEVENTY-FIVE THOUSAND WERE KILLED, AND UNTOLD NUMBERS DIED LATER OF INJURIES, BURNS, AND RADIATION POISONING. TRUMAN PROMISED TO USE THE BOMB AGAIN UNLESS JAPAN SURRENDERED.

Harry S. Truman Library and Museum

Japanese: "We shall continue to use it until we completely destroy Japan's power to make war. Only a Japanese surrender will stop us."

The Japanese government sent its message to the president the very next day. The nation would surrender unconditionally, albeit with the understanding that Emperor Hirohito would remain on the throne.

It was very close to what Stimson had suggested: unconditional surrender on one condition. It was unconditional surrender redefined, and hard-line advisers such as James Byrnes advised the president to turn it down flat. A third atomic bomb was ready now, they pointed out. Use it.

To Henry A. Wallace, the man FDR had asked him to replace as vice president in his fourth-term administration, Truman confessed that he could not stand the thought of killing "all those kids." This time, he meant *Japanese* kids. The president summarily suspended his directive of July 25. From now on, he said, no atomic bombs were to be dropped without his explicit order. Having created a pause in nuclear warfare long enough to ponder the Potsdam Declaration, Truman emerged with another decision, which he summarized in his diary on August 10: "[The Japanese] wanted to make a condition precedent to the surrender. Our terms are 'unconditional.' They wanted to keep the Emperor. We told 'em we'd tell 'em how to keep him, but we'd make the terms."

Replying to the Japanese government on behalf of all the Allies, the Truman State Department agreed that Hirohito would remain on the throne but would be "subject to the Supreme Commander of the Allied Powers," General of the Army Douglas MacArthur. If unconditional surrender could be redefined, so could imperial sovereignty. To ensure a speedy reply, Truman ordered non-nuclear air raids to resume on August 13. Surrender followed on August 14.

"NO 'GREAT DECISION'"

The decision Truman continued to insist to the end of his long life—he died in 1972 at the age of eighty-eight—had been "no 'great decision'" has never ceased to be controversial. It is debated to this day.

Those who agree with Truman insist that the atomic bombs shortened the war and saved lives—not only thousands of American lives, but also millions of Japanese otherwise doomed to fight under the military leadership's death-before-surrender ethos. They point out as well that ending the war in this way saved Japan from Soviet domination, and they conclude their justification by observing that, in any case, Truman had no choice but to use the most powerful weapons he had available. Anything else would have been at the very least an impeachable "high crime" and maybe even outright treason.

Those who disagree with the decision search military history hard for some indication that Japan really was on the verge of giving up, but, failing to find the evidence, they still condemn the thirty-third president of the United States for having committed a war crime and crime against humanity, and, even worse, for creating the precedent of nuclear warfare, initiating a nuclear arms race, and providing the planet's notoriously unstable inhabitants with the means of their own destruction. No motive, they insist, can justify the embrace of Armageddon.

CHAPTER 20

HARRY TRUMAN AND THE BERLIN AIRLIFT: "WE STAY IN BERLIN, PERIOD!"

1948

N THE SPRING OF 1948, BOTH PRESIDENT HARRY S. TRUMAN AND THE CITY OF Berlin were in deep trouble. That year was the president's first chance to be elected to office after taking over when Franklin Roosevelt died three years before. But the Missourian faced tough times with the American people and Congress. Although the war had ended successfully, artificial wartime price controls were now rescinded and inflation had driven the price of ordinary consumer goods up 40 percent. The powerful Southern wing of the Democratic Party was upset by Truman's support of civil rights and the vindictive Republican-controlled Congress stymied his every move.

Truman had made a few miscues on foreign affairs, as well. As the hot war ended and the cold one settled in, Truman had misjudged Soviet leader Joseph Stalin, calling him "honest" and once telling an American audience: "I like old Joe. He is a decent fellow." In the meantime, this "decent fellow" was consolidating his iron grip on Poland, Czechoslovakia, Hungary, Romania, and Bulgaria. Republicans delighted in calling Truman soft on communism, just as Senator Joseph McCarthy's communist witch hunts were ferreting out Red fifth columnists in every Washington closet. Most Americans considered Truman ineffectual (a popular joke of the period went: "I wonder what Truman would do if he were alive?") and he had an approval rating of just over 36 percent—not a happy situation for a president facing a national contest against the young, handsome, and popular Republican, New York Governor Thomas E. Dewey.

The press was already writing the president's political obituary, but, typically outspoken, he was having none of it: "I know every one of these fifty fellows," Truman told a friend. "There isn't one of them has enough sense to pound sand into a rat hole."

Bad as Truman had it, Berlin was much worse.

"THE WORST THAT MODERN CIVILIZATION HAS EVER SEEN"

When World War II ended in May 1945, Berlin was devastated on an epic scale. Five years of bombing had left perhaps 50,000 Berliners dead; in the fierce fighting during the final Russian assault on the city, beginning April 16, more than 100,000 citizens had died and the once-glorious city was now miles and miles of haunted and stinking rubble. Red troops entering the city after the battle subjected Berlin women to an orgy of raping.

By 1948, things had gotten better, but not much. Fifty percent of Berlin buildings were still uninhabitable, and with wreckage being shifted at the rate of 1,000 tons a day—by hand—it was estimated that it would take thirty years to clean up the city. Running water and electricity were rare commodities. The United Nations calculated that adults needed to consume 2,650 calories a day for subsistence; many Berliners were getting only 900 to 1,200.

Former president Herbert Hoover, on a fact-finding humanitarian visit to Berlin, reported back to Harry Truman that living conditions were "the worst that modern civilization has ever seen," and said the death toll among the elderly was "appalling." He recommended that the British and Americans supply Berliners with millions of dollars worth of food, something neither country could afford.

But as possibly the worst of her problems, Berlin was at the epicenter of the growing cold war. In conferences at Yalta, during the war, and Potsdam, afterward, the United States, France, Germany, and the Soviet Union had divided Germany into four zones of influence. The city of Berlin, 110 miles (177 km) inside the Soviet Zone, was divided into four zones, as well, each administered by one of the major powers. By 1948, Great Britain, France, and the United States had decided to combine their German zones of influence into one "Trizone" (which would eventually become West Germany) in an effort to cut costs and stimulate the badly recessionary German economy.

This, however, did not meet with the favor of Joseph Stalin, who wanted to take over a failing Germany. Economic stagnation would lead to civic unrest (as it had after World War I), which the Soviets could stir into a popular communist uprising. The rest would be as easy as subsuming Poland or Romania. He looked for his chance to sabotage the Allied Trizone and saw it. In 1945, General Lucius D. Clay, the military governor of the American Zone in Germany, had agreed when the Russians had set aside only one road and one railroad for Western powers to use in supplying the city. Now, Stalin decreed to his local commanders, those lifelines to Berlin were to be closed.

BERLIN, AROUND 1946. YEARS OF BOMBING HAD LEFT ABOUT 50,000 BERLINERS DEAD AND THE CITY A PILE OF RUBBLE. DURING THE FINAL RUSSIAN ASSAULT ON THE CITY, BEGINNING IN APRIL 1945, MORE THAN 100,000 CITIZENS DIED. RED TROOPS ENTERING THE CITY AFTER THE BATTLE SUBJECTED BERLIN WOMEN TO AN ORGY OF RAPING.

Library of Congress

"UNLESS WE TAKE A STRONG STAND"

On March 31, 1948, the Berlin-based General Clay sent a telegram to his superior, General Omar Bradley, chief of staff of the U.S. Army in Washington. It read, in part:

> Have received a peremptory letter from the Soviet Deputy Commander requiring on 24 hours notice that our military and civilian employees proceeding through the Soviet Zone to Berlin will submit to individual documentation and also will submit their personal belongings to Soviet inspection.

> Likewise is required from Soviet Commander for all freight brought into Berlin by military trains for use of our occupation forces. Obviously these conditions would make impossible travel between Berlin and our zone by American personnel except by air. Moreover, it is undoubtedly the first of a series of restrictive measures designed to drive us from Berlin. . . .

Clay went on to say, "Unless we take a strong stand now, our life in Berlin will become impossible." It was his desire, he told Bradley, to instruct his GIs to open fire if Soviet soldiers attempted to stop their trains and trucks. Bradley refused to give him permission to do this, and so Clay began airlifting supplies into Berlin, although on a limited scale, only enough to supply the roughly 6,000 Western troops in Berlin (troops far outnumbered by the 18,000 Soviet troops in the Soviet Zone outside the city). Truman kept his eye on the situation but was more concerned with the issue or recognizing the newly created State of Israel, which he decided to do on Friday, May 14.

In the meantime, the situation in Berlin was heating up. A Soviet Yak fighter, playing a game of chicken with a British air transport plane, had sheared off its right wing. The Soviet pilot died, as did all eight aboard the British plane. British and American protests over the situation went unheeded. The Soviets did not completely block land traffic into Berlin, but they continued to harass trucks and rail traffic.

At the end of June, Western powers announced plans for a new German deutschmark, because the old one had become worthless. Stability in German currency was the last thing Stalin wanted to see. On June 23, the Russians cut power to the parts of Berlin controlled by the West. On June 24, all rail, road, and water access to Berlin through the Soviet Zone was halted. The Soviets declared further that they would not send any supplies themselves to Berlin, leaving the city with only enough food for thirty-six days and only enough coal for forty-five.

It was time for Harry Truman to step in.

"WE STAY IN BERLIN, PERIOD!"

On June 26, Truman had a meeting in his office with Secretary of Defense Jim Forrestal, Secretary of the Army Kenneth Royall, and Under Secretary of State Robert Lovett. The problem was clear to all of them. They could abandon Berlin—and its 2.5 million people—to the Soviets. Or they could stay—and risk a new world war.

Truman's advisors laid out the options for the bespectacled Missourian. There was talk of closing the Panama Canal to Russian ships as a retaliatory measure, which Truman vetoed. Truman also vetoed a suggestion by General Lucius Clay, relayed through Kenneth Royall—to force an armed convoy through the Russian blockade— as too likely to start a "shooting war."

Then should American forces leave Berlin? asked Royall.

Truman brushed this aside, his steel-rimmed spectacles glinting: "We stay in Berlin, period!" he told the assembled men.

GENERAL LUCIUS CLAY, LEFT, AND LT.
GENERAL WILLIAM TUNNER STAND
DURING THE DEDICATION CEREMONY
OF THE BERLIN AIRLIFT MONUMENT
IN 1959. CLAY, THE MILITARY
GOVERNOR FOR THE AMERICAN
ZONE IN GERMANY DURING WORLD
WAR II, HANDED OVER AIRLIFT
CONTROL TO TUNNER, WHO RAN THE
MASSIVE HIMALAYAN AIRLIFT INTO
BURMA DURING THE WAR.
Time & Life Pictures/Getty Images

Royall pressed the president further—did Truman realize what the consequences of this might be? It was possible that another war would break out, a war America could ill afford after the staggering cost in lives and dollars of the last one.

"We have to deal with the situation as it develops," Truman replied. "We are in Berlin by the terms of the agreement, and the Russians have no right to get us out either by direct or indirect pressure."

That night, Lovett cabled the American ambassador in London: "We stay in Berlin."

On Monday, June 28, Harry Truman ordered a massive airlift of food supplies and other essentials into Berlin. He also sent two squadrons of B-29s to Germany—the B-29 was a plane that the Russians knew very well was capable of dropping the atomic bomb. The particular planes in question had not received the special modifications necessary to carry the bomb, but the Soviets, of course, did not know this.

Interestingly enough, a White House staffer later recalled that Truman's staff "had no direct role whatever in any decisions or in the execution or carrying out of the airlift." In this most charged of political seasons, in other words, Truman had not consulted any of his domestic advisors about whether he might score political points (or lose them) by making this risky decision. He simply went ahead and did what he thought right.

OPERATION VITTLES

Almost immediately, the airlift began. In 1945, the Soviets had ceded the Allies three separate air corridors into Berlin, each about twenty miles (32.1 km) wide. Yet an airlift was not so easy a measure as it might seem. Airlifts as practiced during World War II had never been particularly successful when used on a large scale. During the spring of 1945, it had taken the RAF 650 sorties to drop only 1,560 tons (1,415 t) of food in attempting to supply Holland, where the people were close to starvation. The U.S. Air Force had famously flown supplies over the "Hump" of the Himalayas to feed British troops fighting the Japanese in Burma, but there had been time for close planning and attention to detail.

There was no such time in Berlin, because the city needed food and fuel immediately. There were other problems as well. Three air corridors twenty miles (32.1 km) wide was actually a very tight space for massive American C-54 cargo planes and their British counterparts, the lumbering Yorks and Dakotas of the Royal Air Force. To make matters worse, landings strips and aircraft facilities were poor. The American air field at Tempelhof was in the middle of Berlin and approaches had to be made over both a 400-foot (121.9 m) brewery chimney (which its owner refused to demolish) and seven-story apartment buildings, making things very difficult in bad weather (indeed, one C-54 was to crash into just such a building, killing the crew and the inhabitants of an apartment). The RAF landing field at Gatow had better visibility but only one runway, which was steel mesh laid down over sandy soil.

PRESIDENT TRUMAN, IN 1948, ORDERED A MASSIVE AIRLIFT OF FOOD SUPPLIES AND OTHER ESSENTIALS INTO BERLIN IN JUNE OF THAT YEAR. HE ALSO SENT TWO SQUADRONS OF B-29S TO GERMANY—THE B-29 WAS A PLANE THAT THE RUSSIANS KNEW WAS CAPABLE OF DROPPING THE ATOMIC BOMB.

Popperfoto/Getty Images

There were a few other, smaller airstrips. None had been built with heavy traffic and extremely heavy aircraft in mind, but this is exactly what they got. The first two weeks of the airlift were extremely chaotic. Pilots were pulled in from all branches of the armed services of the two countries, supplies were thrown aboard airplanes, and off they zoomed into the sky. It was early July—midsummer—but the weather was freaky: Heavy thunderstorms turned into snow and ice at higher altitudes, icing wings; fog was heavy; and cloud cover was almost down to 200 feet (61 m), at which point Tempelhoff would be forced to close. Heavy tailwinds sprang up out of nowhere, forcing aircraft to break off their approaches. There was so much rain that the rudimentary landing fields soon became quagmires, forcing crews to labor all night with bulldozers and crushed rock to pave them.

Yet still the aircraft kept coming in the airlift the Americans called "Operation Vittles" and the British referred to as "Operation Plainfare." It was estimated that 2,000 tons (1,814.4 t) of food were needed each day. In July, the most the planes could bring in was 1,480 (1,342.6 t) per day. Yet the tonnage kept rising.

"SOME DASHING LIEUTENANT-COLONEL"

The Soviets were furious as they watched planes lumbering overhead, and there were ominous signs that they were preparing a military response. Soviet fighters continually buzzed the unarmed transport ships, causing highly dangerous situations. Soviet Yak fighters also carried out shooting exercises with live ammunition at towed targets and even made practice bombing runs. The threat of war was becoming less indirect, more pointed, and Secretary of the Army Kenneth Royall decided that he wanted General Clay to go to Washington to meet with Truman and the National Security Council on July 22. Truman thought it was a bad decision and confided so in his diary in characteristic terms: "My mutton-headed Secretary [of the] Army ordered Clay home from Germany and stirred up a terrific how-dy-do for no good reason."

On the morning of July 19, still upset, Truman met with Secretary of State George C. Marshall and Secretary of Defense Forrestal to discuss Berlin. Truman recorded what happened in his diary:

July 19, 1948

Have quite a day . . . A meeting with General Marshall and Jim Forrestal on Berlin and the Russian situation. Marshall states the facts and the conditions with which we are faced. I'd made the decision ten days ago *to stay in Berlin*. Jim wants to hedge—he always does. He's constantly sending me alibi memos which I return with directions and facts. We'll stay in Berlin—come what may. Royall, [Under Secretary of the Army William] Draper, and Jim Forrestal come in later. I have to listen to a rehash of what I know already and reiterate my "Stay in Berlin" decision. I don't pass the buck, nor do I alibi out of any decision I make.

Then, as if to show what a bad mood he was in because of all this second-guessing of his Berlin decision, Truman went on:

Went to [General John J.] Pershing's funeral in the marble amphitheater in Arlington. The hottest damn place this side of hell and Bolivar, Mo . . . This is the fifth time I've prepared to attend the General's funeral. It came off this time.

Truman's mood was not further lifted by his meeting on June 21 with Jim Forrestal, Secretary of the Air Force Stuart Symington, and several others who wanted to convince Truman that the Armed Forces should have "custody" of the atomic bomb—in other words, should decide when and whether to employ the bomb against the Soviets. A Truman aide, David Lilienthal, wrote that night in his diary:

The president . . . looked worn and grim, [with] none of the joviality that he sometimes exhibits, and we got right down to business. It was an important session, and a kind of seriousness hung over it that wasn't relieved a bit, needless to say, by the nature of the subject and by the fact that even at that moment some terrible thing might be happening in Berlin. . . .

Stuart Symington told Truman that the rationale for giving the Air Force control of the weapon was that "our fellas need to get used to handling it," which prompted a lecture from Truman that the atomic bomb "is used to wipe out women and children and unarmed people and not for military uses." When Symington continued to protest, Truman cut him off curtly and abruptly ended the meeting. Later, he sarcastically told Forrestal that he wasn't about to let "some dashing Lieutenant-Colonel decide when would be the proper time to drop one."

By the time General Lucius Clay got to Truman, at a National Security Council meeting on July 22, it had been a hell of a week. Truman had nothing against Clay—in

A U.S. CARGO PLANE CARRIES
SUPPLIES DURING THE BERLIN
AIRLIFT AT TEMPELHOF AIRFIELD
IN 1948. DURING THE ENTIRE
OPERATION, 277,569 PLANES
BEARING FOOD FLEW INTO BERLIN.

fact, he admired the work he had done and would award him with a medal when the Berlin crisis was over—and he listened carefully as Clay once again recommended sending an armed ground convoy through the Soviet Occupation Zone to Berlin—essentially, as a way of testing Stalin's will. Clay estimated the chance that a shooting war would break out at only 25 percent, but this was a chance Truman refused to take, even though the Soviet Union did not, yet, possess the atomic bomb.

He told the assembled generals and Security Council members that he wanted more C-54s sent into Berlin— he wanted Stalin to know his "absolute determination" to keep the airlift going.

GIVING 'EM HELL

Once back in Berlin, Clay ordered another airfield built—in part with the help of 30,000 Berlin citizens, who helped clear rubble and grade the runway. But Truman had one more card to play. He knew that Clay, for all his virtues, was not an airman, and so he handed over control of the airlift to Major General William Tunner, who had been in charge of the massive Himalayan airlift into Burma during the war.

Tunner—nicknamed "Willie the Whip" by subordinates who had felt the lash of his driving personality—assumed control of day-to-day operations of the airlift. He took the extremely logical step of making each of the three air corridors into Berlin run in only one direction, which kept down confusion and fatal accidents. He brought in civilian air traffic controllers from the United States to keep order in the sky and even hired beautiful German women to host runway-side snack bars for weary American fliers, thus immediately improving morale, but also keeping flight crews close to their planes. Within a few weeks, the airlift was bringing in 4,500 tons (4,082.4 t) of food and supplies a day.

Berliners dreaded the oncoming winter of 1948–1949, but Tunner's planes kept on flying, massive waves of them blackening the sky, a symbol to Berliners not of bombs being dropped, as they had been during the war, but of hope and survival in the face of Soviet intransigence. In April 1949, a twenty-four-hour "Easter parade" of planes brought in 13,000 tons (11,794 t) of food. The Soviets knew they were beaten, and they ended the blockade about a month later. In the end, 277,569 planes bearing food flew into Berlin.

Harry Truman was happy to hear the news, but it didn't surprise him. At the time the Berlin blockade ended, the president was entering the first year of his first elected term in office, having, to everyone's surprise but his own, trounced Thomas E. Dewey in the 1948 presidential contest. Truman had won by turning around the impression the American people had of him as a nonentity. Traveling more than 31,000 miles (49,889.7 km) and making an incredible 350 speeches on a whistlestop tour across America, he vowed to the American people that he would "Give 'em hell!" This was directed at Republicans (whom he termed "gluttons of privilege" and "bloodsuckers"), but Americans now knew from the way Harry had handled old Joe Stalin that he was perfectly capable of being the president they needed.

CHAPTER 21

HARRY TRUMAN AND KOREA:
"IT'S HELL TO BE PRESIDENT"

1950

O N THE AFTERNOON OF SATURDAY, JUNE 24, 1950, HARRY TRUMAN'S PLANE, the *Independence*, a prop-driven VC-118 named after the president's hometown, nosed down into Kansas City, Missouri, after a three-hour flight from Baltimore, where the president dedicated a new airport.

Truman was in a relaxed mood. He had no official meetings at all that weekend, and intended, as he told a friend, "to see [his wife] Bess, [his daughter] Margie, and my brother and sister, oversee some fence building—not political—[and] order a new roof for the farm house."

He landed in Kansas City at about 2:00 p.m. and took a car to his home in Independence, where several hundred spectators waited to greet him. Truman waved at them and engaged in some banter before entering his home. The day was baking hot—90°F—and the president did some reading and visiting before sitting down to dinner about 6:00 p.m., afterward chatting with Margaret and Bess on their screened-in back porch until it was time for him to retire, about 9:00 p.m.

At 9:20 he received a phone call from Secretary of State Dean Acheson. "Mr. President," Acheson said. "I have some very serious news. The North Koreans have invaded South Korea." Acheson had already notified the secretary general of the United Nations and asked him to call a meeting of the UN Security Council.

Standing there in his pajamas, Truman immediately replied: "I must get back to the capital."

But Acheson told him: "It isn't advisable to take the risk of a night flight." He said that the president appearing to leave in haste might panic the nation. "Everything is being done that can be done."

He told Truman he would talk to him in the morning and hung up. Truman went to bed, but could not sleep. He was certain—as were most high-ranking American officials—that the first shots of World War III had just been fired.

THE IDEOLOGICAL BATTLEGROUND

Korea had long been a battleground in Asia, a strategically placed peninsula that the Japanese saw as a stepping-stone into China. In 1910, Japan annexed Korea, forcing its factories to produce steel for Japanese munitions and training young men for the Japanese army.

During World War II, Japan's brutal occupation of the country, which included using thousands of Korean women as prostitutes for the Japanese army, cost the lives of hundreds of thousands of Koreans. Hopes by Koreans for independence were dashed as World War II came to a close, even though Franklin Roosevelt, Winston Churchill, and Chiang Kai-shek, meeting in Cairo in 1943, had declared, "Korea should become free and independent." After the Japanese surrender, the new American president Harry Truman suggested to Joseph Stalin that the Soviets receive the surrender of Japanese forces north of the 38th parallel, while the Americans receive the surrender of those south of that point.

In Truman's mind, the 38th parallel was simply an arbitrary line drawn for convenience, but he was far too naïve about Joseph Stalin in those days. The Soviets immediately sealed off the border at the 38th parallel, and now there was a partitioned Korea—and little the Americans could do about it. North Korea, which contained most of the manufacturing might of the country, was ruled by thirty-eight-year-old Kim Il-sung, a former communist partisan fighter in Manchuria during the Chinese civil war, who was seen by most of the world as a Soviet puppet figure. South Korea, mainly agricultural, was led by the American-backed and popularly elected Syngman Rhee.

However, both the People's Republic of Korea (North Korea) and the Republic of Korea (South Korea) were heavily influenced by the Soviets and the Americans, respectively. Both countries provided military backing and advisors to build up North and South Korea's armed forces. In this regard, North Korea, with a Soviet-trained army of 150,000 and 150 T-34 Soviet tanks, was far ahead of South Korea, which had a force of only 65,000 Republic of Korea (ROK) troops, poorly equipped with M-1 rifles and outdated antitank weapons.

President Truman had said as early as July 1946 that Korea was "the ideological battleground on which our entire success in Asia depends," but in fact Truman's eyes were mainly turned to Western Europe and he did not expect an attack on South Korea. By the beginning of 1950, most American advisors were in the process of leaving Korea, having turned over the country's defense almost totally to the ROK army.

Acheson, in a soon-to-be famous speech made in January 1950, did not include the Korean peninsula as part of the "defense perimeter" of the United States and its interests. He did not intend this to mean that South Korea would be left undefended, but Stalin and Kim Il-sung took it that way. And so in the predawn hours of June 25, 1950, Korean time, 90,000 North Korean combat troops, supported by Soviet MIG fighters and Soviet advisors, punched across the 38th parallel, heading straight for the South Korean capital city of Seoul.

"WE'VE GOT TO STOP THE SONS-OF-BITCHES!"

On the morning of Sunday, June 25, Dean Acheson called Truman again at the president's home in Independence. There had been some faint hope that the North Korean attack might be only a probe or a feint, but this had been dashed by reports from Korea and from the headquarters of General Douglas MacArthur in Japan.

"Mr. President," Acheson said, "the news is bad. The attack is in force all along the parallel."

"Dean," Truman exclaimed angrily, "we've got to stop the sons-of-bitches!"

He told Acheson that the secretary needed to assemble the cabinet and heads of the armed forces. He was returning to Washington that day. The press corps following him, having gotten wind of the events in Europe, noted that he was "grim-faced." Although he told one reporter, "Don't make it alarmist!"—meaning, don't report that the attack on South Korea was a panic moment for the public—a presidential aide whispered to another pressman: "The boss is going to hit those fellows hard."

While Truman flew to Washington, the United Nations Security Council met and voted 9-0 to demand an immediate cessation of hostilities by the North Koreans (the Soviets did not vote because the Soviet ambassador to the UN had walked out earlier that year when the UN refused to unseat nationalist China). Once in Washington, Truman went immediately to Blair House, where he was temporarily living during repairs to the White House, and met with advisors, including Acheson; Dean Rusk, the influential assistant secretary of state for Asian affairs; Secretary of Defense Louis Johnson; Secretary of the Army Frank Pace Jr.; the heads of the U.S. Army, Air Force, and Navy; and General Omar Bradley, chairman of the Joint Chiefs of Staff, a fellow Missourian and the soldier whom Truman trusted most.

The group met, the *New York Times* reported, "as an atmosphere of tension, unparalleled since the war days, spread over the capital." John Foster Dulles, an influential Republican and future secretary of state who was visiting Korea at the time of the invasion, had telegrammed Acheson and Rusk:

A MAP OF KOREA DURING THE WAR SHOWING THE 38TH PARALLEL, WHICH DIVIDED THE NORTH, CONTROLLED BY THE SOVIET UNION, AND THE SOUTH, OVERSEEN BY THE UNITED STATES. IN TRUMAN'S MIND, THE 38TH PARALLEL WAS SIMPLY AN ARBITRARY LINE DRAWN FOR CONVENIENCE, BUT HE WAS FAR TOO NAÏVE ABOUT JOSEPH STALIN IN THE DAYS FOLLOWING WORLD WAR II.

Harry S. Truman Library and Museum

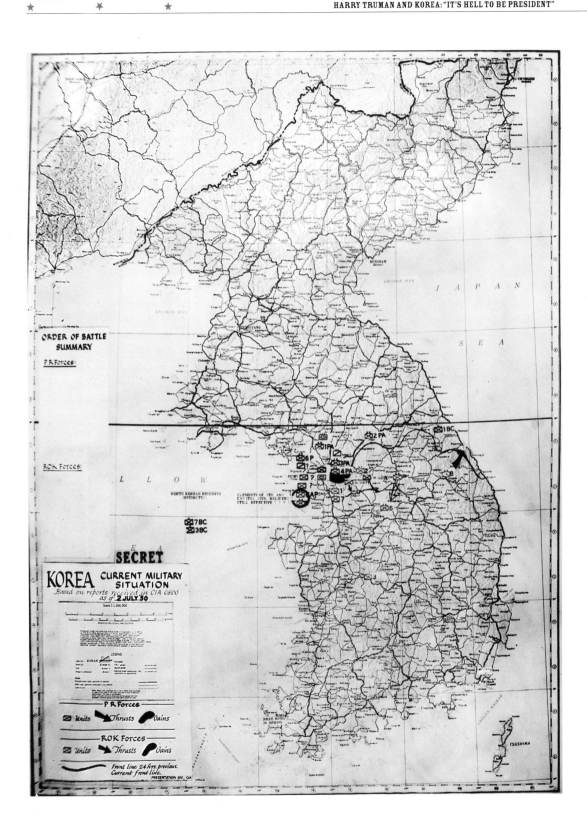

> To sit by while Korea is overrun by unprovoked armed attack would start a disastrous chain of events leading most probably to world war.

This was what most people in the room thought—or perhaps feared. A Korea occupied by communists was "a dagger pointed at the heart of Japan" (which was now the United States' chief military stronghold in the Far East), Acheson said. Omar Bradley chimed in that "we must draw the line somewhere" against communism. Truman listened to all of them.

To understand his thinking—and the thinking of the rest of the men in the room—one must understand that the attack on Korea came at a time when Americans felt they were being surrounded by the dark forces of communism everywhere. The Soviet Union had exploded its first test atomic bomb in 1949. Stalin had intervened in civil unrest in Greece and Turkey. In Asia, Mao Zedong had won a crushing victory over the American-backed forces of Chiang Kai-shek, and the Truman administration was facing criticism from Republicans that it had "lost" China.

Domestically, Joseph McCarthy, the right-wing senator from Wisconsin, had begun his hunt for communists within the U.S. government. This put pressure on Truman not to appear "soft" on communism.

Darkness fell over Washington and still the meeting at Blair House continued. Truman asked for an intelligence report on "possible next moves" by Stalin in other regions of the globe, fearing that the shots fired in Korea were only the first in a possible series of attacks. When the group finally broke up at 11 p.m.—leaving by the back door to avoid reporters—Truman reserved decision, but, he later wrote, he knew in his heart that he had "the complete, almost unspoken acceptance that whatever had to be done to meet aggression had to be done."

"A POLICE ACTION"

The next day, Truman assembled what was even then being called "his war cabinet" and made a decision to evacuate Americans from Seoul, as well as provide immediate air and naval support to ROK forces fighting against overwhelming odds. He still did not endorse sending in American ground troops. He told those assembled at Blair House that he did not want to go to war.

"Everything I have done in the past five years has been to try to avoid making a decision such as I had to make tonight."

The next day, June 27, North Korean forces swept into Seoul and North Korean premier Kim Il-sung made a radio speech in which he proclaimed that he would "crush"

South Korea. Truman issued a statement that began: "The attack on Korea makes it plain beyond all doubt that communism has passed beyond the use of subversion to conquer independent nations . . ." An enthusiastic Congress—for once, even the Republicans were on Truman's side—voted to extend the draft law by one year. More important, the United Nations voted to back the American decision to go to war—the first time in its short history that the UN had voted to back its sanctions with force.

On June 30, General MacArthur cabled Secretary of the Army Pace with an urgent request for American ground combat troops—two divisions of them—without which, MacArthur said, American efforts to save South Korea would be "doomed to failure." Pace called Truman at 5 a.m. (Truman noted in his diary, however, that he "was already up and shaved") to pass on the request. Truman immediately authorized a regiment, and then, the next morning, approved the use of two divisions. He was now sending American boys into war for the first time since he became president. It was, he said later, a harder decision to make than that of dropping the atomic bomb on Japan.

That afternoon, Truman held a press conference. A reporter asked him: "Are we or are we not at war?"

Truman replied: "We are not at war."

Another reporter suggested: "Would it be possible to call this a police action under the United Nations?"

Truman, his gray-blue eyes flashing beneath his spectacles, answered: "Yes, that is exactly what it amounts to."

PRESIDENT TRUMAN, RIGHT, MEETS WITH SECRETARY OF STATE DEAN ACHESON, LEFT, AND GENERAL GEORGE MARSHALL, CENTER, IN 1950. IT WAS ACHESON WHO INFORMED THE PRESIDENT, WHO WAS STAYING AT HIS MISSOURI HOME, OF THE NORTH KOREAN INVASION OF SOUTH KOREA.

Abbie Rowe, National Park Service, courtesy Harry S. Truman Library and Museum

"BUG-OUT FEVER"

Despite rushing two divisions and then four—for a total of 30,000 American troops—to South Korea, the war went badly for the United States during the summer of 1950. American industry had stopped making war materials after World War II, following the country's practice of severely curtailing arms production when no longer needed in active war. The army was at a low ebb as well, and many of the American GIs sent to fight in Korea were inexperienced and fat from garrison duty in Japan and elsewhere. As hardened North Korean fighters pushed south, many American GIs were gripped by "bug-out fever," and throwing away their arms, fled for their lives. (Later in the war,

GENERAL DOUGLAS MACARTHUR, RIGHT, INSPECTS THE WESTERN FRONT NEAR SUWON, KOREA, IN JANUARY 1951. STANDING NEXT TO HIM ARE MAJOR GENERAL FRANK MILBURN, LEFT, AND MAJOR JAMES LEE, CENTER. MACARTHUR, TRUMAN, AND THE U.S. STATE DEPARTMENT WOULD GREATLY MISCALCULATE THE CHINESE DURING THE WAR.

Associated Press

the epidemic lessened as GIs became better trained and equipped and in nearly all instances stood their ground and fought heroically.)

But even more Americans, UN forces, and their ROK counterparts stood and fought rear-guard actions on hundreds of nameless hills, sacrificing their lives to delay the oncoming North Koreans so that American and UN forces could establish a last-ditch defense perimeter around the port of Pusan, in southeastern Korea. By early September, 87,000 Americans and 91,000 ROK troops had inflicted 58,000 casualties on North Korea, blunting their advance. But more than 12,000 GIs had been killed, wounded, or taken prisoner. Reporters and some in Congress were beginning to scoff at the phrase "police action" to describe a bloody war.

Truman was already having problems with the arrogance and Napoleonic qualities of his commander in chief, General Douglas MacArthur, who was in the habit of issuing statements to the press about political matters—statements that Truman naturally assumed to be his territory and that, onlookers reported, turned Truman rigid with anger, "his lips white and compressed."

Still, he approved MacArthur's daring amphibious invasion of Korea at Inchon, on the west coast of South Korea, on September 15, 1950, a plan that turned the tide of the war completely. With Americans advancing down the Korean peninsula from the rear, the North Korean army was forced to break off its investment in Pusan and flee north. The American and UN forces at Pusan broke out and now the North Koreans were caught in a pincher movement. The war seemed to have made a sudden and providential turn—and Truman, perhaps carried away with MacArthur's success, allowed him to pursue the North Korean forces beyond the 38th parallel, although with the caveat that if any large Chinese or Soviet forces were spotted, MacArthur would break off contact.

When the Chinese protested, Truman and the State Department ignored them. After meeting with MacArthur at Wake Island in the Pacific—a meeting that confirmed MacArthur's arrogance, but also convinced Truman that the war was going well—Truman returned home. All seemed to be going well, even though, on November 1, two weeks after the Wake Island meeting, a couple of Puerto Rican nationalists attempted to shoot their way into Blair House and kill Truman. One White House police officer died in the barrage of bullets, and two others were wounded.

Publicly, Truman was stoic: "A president has to expect these things," he told the press, but to his diary he griped that the Secret Service no longer wanted him to take his usual walk. "It's hell to be president," he wrote.

"AN ENTIRELY NEW WAR"

The hell of the presidency was about to get even worse for Truman. Everyone—he, MacArthur, the State Department—had made a major miscalculation about the Chinese. On November 3, 300,000 Chinese troops poured across the Yalu River, bordering China and North Korea, and fiercely attacked American and UN forces, driving them southward in some of the worst fighting of the war. Mao Zedong had signaled that he was not about to allow the presence of American forces so close to his border. MacArthur cabled Truman: "We face an entirely new war."

As Truman often said, the buck stopped with him, however. The reporter and author John Hersey noted in a *New Yorker* profile of the president that he seemed completely "alone" when he heard the news of the massive communist Chinese invasion. "His mouth drew tight, his cheeks flushed. For a moment, it seemed as if he would sob. Then in a voice that was incredibly calm and quiet, considering what could be read on his face . . . he said: 'This is the worst situation we have had yet. We'll just have to meet it as we've met all the rest.'"

U.S. and UN forces—troops from Great Britain, Australia, Greece, Turkey, Ethiopia, Canada, France, Belgium, and the Philippines, among others—fought one of the most extraordinary rear-guard actions in history all throughout the bitter winter of 1950–1951, and even though

NORTH KOREAN PRESIDENT KIM IL SUNG, A FORMER COMMUNIST PARTISAN FIGHTER IN MANCHURIA DURING THE CHINESE CIVIL WAR, SEEN BY MOST OF THE WORLD AS A SOVIET PUPPET FIGURE.

AFP/Getty Images

AMERICAN WARSHIPS ARE
SHOWN MOORED BY THE BEACHES
OF INCHON IN SEPTEMBER 1950
AFTER THEIR BOMBARDMENT
AND INVASION OF THIS CRITICAL
PORT DURING THE WAR.
Getty Images

Seoul fell to the Chinese in January, American and UN troops were able to rally and drive them out by March. The Chinese were now forced to withdraw, in part because of their primitive supply system, which permitted operations for no more than a week or two before the army needed to halt for resupplying. The Chinese depended a good deal on mules and manpower to bring up supplies, and these slow-moving columns were vulnerable to American air attack.

But the Korean War now settled into a long, protracted stalemate, with fighting up and down the peninsula. As the stalemate continued, Truman's popularity in America ebbed. He had the misfortune to become the first American president of the modern era to be forced to fight a "limited war," and he was caught in the kind of trap that would ensnare American chief executives during the Vietnam War.

He had not gone to Congress to get a resolution of war—in part because he was afraid this precedent would adversely affect future presidents—but now he was criticized by that very same Congress for allowing an undeclared war to drag on and on, with serious cost to American lives. When asked by a reporter, around the time of the Chinese attack across the Yalu, whether he would "include the atomic bomb" in America's response to the Chinese, Truman said: "There has always been active consideration of its use."

The reporter then asked whether America would use the atomic bomb only under "United Nations authorization." To which Truman replied: "No, the military commander in the field will have charge of the use of weapons, as he always has." By this, the president meant that the United States would not cede control of the bomb to the United Nations, but his reply was so clumsily phrased that it sounded as if he meant that U.S. field commanders would have the discretion to decide whether to use nuclear force. Because Truman had decided during the Berlin Airlift crisis that sole authority over the use of the bomb would rest with the executive branch, he had driven himself into a corner and his aides were forced to scramble to issue a statement saying only the president would authorize deployment of nuclear weapons.

"RIGHT AND WRONG AND LEADERSHIP"

Harry S. Truman decided not to run again for another term and left the Oval Office in 1953, to be replaced by Dwight David Eisenhower. The Korean War, which cost 35,576 American lives, 140,000 South Korean military and civilian lives, and the lives of an estimated 1,500,000 military and civilian North Koreans and Chinese, was halted in 1954 by an armistice, but in a very real sense, it never really ended. Armed forces of the North and the South, as well as those of the United States, still face each other across the demilitarized zone of the 38th parallel today.

Because of the Korean War, the United States never again stood down as completely from arms production as it did after World War II, and the United States began its first peacetime program of military preparedness. Ironically, although the war had become highly unpopular for the American public, it stimulated the stagnant post–World War II economy, helping bring about the prosperity of the 1950s.

Should Harry Truman have jumped to South Korea's aid in 1950? Would Stalin have taken a tepid American response as an open invitation to seize other parts of the world? We'll never completely know the answers to these questions, but certainly Truman scored a success by making the war a United Nations' effort and by assuring other countries that the United States would come to their aid if they were attacked.

Truman himself never doubted that he had done the right thing. He was to write in his diary: "It isn't polls or public opinion of the moment that counts. It is right and wrong and leadership—men with fortitude, honesty, and a belief in the right that makes epochs in the history of the world."

CHAPTER 22

DWIGHT EISENHOWER AND THE INTERSTATE HIGHWAY SYSTEM: "BROADER RIBBONS ACROSS THE LAND"

1956

O N THE SULTRY MORNING OF MONDAY, JULY 7, 1919, THE LARGEST CONVOY OF military motor vehicles the world had ever known rumbled through the streets of Washington, D.C., making such a roar that flowerpots fell off windowsills, cats ran for cover, and, in more than one instance, an elderly person fainted. The First Transcontinental Motor Convoy (FTMC), as it was known, comprised eighty-one vehicles. This number included two fuel tankers carrying 750 gallons (2,838.2 l) of gas apiece, a water tanker, eleven passenger cars, nine motorcycles, five ambulances, two kitchen service trucks, a truck carrying a pontoon bridge, another truck carrying a three-million-candlepower searchlight, and, last but not least, a custom-built (to the tune of $40,000) wrecker truck with a winch for hauling stuck vehicles from ditches or quicksand.

Accompanying these vehicles were two hundred and fifty-eight enlisted men and thirty-seven officers of the U.S. Army. This procession, more than two miles (3.2 km) long, wended its way through Washington to the area known as the Ellipse in Potomac Park, south of the White House. There the vehicles were arranged in a semicircle around a "Zero Milestone" marker and Secretary of War Newton Baker gave a short address, telling the men of the convoy that the journey they were about to make signified "the beginning of a new era." For he was sending the FTMC on a trip all the way across the United States to San Francisco in order, as Baker wrote, "to service-test the special purpose vehicles developed for use in the [just ended] World War, not all of which were available in time for such use."

By noon, the trucks of the FTMC had rumbled out of Washington, leaving the city in blessed peace; their first stop, forty-eight (77.2 km) miles and seven and a half hours later, was Frederick, Maryland, where the convoy was joined by a twenty-eight-year-old army lieutenant colonel named Dwight David Eisenhower, who had signed on as an observer. The next morning the trucks set off in earnest on their epic cross-country trip.

"TWO RUTS ACROSS THE PRAIRIE"

In 1919, although 6.5 million Americans had cars, the country's road system was abysmal. There were few miles of paved highways outside of the cities and those few were not properly maintained. In short, writes historian Pete Davies, "when the car appeared there was nothing for it to drive on." The only cross-country automobile journeys were ones sponsored by automobile companies trying to sell their cars. These took months, one contemporary writer wrote, and the intrepid motorist needed to first "lay in a stock of supplies only slightly less comprehensive, expensive, and cumbersome than Captain Amundsen would require for a dash to the Pole." Much of the travel through the Plains states was done on what one motorist called "two ruts across the prairie."

However, beginning in 1912, several American car enthusiasts, chief among them auto dealer and early headlight manufacturer Carl Fisher, banded together to build, with contributions from private individuals and automobile companies, a cross-country road they called the "Lincoln Highway," which stretched from New York City to San Francisco. It sounded grand, but in truth, as a reporter of the time wrote, the Lincoln Highway was more "an imaginary line, like the equator," linking together numerous poor stretches of country road with newly paved ones.

It was this Lincoln Highway that the FTMC, and Dwight Eisenhower, were to follow to test their vehicles against the rigors of the American countryside. However, an even more important purpose of the journey was Secretary of War Baker's desire to support the "good roads movement" started by Fisher and others—a movement pushing for a unified interstate highway system. The young Eisenhower was an early automobile owner (his first car was a 1912 Pullman Roadster) and a proponent of good roads. He had spent the war at Camp Colt in Gettysburg, Pennsylvania, helping establish a tank corps whose "mechanical dinosaurs lumbered over the field where once Union and Confederate soldiers had clashed," as one Eisenhower biographer wrote. However, the war ended before he and his unit made it overseas, and young Eisenhower faced an uncertain future in the army. He was considering resigning to take a job in the civilian world when the opportunity to join the FTMC came along. He leaped at it—and it's a good thing for America, and America's highways, that he did.

"BROADER RIBBONS ACROSS THE LAND"

Eisenhower would write years later about his journey across America in 1919: "To those who have known only concrete and macadam highways of gentle grades and

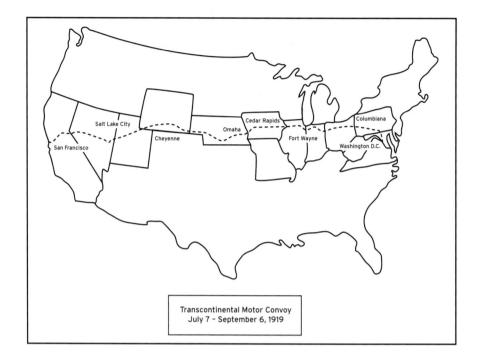

Transcontinental Motor Convoy
July 7 – September 6, 1919

THE MAP SHOWS THE ROUTE OF
THE FIRST TRANSCONTINENTAL
MOTOR CONVOY IN 1919. PART OF
THE ROUTE, FROM NEW YORK TO
SAN FRANCISCO, WAS ACROSS THE
LINCOLN HIGHWAY, WHICH WAS,
IN REALITY, NUMEROUS POOR
STRETCHES OF COUNTRY ROAD
LINKED WITH NEWLY PAVED ONES.

The Dwight D. Eisenhower
Presidential Library and Museum

engineered curves, such a trip might seem humdrum. In those days, we were not sure it could be accomplished at all." By the time, sixty-two days later, that the FTMC reached San Francisco, the convoy had traveled 3,251 miles (5,232 km), averaging 58.1 miles (93.5 km) per day and 6.07 miles (9.8 km) an hour.

> **By the time, sixty-two days later, that the FTMC reached San Francisco, it had traveled 3,251 miles (5,232 km), averaging 58.1 miles (93.5 km) per day and 6.07 miles (9.8 km) an hour.**

Nine vehicles, the expedition's official report said, "were so damaged as to require retirement en route." The convoy destroyed or severely damaged eighty-eight "mostly wooden bridges or culverts" and was involved in "two hundred and thirty . . . instances of road failure and vehicles sinking in quicksand or mud, running off the road . . . or other mishaps due entirely to the unfavorable and at times appalling traffic conditions that were encountered."

In November 1919, Eisenhower filed his official "Report on the Trans-Continental Trip." Although there were stretches of smooth road, particularly in California, many of the roads were so rough that "portions of the train did not move for two hours." And even some of the good roads had been ruined within a few years of being laid down because they "had since received no attention whatsoever" in terms of maintenance. "It seems evident," wrote Eisenhower, "that a very small amount of money spent at the proper time would have kept the road in good condition."

After his journey with the FTMC, Dwight Eisenhower stayed in the army and, during World War II, rose to become the supreme commander of the Allied Expeditionary Force in Europe. In early 1945, he watched admiringly as his American armored forces—after becoming bogged down in other parts of Europe—entered Germany's superb autobahn system and immediately raced across the country. This and his FTMC experiences helped form his vision of how effective and essential a national highway system could be.

"The old convoy [the FTMC] had started me thinking about good, two-laned highways," Eisenhower wrote, "but Germany had made me see the wisdom of broader ribbons across the land."

"GET THE HELL OUT OF THE ROAD-BUILDING BUSINESS"

Eisenhower was not the only one who saw this wisdom. Early planning for a national highway system began in 1921 when the Bureau of Public Roads (BPR—the predecessor of the Federal Highway Administration) asked the army for a list of roads necessary for national defense. Later, Franklin Roosevelt marked out eight superhighway corridors for the BPR to study, and in 1944, the BPR presented Congress with a proposal for a system of interstate highways, which Congress approved in the Federal Aid Highway Act that same year. This called for a National System of Interstate Highways of up to 40,000 miles (64,373.8 km). In 1947, the BPR selected the routes that made up the first 37,700 miles (60,672.3 km) of this system. However, Congress had appropriated such woefully inadequate funds for construction that progress was slow. President Harry Truman, busy at a time of postwar inflation, housing shortage, and the Korean War, was unable to spend much time on the nation's highways.

When Dwight Eisenhower became president in January of 1953, the Bureau of Public Roads reported that 6,400 miles (10,299.8 km) of "Interstate System improvements" had been completed since the end of World War II. However, these improvements were basically upgrading and maintaining existing roads, not building new ones. Almost immediately, Eisenhower decided that his administration needed "to put an emphasis" on pushing through a major overhaul to the U.S. highway system.

There were numerous reasons why he felt the time was ripe. The Detroit automotive industry was now selling nearly eight million cars per year; 70 percent of

American families owned cars. Yet, aside from New York, Chicago, and Los Angeles, there were no high-speed expressways in or near major cities. With the exception of a few toll roads like the Pennsylvania Turnpike, there were no four-lane highways that connected major urban areas. Despite the passage of laws like the Federal Aid Highway Act, construction had been slowed by lack of funding and congressional disputes over who should pay for a new highway system and whether it should be funded through taxes or tolls or a bond issue, or a combination of all three. As with any major public works project, there were numerous factions pushing their own ideas about how highways should work—the trucking industry, the American Automobile Association, and the National Automobile Dealers Association, to name just a few.

Most of the states wanted the federal government to stay out of the picture when it came to laying down highways—they wanted no part of federal bureaucracies and raised taxes. At one governor's conference in 1952, Governor Val Peterson of Nebraska said: "How many governors would oppose a resolution telling the federal government to get the hell out of the road-building business?"

This utterance was met by great applause.

"OUR UNITY AS A NATION"

Coming into office, Eisenhower knew he had a fight on his hands when it came to interstate roads, but it was a fight he would relish. Although he is often portrayed as a mild-mannered chief executive with a hands-off policy on most matters, Eisenhower battled fiercely for what he believed in. And he believed firmly that there were four main reasons the federal government needed to lead the way on building an interstate system.

One, no one could deny that the need was present for such a system.

Two, only the federal government could build a unified system—leaving it up to individual states, as some governors wished, would end in chaos.

Three, such a massive public works program would provide numerous jobs and a huge boost to the economy.

Fourth—possibly most important to Eisenhower and his administration in the middle of a tense cold war—these highways would provide means by which to evacuate cities and move massive amounts of military vehicles and personnel in case of war.

In early 1954, the president welcomed 2,500 delegates to the White House Conference on Highway Safety. He told them that it was estimated that 80 million vehicles would travel America's highways by 1975. (There would actually be 133 million.) "The federal government is going to do its part in helping to build more highways," he said. "It is going to be a job. But that [80 million] figure means this: We don't want to stop that many vehicles from coming. We want them."

Eisenhower was able to push the Democratic-controlled Congress to extend the Federal Aid Highway Act in the spring of 1954, but the funds allocated now—$2 billion—were still not enough, in his opinion, because "the needs are so great that continued efforts to modernize and improve our obsolescent highway system are mandatory." The use of highway building as a way to pull the nation out of the post–Korean War recession was much on his mind. He told his aides, according to his biographer, Steven Ambrose, that he did "not want to get tagged like [Depression-era President Herbert] Hoover did . . . [for] not doing anything to help in economic bad times."

Eisenhower decided that what he wanted was a massive overhaul of the highway system to the tune of $50 billion. He had planned to announce what he called his "grand plan" at the annual Governor's Conference at Lake George, New York, on July 12, 1954, but when his sister-in-law died unexpectedly, the president sent Vice President Richard Nixon to make the speech in his stead. Nixon told the nation's governors: "Our highway net is inadequate locally and obsolete as a national system." He pointed out that the annual death toll from road accidents was nearing 40,000, the equivalent of "the casualties of a bloody war." (By comparison, the number of deaths from traffic accidents in the United States in 2008 was 41,059, with 250,000,000 vehicles on the road compared to 61,000,000 vehicles in 1955.)

After some initial resentment, the governors came cautiously on board. In 1955, to garner further support, Eisenhower commissioned his old subordinate, U.S. Army General Lucius Clay (Ret.), to head a panel studying the issue; accepted Clay's proposal for a ten-year, multibillion-dollar building program (financed by federal gasoline and tire taxes and a bond issue); and presented it to Congress on February 22, 1955, as an administration-backed bill. "Our unity as a nation is sustained by free communication of thought and easy transportation of people and goods," Eisenhower told Congress. The United States, he said, needed "comprehensive, quick and forward-looking action."

The administration's bill passed in the Senate, but became bogged down in the House, the victim of Democrats who wanted the trucking industry to pay more of the cost of building highways. This bickering "would be funny," wrote one newspaper, "if we didn't need the roads so badly."

Still, Eisenhower pressed on. It was a congressional election year and he traveled the country delivering speech after speech in support of Republican candidates and

A YOUNG LT. COLONEL DWIGHT EISENHOWER STANDS WITH THE MOTOR CONVOY IN 1919. "THE OLD CONVOY HAD STARTED ME THINKING ABOUT GOOD, TWO-LANED HIGHWAYS," EISENHOWER WROTE, BUT A TRIP TO GERMANY AND ITS AUTOBAHN SYSTEM "MADE ME SEE THE WISDOM OF BROADER RIBBONS ACROSS THE LAND."

National Archives

MEMBERS OF THE CONVOY STOP AT AN UNKNOWN SPOT IN 1919, POSSIBLY HAVING PULLED THE TRUCK OUT OF THE TWO RUTS IN THE FOREGROUND OF THE PICTURE. DESPITE THE FACT THAT ABOUT 6.5 MILLION AMERICANS HAD CARS AT THIS TIME, THE ROADS ACROSS THE COUNTRY WERE ABYSMAL.

pushing for the interstate system, which he called "a road program that will take this nation out of its antiquated shackles of secondary roads all over this country and give us the types of highways that we need for this great mass of motor vehicles."

Without the interstate highways, Eisenhower cautioned, the United States "will certainly end up in a hopeless traffic jam."

"AS FAST AS WE CAN GET THEM"

The Republicans would lose control of the Congress that year (as they would in the next two congressional elections), but Eisenhower had finally gotten his point across to the American people. In the winter of 1956, he sent a message to Democrats in Congress that "we want the roads as fast as we can get them." As he later told a biographer, he had grown "restless with the quibbling over methods of financing" and was ready to compromise. At the same time, in a clever political move, the administration released a map showing the routes of the proposed interstates; people, especially near urban centers, could now envision the amount of revenue—through highway building, tolls, tourist dollars, and the like—that would come into their areas and see the ease with which they could travel.

With the American people now solidly behind the idea of an interstate system, the Federal Aid Highway Act of 1956 was finally passed on June 26. It called for roads to be funded with an increase in gasoline and tire taxes and for a Highway Trust Fund to be set up for these revenues. The Federal Aid Highway Act of 1956 called for the creation of 42,000 miles (67,592.5 km) of modern and limited access highways (toll roads like the New York State Thruway). The federal government would foot 90 percent of the bill, with states providing the other 10 percent. Road standards were set. Lanes were required to be 10 feet (3 m) wide, shoulders 12 feet (3.7 m) wide, bridges a minimum of 14 feet (4.3 m) high, and road grades less than 3 percent. The highways needed to be able to sustain travel at speeds up to 70 miles (113 kph) per hour. And all of this was to be completed within sixteen years.

On June 29, President Eisenhower, still recovering from an operation for ileitis (Crohn's disease), signed the bill into law without fanfare and even without photographers. Yet, said an aide, "he was highly pleased." The next year, as he campaigned successfully for his second term in office, he often reminded voters about "the mighty network of roads" that he had caused to be spread across the land.

However, there were problems to be faced. The cost of running the highways through urban centers, which necessitated tearing down buildings and relocating people, was greater than anticipated. A recession in 1958 slowed down funding, and it was apparent that the interstate system would not be "self-liquidating" (i.e., self-supporting through revenues), as Eisenhower had once hoped. In 1959, Eisenhower was forced to increase the federal gas tax, something he had not wanted to do, "in order to avoid a serious disruption of the highway program."

Despite this—and despite charges of corruption that would be leveled in the next few years against those administering the funds for building the highways—the Interstate Highway System continued to be built. It would take thirty-seven years to complete the system, not sixteen, with the last link, Interstate 105 in Los Angeles, not completed until 1993. The Interstate Highway System created a number of unforeseen complications, including urban sprawl, noise and air pollution, the decay of downtown areas in cities, and the decline, in some areas, of mass transit. However, it did connect the country and has given Americans a freedom and rapidity of movement they could never have dreamed of in the days that the FTMC convoyed across the nation at 6 miles (9.7 km) an hour.

The Interstate Highway System was President Dwight Eisenhower's favorite domestic program. As he later wrote: "This was one of the things that I felt deeply about, and I made a personal and absolute decision to see that the nation would benefit by it." Therefore it was fitting, in 1990, that Congress would enact a law, signed by President George H. W. Bush, renaming the system the Dwight David Eisenhower National System of Interstate and Defense Highways.

CHAPTER 23

JOHN F. KENNEDY AND THE BAY OF PIGS: "HOW COULD WE HAVE BEEN SO STUPID?"

1961

A MONTH OR SO AFTER HE HAD MADE THE DISASTROUS DECISION TO GREEN-light the invasion of Cuba by 1,400 CIA-trained Cuban exiles, John F. Kennedy turned to *Time* magazine reporter Hugh Sidey and said, "I want to know how all this could have happened. There were fifty or so of us, presumably the most experienced and smartest people we could get, to plan such an operation. Most of us thought it would work . . . But five minutes after it began to fall in, we all looked at each other and asked, 'How could we have been so stupid?'"

In the days and weeks following the April 17–20, 1961, Bay of Pigs invasion, Kennedy did a great deal of breast-beating of this nature. "How could I have done it?" he said to his close friend, Charles Spalding, and told advisor Theodore Sorenson: "All my life I've known better than to depend on the experts."

Some of this anguish was no doubt disingenuous—the handsome young president deliberately letting down his guard for sympathetic reporters and select advisors, to show his humility and desire to do better—but there is enough of it to indicate that Kennedy really did feel as if he had made a profound mistake. He had hoped for a grand start to his so-called "New Frontier," wanted a fresh wind to blow out all the stale and noxious cobwebs of eight years of Dwight Eisenhower, and instead had fallen prey to a scheme hatched by CIA spooks and Republican politicos.

Damn, but it was galling. Above all things, John F. Kennedy considered himself a smart guy—and here he had gone and done a very dumb thing.

"A PARAMILITARY FORCE"

In 1956, Fidel Castro, the darkly handsome, bearded, illegitimate son of a wealthy plantation owner, took eighty-one men and women into the mountains of Cuba to wage a revolution against corrupt Cuban dictator Fulgencio Batista. Over the course of three years (and aided by the United States, which had extensive business interests in Cuba), Batista's 30,000-man army waged war against Castro's band of guerillas, which, for most of the campaign, numbered no more than 800. In January 1959, Castro—who called himself "the Maximum Leader"—swept down from the mountains and, with popular support behind him, took Havana while Batista fled to exile in Spain.

The administration of Dwight Eisenhower recognized Castro's government, but became concerned the following year when it emerged that Castro was not a nationalist, but in fact a communist, a "Marxist-Leninist," as he referred to himself. To have a communist country sitting ninety miles (144.8 km) off the coast of Florida was not in the best interests of the United States, Eisenhower and the State Department decided. Yet the public steps Eisenhower took—boycotting Cuban sugar imports and protesting when Cuban land owned by American corporations was distributed to peasants—only drove Castro closer to Russia.

The private steps were even worse. In March 1960, Eisenhower approved a top-secret anti-Castro plan drawn up by Richard Bissell, head of the CIA's Directorate for Plans (DDP), which was more generally known as Black Operations. Bissell's program, titled "A Program of Covert Action Against the Castro Regime" (code-named JMARC), called for the creation of "a paramilitary force outside of Cuba for future guerilla action." Cuban exiles were recruited for the force and trained for an invasion in secret CIA bases in Guatemala. Other parts of JMARC called for the assassination of Castro by hit men employed by the Mafia (which had lost out heavily when Castro nationalized mob holdings in Cuba). At the very least, he was to be humiliated: Schemes were hatched to pass him powder that would cause his trademark beard to fall out, or slip him hallucinogens before television appearances.

A few weeks after his close defeat of Richard Nixon in the presidential election of 1960, Kennedy was briefed on the plan. Eisenhower left office in January 1961. On January 28, eight days after his inauguration, Kennedy directed the Joint Chiefs of Staff to examine the feasibility of the invasion.

"YOU CAN'T *MAÑANA* THIS THING"

Theodore Sorenson, a close Kennedy advisor who almost always viewed the president in a highly sympathetic light, claimed that JFK was "wary and reserved" about the Cuban invasion, but that Kennedy was sold heavily on the operation by CIA director Allen Dulles, a friend of JFK's father, Joe Kennedy, who played on the young president's fear of not seeming macho enough in the face of communism.

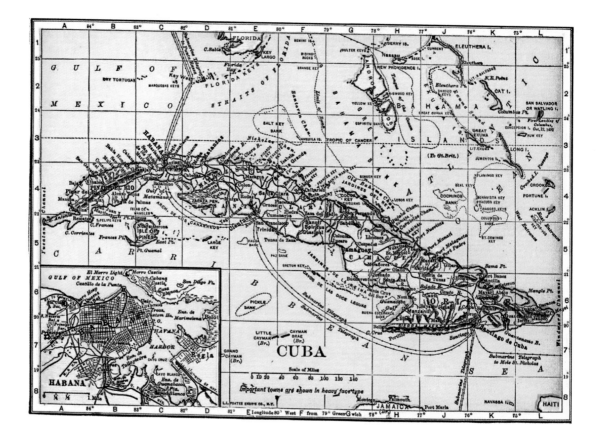

A MAP OF CUBA SHOWS THE BAY OF PIGS. AMERICAN OFFICIALS DIDN'T REALIZE THE BAY WAS A FAVORITE FISHING SPOT OF CASTRO, AND THE PEASANTS THERE WERE ESPECIALLY LOYAL TO HIM. WHEN HE ARRIVED, PERSONALLY, TO TAKE CHARGE OF THE COUNTERATTACK, THEY CHEERED.

Dulles related to Kennedy a scene that had occurred in the Oval Office in the early days of the Eisenhower administration. In 1954, Dulles had overseen the successful CIA overthrow of the Left-leaning government in Guatemala. He now told Kennedy that before that operation: "I stood right here at Ike's desk and I told him I was certain our Guatemalan operation would succeed . . . Mr. President, the prospects for this plan are even better than they were for that one."

Richard Bissell—described by contemporaries as "a persuasive briefer"—got to Kennedy by telling him that the window for such an invasion was closing rapidly. Castro's government was about to take possession of a shipment of Soviet MIG fighters along with their Soviet-trained Cuban pilots, a move that would drastically increase the size and effectiveness of Castro's small air force. Not only that, but word of the plan had leaked out.

There were reports of a possible U.S. invasion of Cuba in the Latin American press, causing the president of Guatemala, embarrassed to be seen in such close cooperation with the Yankees, to demand that the CIA move the Cuban exile force elsewhere. The *New York Times* speculated on just such an invasion in early January, quoting one Cuban exile leader as saying: "I expect to be in Cuba beginning in February." And Castro himself was expecting a move on the part of the United States, saying publicly: "President Kennedy has taken off the mask. This is a new attack on Cuba by the United States."

By March, Bissell had told Kennedy repeatedly: "You can't *mañana* this thing."

BAHIA DE COCHINOS

Kennedy could, in fact, have *mañana*-ed the invasion forever, but instead he allowed himself to succumb to pressure. Even so, he was fearful of the high U.S. profile of the invasion. The original attack, as Bissell had envisioned it, was to consist of landing near the port of Trinidad, on the south coast of Cuba, which the CIA claimed was chock-full of anti-Castro sympathizers. These would no doubt swell the ranks of the invading army, which could, if need be, move into the Escambray Mountains to wage guerilla warfare against Castro. This was a likely eventuality, given that the Cuban premier had armed forces numbering about 20,000 and a militia of about 200,000.

But on March 11, Kennedy told Bissell to go back to the drawing board, that he wanted something "less spectacular," preferably a night landing, and no involvement of U.S. military at all. Interestingly, no one in these discussions with the president reminded him of an obvious fact—that a night landing in a remote area would lessen the dramatic effect of the invasion and would not be as likely to stir an aroused citizenry to rise up against Castro. Instead, Bissell came back with another plan, this time stipulating that the invasion take place in an area known as the *Bahia de Cochinos*, or the *Bay of Pigs*, which was a hundred miles (160.9 km) west of Trinidad. Facing the exile army would be a huge swamp, impenetrable in places, and filled, as Bay of Pigs historian Howard Jones wrote, "with alligators *and* crocodiles, ferocious pigs, poisonous snakes, voracious insects, and millions of sharp-shelled, toxic red land crabs."

The guerillas would be exposed here—the Bay of Pigs was some eighty miles (128.7 km) from the Escambray Mountains—with little chance of hiding to wage a guerilla war. Even the CIA understood that the chances of the invasion's success, small to begin with, had just gotten smaller. But Dulles had factored that in. He said later that he and Bissell and others in the CIA felt that "when the chips were down, when the crisis arose in reality, any action required for success would be authorized, rather than permit the enterprise to fail."

In other words, Dulles was certain that in the event of failure, the president would run out of options and have no choice but to fully commit U.S. military might. In fact, some scholars believe that Dulles and Bissell, with their revised plan, were deliberately trying to force Kennedy into a corner that would result in a full-scale American attack on Cuba.

"LET 'ER RIP!"

There were cooler heads within and outside of the Kennedy administration who attempted to stop the CIA from convincing the president of the rightness of the attack. On March 30, Senator William Fulbright, head of the Foreign Relations Committee, sent a memorandum to Kennedy, which said that an attack on Cuba, even if successful, "would be denounced from the Rio Grande to Patagonia as an example of imperialism."

Under Secretary of State Chester Bowles sent a memo to Secretary of State Dean Rusk (who was traveling overseas) pointing out that such an attack on a sovereign state by another would violate the charter of the Organization of American States (OAS), of which the United States was a signatory. Bowles told Rusk: "Our national interests are poorly served by a covert operation of this kind at a time when our new president is effectively appealing to world opinion on the basis of high principle."

In other words, how could a nation that held itself up as the bastion of the free world turn around and make an unprovoked attack on another nation? But Rusk refused to be swayed by Bowles's arguments and would not allow him to bring his objections directly to Kennedy.

Finally, on April 4, only two weeks before the projected date set for the invasion, Kennedy held a final meeting on the Bay of Pigs. It was attended by Bissell, Dulles, William Fulbright (there at Kennedy's invitation), Dean Rusk, Robert McNamara, Adolf Berle, a State Department Latin America expert, and Arthur Schlesinger. Schlesinger, who had misgivings about the invasion, was silent during the meeting, as were several others. It was Schlesinger's opinion that those, like himself, who did not speak at the meeting were afraid of being seen as "soft" on Castro and communism. Among the vocal enthusiasts for the attack was Berle, who said at one point: "I say, let 'er rip!"

A few days later, Kennedy gave Bissell and Dulles the go-ahead and preparations for the invasion began. The 1,400 officers and men of Brigade 2506 received their final instructions in Guatemala. They were told that the small Cuban air force would be neutralized by two days of bombing by U.S. B-26s based in Nicaragua and that the invasion itself, scheduled for early in the morning of April 17, would have U.S. fighters flying overhead as cover, and U.S. Marines ready to storm ashore after the brigade.

Of course, the Cuban exiles were not the only ones who knew about the coming attack. Security was so poor that the *New York Times* ran an article on its front page essentially detailing plans for the invasion, while Cuban exile leaders hinted to their followers that an attack on their homeland was "imminent." Kennedy himself contributed to the problem during a news conference on April 11 when he told a reporter: "I think Latin America is in a most crucial period in its relation with us. Therefore if we don't move now, Mr. Castro may be a greater danger than he is today."

A CRIMINAL IMPERIALISTIC ATTACK

And yet, despite this kind of blunt talk, Kennedy kept softening the blow of the invasion. When Bissell reminded the president that the CIA was planning two days of preinvasion strikes with sixteen B-26s, to incapacitate Castro's small air force, Kennedy cut the number of planes to six, telling Bissell he wanted things on a "minimal" scale. As it turned out, six B-26s piloted by CIA-trained Cuban exiles attacked three Cuban air bases, destroying five planes. All that the first attack did was warn Castro that he was about to be invaded, and he responded by putting the country on full military alert, proclaiming: "Our country has been the victim of a criminal imperialistic attack."

Castro, with his arms stores full of Eastern bloc weapons, and his 220,000 men (both regular army and militia) in uniform, was more than prepared to meet the threat posed by 1,400 Cuban exiles, however brave they were. In the meantime, things were getting hot for Jack Kennedy. The bombing was widely seen for what it was—a U.S. attack on Cuba. Castro told his people: "If President Kennedy has one atom of decency, he will present the planes and pilots before the United Nations. If not, then the world has a right to call him a liar."

Kennedy decided now to cancel the second bombing attack, much to the frustration of the military, but the CIA and the administration were now becoming exceedingly nervous about being found out: "I know everybody is grabbing their nuts on this," Kennedy told an advisor. But it seemed too late to back out now. Early on the morning of Monday, April 17, Brigade 2506 stormed ashore at the Bay of Pigs, while a parachute battalion was dropped farther inland, with the intention of cutting off the three causeways that led to the beach. Things began to go wrong immediately. A radio station near the beach broadcast a warning of the attack—a station that should have been immediately marked for destruction. The paratroopers were dropped too

A GROUP OF FIDEL CASTRO'S REVOLUTIONARIES ARE PICTURED AFTER DEFEATING THE U.S.-BACKED BAY OF PIGS INVASION. LONG TERM, THE BAY OF PIGS INVASION HAD THE OPPOSITE EFFECT FROM WHAT AMERICAN PLANNERS INTENDED— IT STRENGTHENED CASTRO'S STANDING BOTH IN CUBA AND THE REST OF LATIN AMERICA AND DAMAGED THE REPUTATION OF THE CIA.

Getty Images

close to the shore and thus did not cut off the causeways, allowing Castro's troops and, especially, tanks, to race down them toward the battalion.

But mainly it was the lack of air cover. The Cuban jet fighters that had survived the B-26 bombing pounded the invasion force at will as it cowered on the beach. José Alfredo Pérez San Román, the leader of the attack force, called the CIA over and over as his men were slaughtered by jet cannon fire and pounded by artillery that the Cubans had brought in close to the beach: "We do not see any air cover as you promised," he told them. "Need jet cover immediately." When he was told it would not be forthcoming he replied: "You, sir, are a son-of-a-bitch."

All through the day on April 17, the Cubans pressed closer to the men trapped on the beach. Another bit of bad luck: The Bay of Pigs was a favorite fishing spot of Castro, and the peasants there were especially loyal to him. When he arrived, personally, to take charge of the counterattack, they cheered.

"PROFILE IN TIMIDITY AND INDECISION"

A TRIUMPHANT FIDEL CASTRO TALKS WITH THE MEDIA AFTER THE FAILED INVASION. HE FINALLY AGREED TO RELEASE THE AMERICAN-BACKED CUBAN EXILES HE HELD PRISONER IN EXCHANGE FOR MILLIONS IN FOOD AND MEDICINE FROM THE UNITED STATES.

Getty Images

Back in Washington, the CIA realized immediately that all was lost. Bissell went to Kennedy on April 18 and begged for air support. He was surprised when Kennedy initially turned him down. Finally relenting, the president authorized only six unmarked jets from an American aircraft carrier, the *Essex*, which were to rendezvous over the Bay of Pigs with a flight of B-26s from Nicaragua. Because of an air force mix-up over a time zone change, the flights failed to meet up as planned. The jets returned to the *Essex* without having fired a shot, while the B-26s, unescorted, ran into heavy ground fire and air attack. They were piloted by American employees of the CIA, four of whom were killed in the attack.

On April 19, Brigade 2506 surrendered. Almost 140 of its men were killed; the rest were dragged off into prison. Back at the White House, Kennedy was already beginning to wonder how he had allowed himself to get trapped into such a hubristic affair. He met with Cuban exile leaders flown in from Miami, telling them: "I lost a brother and a brother-in-law in the war. I know something of how you feel." Kennedy still refused, publicly, to acknowledge the United States' role in the Bay of Pigs affair, but privately he was distraught. Kennedy family confidant Richard Cardinal Cushing later wrote: "It was the first time I saw tears in his eyes."

Kennedy would later do his best for the men of the Cuban brigade and their families. He first agreed to give Castro $30 million worth of tractors and farm equipment, but this humiliating deal—for which he was roundly criticized, once again, as being too "soft" on communism—fell through. Finally, in December 1962, he was able to get the prisoners returned to America by giving Castro millions in food and medicine—all of which was a tacit admission that the United States had been involved after all.

Many historians feel that the silver lining in the dark cloud of the Bay of Pigs was that Kennedy was able to deal more forcefully with Castro and Nikita Khrushchev when the far more serious Cuban Missile Crisis occurred the following fall. Others point out that had there been no American bumbling at the Bay of Pigs, there might have been no Cuban Missile Crisis. No one knows for sure, but it was apparent that in Jack Kennedy's first major test as president, he had failed miserably.

Long term, the Bay of Pigs invasion had the opposite effect from what American planners intended—strengthening Castro's standing both in Cuba and the rest of Latin America as he fought off the very public aggression of the United States. The CIA had once been seen by many Americans as a heroic force fighting the cold war in Europe. Its machinations close to home against Castro sullied the name of the agency, turning it into what one historian called "a sinister, nefarious force." The ultimate failure of the invasion, of course, can be seen in the fact that Castro, though enfeebled, is still in a powerful force in Cuba, while the Kennedy brothers are long gone.

Former president Dwight Eisenhower, visiting Kennedy at Camp David shortly after the failed invasion, found Kennedy "subdued and more than a little bewildered."

Eisenhower was shocked that the president was naïve enough to think that American involvement might go unnoticed. Shaking his head, the former president went on to write that the young president, far from presenting a "profile in courage" such as the ones Kennedy had written about in his Pulitzer Prize–winning book of the same name, had instead displayed a "profile in timidity and indecision."

PRESIDENT KENNEDY HONORS MEMBERS OF BRIGADE 2506 IN DECEMBER 1962, FOLLOWING THEIR RELEASE FROM CUBA. FORMER PRESIDENT DWIGHT EISENHOWER LATER SAID THAT FAR FROM PRESENTING A "PROFILE IN COURAGE" SUCH AS THE ONES KENNEDY HAD WRITTEN ABOUT IN HIS PULITZER PRIZE–WINNING BOOK OF THE SAME NAME, KENNEDY HAD INSTEAD DISPLAYED A "PROFILE IN TIMIDITY AND INDECISION."

John F. Kennedy Presidential Library and Museum

CHAPTER 24

JOHN F. KENNEDY ANNOUNCES THE UNITED STATES WILL PUT A MAN ON THE MOON BY THE END OF THE DECADE

1961

GORDON HARRIS, THE PUBLIC AFFAIRS DIRECTOR FOR AMERICA'S STRUGGLING space program, was talking to Dr. Wernher von Braun, the nation's top rocket scientist. He was telling him what he, along with hundreds of millions in the United States and the rest of the world, had just heard broadcast over the radio.

"Beeps," Harris said. "Just beeps. Over and over. That's all. Beeps."

It was October 4, 1957, and the beeps were emanating from a 184-pound (83.5 kg) ball of metal orbiting the Earth, launched by the Soviet Union.

At a news conference a few days later, President Dwight D. Eisenhower, nearing the end of his first term presiding over a nation basking in the complacency of its prosperity, did his best to dismiss the achievement.

"After all, the Russians have only put one small ball in the air," he told reporters.

Not surprisingly, Soviet premier Nikita Khrushchev had a different slant on his nation's achievement. "People of the whole world are pointing to the satellite," he stated. "They are saying the U.S. has been beaten."

Khrushchev had said a lot of things about the United States since the early 1950s. Most of it could be chalked up to so much hollow propaganda. This time, however, the fact was that the world's democratic superpower had not taken the first step off of its home planet. *Sputnik I* (the name meant "satellite," but could also be translated as "fellow traveler," the very phrase used to identify anyone friendly to Soviet communism) was a triumph of Soviet communist science. Just beeps? Many who heard them believed they were listening to an elegy for American democracy.

CRISIS OF CONFIDENCE

The Americans had entered World War I late, nearly three years after the conflict had begun, but when the shooting stopped on November 11, 1918, they felt they had won the war and had made, in Woodrow Wilson's ringing phrase, "the world safe for democracy." The United States emerged from the war a world power, and President Wilson hoped to dictate a peace that would ensure it would be the "war to end all wars."

He fell far short. The peace that followed the First World War proved to be nothing more than a twenty-year truce culminating in a second, far deadlier, world war. But then Americans emerged from that one even more convinced that their nation and its military might, economic muscle, and technological know-how had put them once again on top of the world. It was American science, after all, that had found a way to harness the power of the elementary forces of the universe, put them into a bomb, and use that bomb to win the war. And no one else but the United States had that bomb.

The exhilaration of peace and the comfort that came with the knowledge of possessing a nuclear monopoly did not last long. The Soviets built an atomic bomb well before anyone thought they could, and the United States found itself in a "cold war" with Russia and its various puppet states. Yet most Americans still found it surprisingly easy to ignore their growing anxiety. Democratic capitalism seemed obviously superior to Soviet communism. The Soviets "got the bomb" not through their own ingenuity (Americans believed) but by espionage. When panicky rumors began to circulate that a Soviet agent could carry an atomic bomb into the United States in a suitcase, one waggish government official assured his fellow Americans that it would never happen because the Russians had yet to perfect the suitcase.

The Soviets launched another satellite, *Sputnik II*, just a month after the first. This time, it carried more than a radio. They had put Laika, a mongrel dog, into orbit and broadcast her heartbeats back to Earth. The new satellite weighed in at a stunning 1,120 pounds (508 kg) and reached an unprecedented altitude of 1,031 miles (1,659.2 km). The American space program at this time was struggling to loft its puny, three-pound (1.4 kg) *Vanguard* satellite into orbit. On December 6, 1957, one month after *Sputnik II*, *Vanguard* was finally launched from Cape Canaveral, Florida. Harry Reasoner of CBS News broadcast what he believed was the liftoff.

"It was so quick," he panted into the microphone, "I really didn't see it."

That was because the rocket had risen only a few inches from the launchpad before it fell backward, crumpled, and burst into a fireball. The *Vanguard* satellite, all three pounds of it, blasted off the nose of the disintegrating rocket and was hurled like a basketball onto a piece of Florida earth, strewn with debris. Its radio transmitter, still intact, broadcast beeps, just beeps, over and over.

THE TORCH IS PASSED

Through most of the Eisenhower administration, Americans were (in a phrase favored by soldiers) "fat and happy." But in 1960, by the slimmest of margins, they rejected Eisenhower's two-term vice president, Richard M. Nixon, and elected instead Democratic candidate John F. Kennedy. Americans viewed Nixon as the champion of the comfortable status quo. Kennedy, however, offered youth and glamour but, more important, a hard-edged challenge to his fellow citizens: that they strive for more than comfort and complacency.

In his inaugural address, Kennedy underscored the challenge as not merely an opportunity, but a duty. "The torch," he said, "has been passed to a new generation of Americans" who were willing to "pay any price, bear any burden, meet any hardship . . . to assure the survival and success of liberty."

Little more than three months after this stirring speech, on April 12, 1961, the Soviet Union orbited the first man in space, cosmonaut Yuri Gagarin. If anything, it stung harder than *Sputnik* had. U.S. military leaders spoke ominously of the Soviets winning the "high ground" of outer space, gaining a platform, as it were, from which they could launch anything anywhere, including against the United States. It was upsetting talk, but it didn't get at the heart of what bothered most Americans, which was a fear that ran deeper than a fear of military attack.

By 1961, the Cold War was nearly fifteen years old, and its end appeared to be nowhere in sight. It was largely an ideological and economic fight for the hearts and minds of the planet's people. Most Americans believed that the United States, champion of democratic liberty, would ultimately prevail over the Soviet Union, whose system of government was the exact opposite of freedom. Yet the facts, as of April 12, 1961, were trending against the faith. On May 5, 1961, less than a month after Gagarin's orbital flight, the United States successfully put astronaut Alan B. Shepard into space—though only for a quarter hour and without attempting even a single orbit. No one could deny that Shepard's achievement fell short of Gagarin's, but the American people regarded Shepard as a hero nonetheless, and President Kennedy embraced him. He saw in the brief flight of Shepard's *Freedom 7* not an also-ran in what was popularly called "the space race," but the promise of something far greater.

TO CREATE THE FUTURE

The Gagarin mission sent through the corridors of American technological and political power a leaden wind of defeatism. The head of the president's influential Science Advisory Committee recommended to President Kennedy that he instruct the recently created National Aeronautics and Space Administration (NASA) to drop out of the race, which, he pointed out, had already been lost. MIT professor Jerome B. Wiesner's advice was to focus instead on the "aeronautics" in NASA's name and drop "space" altogether.

The first move, he said, should be to cancel Project Mercury, which was the initial phase of the manned space program, and devote all resources to unmanned satellite experimentation, not only to derive general scientific knowledge but also to quickly realize practical gains in global communications and military intelligence and weaponry. These areas were the "winners," and, trailing as it was in the race against the Russians, the United States should definitely "go with the winners," Wiesner told JFK.

It was a cogent and persuasive argument. Wiesner was proposing not only an alternative to scientific and technological defeat but also a fast track to creating practical, profitable uses for space exploration. The president listened but what he could not bring himself to ignore was that Alan Shepard had reached the edge of space. It was a battle won, and no commander in chief likes to retreat from a victory.

There were risks to the continuied pursuit of a manned space program. The costs were literally astronomical, American prestige was on the line (and with each Soviet triumph, the line grew thinner), and some of the nation's best and brightest people could get killed. The risks were grave, and Kennedy understood that Wiesner certainly knew more than he did about the potential scientific rewards. In strictly pragmatic terms, devoting NASA to making communication and military spacecraft almost certainly promised bigger and quicker rewards than continuing to send men into space.

Yet Kennedy believed that victory in the Cold War would be decided not by the United States or the Soviet Union, but by the world—by how the world chose to spend its precious store of loyalty, confidence, and faith. The world would judge the United States and Soviet Union not by what they said they stood for, Kennedy reasoned, but

COSMONAUT YURI GAGARIN, 27, JUST BEFORE MAKING HISTORY AS THE FIRST MAN TO TRAVEL IN SPACE. THE GAGARIN MISSION SENT THROUGH THE CORRIDORS OF AMERICAN TECHNOLOGICAL AND POLITICAL POWER A LEADEN WIND OF DEFEATISM, WITH SOME SCIENTISTS AND PROFESSIONALS SUGGESTING AMERICA ABANDON ITS SPACE PROGRAM TO FOCUS ON AERONAUTICS ALONE.

AFP/Getty Images

KENNEDY STANDS WITH ASTRONAUT ALAN SHEPARD IN MAY 1961 FOLLOWING THE SUCCESSFUL *FREEDOM* 7 MISSION. NO ONE COULD DENY THAT SHEPARD'S ACHIEVEMENT FELL SHORT OF COSMONAUT YURI GAGARIN'S, BUT THE AMERICAN PEOPLE REGARDED SHEPARD AS A HERO NONETHELESS.

Time & Life Pictures/Getty Images

by what they actually achieved. The world would weigh democracy against communism on the success or failure of spectacular undertakings. About the science, Wiesner was undoubtedly right. But Kennedy decided that although the space race was run on science, it was not primarily about science. It was about whom the world would choose to create its future.

"SPECIAL MESSAGE ON URGENT NATIONAL NEEDS"

Call this insight "visionary." But the visionary Kennedy was also a hard-nosed realist. He couldn't deny the fact that the United States had lost the race into space and then the race to put a *person* into space. He also acknowledged that the Soviets had created bigger and more powerful rocket boosters than the United States had.

As he explained in what he titled a "Special Message on Urgent National Needs," delivered as a speech to Congress on May 25, 1961, just twenty days after Shepard's flight, the Soviet Union's bigger boosters meant that, in the near term, that country would almost surely orbit bigger and more impressive payloads than the United States could match, let alone surpass. Bigger Soviet space vehicles would carry more Soviet men around the Earth.

The Soviets had won the orbital race. Therefore, the president told Congress, the time had come to move on to a new undertaking, one that would do no less than capture the imagination of all humankind.

"Now it is time to take longer strides—time for a great new American enterprise—time for this nation to take a clearly leading role in space achievement, which in many ways may hold the key to our future on Earth."

He assured Congress of his belief that "we possess all the resources and talents necessary" for this new enterprise, but admitted the country had not made the necessary "national decisions or marshaled the national resources required" to achieve this great thing, which he had yet to identify.

> Recognizing the head start obtained by the Soviets with their large rocket engines, which gives them many months of lead-time, and recognizing the likelihood that they will exploit this lead for some time to come in still more impressive successes, we nevertheless are required to make new efforts on our own. For while we cannot guarantee that we shall one day be first, we can guarantee that any failure to make this effort will be our last. We take an additional risk by making it in full view of the world, but as shown by the feat of astronaut Shepherd, this very risk enhances our stature when we are successful. But this is not merely a race. Space is open to us now; and our eagerness to share its meaning is not governed by the efforts of others. We go into space because whatever mankind must undertake, free men must fully share.

Before he had stepped into the well of the House of Representatives to make his speech, the president had made his decision. For this to be a realistic as well as spectacular goal, getting to it would have to consume enough time to permit U.S. technology to catch up to and surpass that of the Soviets, and the goal had to be in a field in which Soviet space science had no definite head start.

So Kennedy came to the climax of his speech: "I believe that this nation should commit itself to achieving the goal, before this decade is out, of landing a man on the

MEMORANDUM FOR

VICE PRESIDENT

In accordance with our conversation I would like for you as Chairman of the Space Council to be in charge of making an overall survey of where we stand in space.

1. Do we have a chance of beating the Soviets by putting a laboratory in space, or by a trip around the moon, or by a rocket to land on the moon, or by a rocket to go to the moon and back with a man. Is there any other space program which promises dramatic results in which we could win?

2. How much additional would it cost?

3. Are we working 24 hours a day on existing programs. If not, why not? If not, will you make recommendations to me as to how work can be speeded up.

4. In building large boosters should we put our emphasis on nuclear, chemical or liquid fuel, or a combination of these three?

5. Are we making maximum effort? Are we achieving necessary results?

I have asked Jim Webb, Dr. Weisner, Secretary McNamara and other responsible officials to cooperate with you fully. I would appreciate a report on this at the earliest possible moment.

A MEMO FROM PRESIDENT KENNEDY TO VICE PRESIDENT LYNDON JOHNSON ASKING HIM, AS CHAIRMAN OF THE SPACE COUNCIL, TO PROVIDE KENNEDY WITH AN ASSESSMENT OF THE COUNTRY'S SPACE PROGRAM. IN THE SPACE RACE, AMERICAN PRESTIGE WAS ON THE LINE AND WITH EACH SOVIET TRIUMPH, THE LINE GREW THINNER.

John F. Kennedy Presidential Library and Museum

Moon and returning him safely to the Earth. No single space project in this period will be more impressive to mankind or more important for the long-range exploration of space; and none will be so difficult or expensive to accomplish." With this, he asked Congress for the funds.

WE CHOOSE TO GO TO THE MOON

In the period following the speech, the president was deluged with questions from politicians, the public, and even scientists. Was it wise—did it even make sense—to lavish money on space when the earth was faced with many and urgent problems?

Kennedy always answered that it not only made sense, but it was also the very wisest of investments—for the reasons he had given to Congress. While the naysayers persisted, JFK remained upbeat, gathering substantial crumbs of comfort from a 1962 *Aviation Week* poll reporting that 56 percent of Americans believed the lunar mission was "questionable" but "perhaps necessary" in light of the Cold War. A pessimist would see this as revelatory of national doubt. Kennedy, however, interpreted it as a sign that most Americans understood what going to the moon entailed.

Congress seemed to understand it, too. This president, whose record of success with the legislative branch was dicey at best, received all the funding necessary, so that, on September 12, 1962, in an address at Rice University, he was in a position to create a full national context of understanding for what was now officially and formally a national goal.

With America just barely into space, he admitted, getting to the moon in fewer than ten years seemed unrealistic, yes, but Americans have always embraced what seemed unrealistic. "William Bradford," Kennedy observed, "speaking in 1630 of the founding of the Plymouth Bay Colony, said that all great and honorable actions are accompanied with great difficulties, and both must be enterprised and overcome with answerable courage . . . no nation which expects to be the leader of other nations can expect to stay behind in the race for space."

Indeed, he continued, all Americans "who came before us" had seen to it that America was always ahead in science, industry, and technology, "and this generation," Kennedy pledged, "does not intend to founder in the backwash of the coming age of space. We mean to be a part of it—we mean to lead it."

He rephrased what he had told Congress: that "the eyes of the world now look into space, to the moon and to the planets beyond, and we have vowed that we shall not see it governed by a hostile flag of conquest, but by a banner of freedom and peace. We have vowed that we shall not see space filled with weapons of mass destruction, but with instruments of knowledge and understanding."

We choose to go to the moon. We choose to go to the moon in this decade and do the other things, not because they are easy, but because they are hard, because that goal will serve to organize and measure the best of our energies and skills, because that challenge is one that we are willing to accept, one we are unwilling to postpone, and one which we intend to win, and the others, too.

LUNAR LEGACY

The president admitted to his Rice audience that the United States was behind the Soviet Union "and will be behind for some time in manned flight." But he declared that the nation did not intend to stay behind, but would "in this decade . . . make up and move ahead." Cut down by an assassin's bullet on November 22, 1963, John F. Kennedy did not of course live to see *Apollo 11* land on the moon on July 20, 1969—six months before the decade was out. Five of six (*Apollo 13* had to turn back) subsequent Apollo missions also landed on the moon, the last, *Apollo 17*, on December 11, 1972.

Since then, the American space program has focused primarily on achieving the scientific, communications, and military objectives Wiesner had advocated in 1961. The Soviets never landed men on the moon, and, after December 1972, the United States never again tried (at least so far). Although some politicians and scientists continue to debate the relative value of the Apollo missions and of the manned space program generally, no one among the 450 million occupants of planet Earth who watched the *Apollo 11* landing via live television broadcast that July day could or can deny the profound exaltation it produced.

The moon landing's effect on the course of the Cold War is harder to determine and certainly impossible to measure precisely. No one in 1969 would have guessed that

the Soviet Union had scarcely more than two decades of life left to it. Did the moon shot's vindication of the science, technology, and spirit of courageous inquiry born of democratic capitalism shorten the life of that totalitarian communist state? We do not know. We probably cannot know. But neither can we know what the outcome of the contest between the two systems of government would have been had the United States conceded the space race to the Soviet Union in 1961.

Those who believe in the historical benefits of the space race argue that, thanks to JFK and other visionary American leaders, it served as a powerfully effective weapon in the Cold War, yet one that brought to the world knowledge and the unity of shared achievement instead of destruction and death. Others dispute the magnitude of the benefits and suggest that the space race was actually little more than a covert extension of the arms race, an apparently "scientific" excuse for building rockets and other space systems designed to deliver more thermonuclear weapons to more targets more effectively.

There is one use for the moon shot on which everyone agrees. It is as an enduring and indelible benchmark of human and national achievement. Today, in a nation faced with environmental, economic, political, and spiritual crises, some use it to mark a lamentable national decline. Yet others, today, cite the flag Neil Armstrong and Buzz Aldrin planted on the lunar surface more than forty years ago as a banner of what is yet possible for the United States and the other people of planet Earth.

BUZZ ALDRIN TAKES A STEP ON THE MOON IN 1969, SEVEN YEARS AFTER JFK VOWED TO PUT A MAN ON THE MOON BEFORE THE END OF THE DECADE. CUT DOWN BY AN ASSASSIN'S BULLET ON NOVEMBER 22, 1963, JOHN F. KENNEDY DID NOT LIVE TO SEE *APOLLO 11* LAND ON THE MOON, SIX MONTHS BEFORE THE DECADE WAS OUT.

CHAPTER 25

JOHN F. KENNEDY RESOLVES THE CUBAN MISSILE CRISIS, AVERTING THE THREAT OF A NUCLEAR WAR WITH THE SOVIET UNION

1962

WHEN PRESIDENT JOHN F. KENNEDY'S PREDECESSOR, DWIGHT D. EISENHOWER, wanted a window on the Soviet Union, the maverick aircraft designer Clarence "Kelly" Johnson convened his legendary "Skunk Works" group at Lockheed and emerged with a plane that mated glider wings to the fuselage of an already-existing advanced jet fighter, the F-104. He called it the "CL-282," but the CIA dubbed it the "U-2," the "U" vaguely referring to "utility" and the "2" chosen entirely at random.

In the days before anyone even dreamed of surveillance satellites, the U-2, with its nearly stratospheric ceiling of 85,000 feet (25.9 km) and its ability to glide silently on its long, delicate wings, could snap miles of pictures over any hostile airspace. Eisenhower had intended it to spy on the Soviets, but on October 14, 1962, its subject was Fidel Castro's Cuba, just ninety miles (144.8 km) from the streets of Miami.

The pictures the U-2 brought back later that day to a team of CIA photointerpreters working out of a drab building at 5th and K streets, Washington, revealed dozens of Soviet SS-4 medium-range ballistic missiles (MRBMs), each capable of delivering a nuclear warhead a distance of 1,300 miles (2,092.1 km), which meant that the likes of Dallas, New Orleans, Atlanta, Miami, St. Louis, Cincinnati, and Washington, D.C., were within range of annihilation. Some of the missiles were still crated, but others were already unpacked and laid out on the ground, awaiting completion of the launch facilities that were visible in varying stages of construction. On the evening of October 15, Kennedy's national security adviser, McGeorge Bundy, was hosting a dinner party with his wife when he was called to the phone. It was Ray Cline, the CIA's deputy director for intelligence.

"Those things we've been worrying about," he said, "it looks as though we've really got something."

That was the whole conversation, but it was enough. Bundy understood. Deciding that there was no point in calling the president at that late hour, he returned, with or without appetite, to his dinner guests. On the morning of October 16, at about 9:00 a.m., Bundy informed the president as he ate breakfast over the morning papers in the private quarters of the White House. Kennedy told Bundy to gather his top advisers for a secret meeting at 11:45 a.m.

LEGACY OF FIASCO

On November 18, 1960, CIA director Allen W. Dulles and Richard Bissell, the agency's director for plans, called on president-elect Kennedy in Palm Beach, Florida, to brief him on JMARC, the plan the agency had produced for the outgoing Eisenhower administration to invade Cuba and foment a coup d'etat against Fidel Castro. Kennedy went along, but never supported the dubious plan wholeheartedly, and when it began to fail in the execution, the president, hoping to minimize his losses, abruptly cut the operation loose.

In April 1961, barely four months after Kennedy had taken office, the Bay of Pigs invasion (see chapter 23) lurched from probable failure to certain failure. Among those watching the fiasco was Soviet premier Nikita Khrushchev. He had long fretted over a balance of power that tilted heavily toward the United States, whose European and Turkish allies provided bases for medium-range missiles targeting major Soviet cities. Russia, however, had no similar advantage, and could target the United States with only a handful of long-range, complex, and costly intercontinental ballistic missiles (ICBMs), launched from Soviet territory.

Kennedy's display of cold feet at the Bay of Pigs convinced Khrushchev that the new American president was so weak that he would probably do nothing if the Soviet Union put medium-range missiles in Cuba and aimed them at America's major cities.

"I DON'T THINK WE HAVE ANY SATISFACTORY ALTERNATIVES"

At his 11:45 a.m. meeting on October 16, 1962, the president created an executive committee of advisers—"EX-COMM"—and assigned it to formulate advice on the best way to respond to the missile crisis. Unwilling to blunder into another impulsive move in Cuba, JFK withheld the U-2 intelligence from the public until he had decided on a course of action. He was determined—this time—to appear strong, confident, and resolute. So, while EX-COMM worked on the problem, Kennedy adhered to his public routine, as if nothing unusual were happening.

On the evening of October 18, the president summoned EX-COMM, along with other advisers, including the venerable Dean Acheson, former secretary of state under President Truman. A "cold warrior" from the inception of the Cold War, Acheson did not hesitate to recommend an immediate air strike aimed at taking out the missiles before they became operational. To delay, he warned, was to invite a nuclear attack. Once that happened, there would be no option but to respond in kind, and that, in turn, would bring a full-scale nuclear response from the Soviet Union against the United States as well as its European allies. World War III would surely be a short war, ending with the end of civilization itself.

Like Acheson, Robert Lovett, a former secretary of defense, had been brought in for advice from outside of EX-COMM and the Kennedy administration. He disagreed with Acheson, however, proposing a strong naval blockade of Cuba to intercept and turn back—by force, if necessary—inbound Soviet cargo vessels that carried missiles and other weapons.

National Security Adviser McGeorge Bundy proposed yet a third course: wait and watch. He cautioned that an immediate air strike had as much chance of provoking as it did of heading off a civilization-ending world war. Yet, he added that even a blockade could push Khrushchev into a move against West Berlin, that precarious bastion of Western-allied democracy situated deep in the Soviet satellite state of East Germany. A communist takeover

AMERICAN AERIAL SURVEILLANCE PICTURES SHOW THE BUILD UP OF SOVIET MISSILES IN CUBA. STILL REELING FROM THE BAY OF PIGS FIASCO AND UNWILLING TO BLUNDER INTO ANOTHER IMPULSIVE MOVE IN CUBA, JFK WITHHELD THE U-2 INTELLIGENCE FROM THE PUBLIC UNTIL HE HAD DECIDED ON A COURSE OF ACTION.

of West Berlin could not go unanswered—and the answer was likely to come in the form of a thermonuclear apocalypse. Kennedy, Bundy, and the others knew that Kremlin hardliners saw West Berlin as an intolerable incursion into the Soviet sphere of influence, and they also understood that Khrushchev regarded it as an American vulnerability.

"Berlin is the testicle of the West," the Soviet premier once quipped. "When I want the West to scream, I squeeze on Berlin." The best course, Bundy therefore advised, was to wait and determine whether the Cuban missiles were just one phase of a much wider Soviet offensive, including action against West Berlin, or an isolated move. Only after verifying this information could they make the most informed response.

President Kennedy walked out of the October 18 meeting having made three decisions. First, an air strike at that point was too likely to provoke an aggressive Soviet response, if not in Cuba, then in Europe—probably against West Berlin. Second, watchful waiting was unacceptable because it displayed indecision and weakness to Americans, Soviets, and Cubans alike. These two decisions pointed the way to the third: creating a naval blockade to turn back incoming ships potentially carrying missiles or other offensive cargoes.

On the next day, October 19, Kennedy brought together Secretary of Defense Robert McNamara and the members of the Joint Chiefs of Staff. General Maxwell Taylor, whom Kennedy had appointed chairman of the Joint Chiefs just eighteen days earlier, told the president that the chiefs initially agreed that air strikes combined with a blockade was the only effective response to the missiles, but, he continued, after further discussion, they decided they could not guarantee that air strikes would destroy all of the missiles. Furthermore, the chiefs believed that the strikes would provoke a launch of whatever missiles survived. As if this were not a sufficiently steep downside, Taylor went on to point out that the air strikes might alienate U.S. allies. At this, the president jumped in, agreeing with Taylor by observing that an air strike would give the Soviets an excuse—"a clear line," he called it—to occupy West Berlin even as America's allies were decrying the actions of a gang of "trigger-happy Americans," who were letting Berlin slip away because they could not stand the heat in Cuba.

The pressures on John F. Kennedy to pull the trigger on Cuba were both political and personal. Politically, his leadership reputation, badly wounded by the Bay of Pigs, hung in the balance. Personally, there was the burden of his inheritance. He was the son of Joseph P. Kennedy, who, as U.S. ambassador to Britain in the years leading up to World War II, had been an outspoken advocate of "appeasement," of yielding to Adolf Hitler's early territorial demands in Czechoslovakia instead of taking an

U-2 SURVEILLANCE IN OCTOBER 1962 REVEALED THE PRESENCE IN CUBA OF SOVIET MISSILES, EACH CAPABLE OF DELIVERING A NUCLEAR WARHEAD A DISTANCE OF 1,300 MILES (2,092.1 KM), WHICH MEANT THAT THE LIKES OF DALLAS, NEW ORLEANS, ATLANTA, MIAMI, ST. LOUIS, CINCINNATI, AND WASHINGTON, D.C., WERE WITHIN RANGE OF ANNIHILATION, AS SHOWN IN THIS DECLASSIFIED CIA MAP, WHICH ALSO SHOWS THE DESTRUCTIVE POTENTIAL OF THE EVEN LONGER-RANGE MISSILES DISCOVERED LATER IN THE CRISIS.

aggressive stand against him. The outbreak of World War II thoroughly discredited the appeasement policy and Ambassador Kennedy for having championed it. JFK could not help but hear the insinuating murmurs behind his back: Like father, like son.

But the president refused to be blinded by politics, personal heritage, or even the looming specter of missiles just ninety miles (144.8 km) off the Florida coast. Instead, at the height of the crisis, he looked beyond the immediate threats to see directly into the world situation. Everything in international politics was interconnected. He had recently finished reading a new best seller by historian Barbara Tuchman, *The Guns of August*. It was a brilliant study of the outbreak and first month of World War I, which had begun with Austria's delusion that it could fight a short, contained punitive war against Serbia, a thorn in its side, without provoking a larger conflict. This inability to look beyond the immediate situation triggered the most destructive war fought on the planet to that time, and Kennedy was determined not to make the same mistake now, a mistake that would have far graver consequences than those of 1914.

He remarked that Cuba might be ninety miles (144.8 km) from American, but it was six thousand miles (9,656.1 km) from America's European allies, who therefore "don't give a damn about it." America could expect no help from Europe if it attacked Cuba. Even worse, if the Soviets, seeing the United States isolated and friendless, were emboldened to respond to an air strike on Cuba by overrunning West Berlin, he, as president, would be left with "only one alternative, which is to fire nuclear weapons— which is a hell of an alternative—to begin a nuclear exchange."

The president's closest adviser, his brother, Attorney General Robert F. Kennedy, spoke up at this point. What he said was chilling: "I don't think we have any satisfactory alternatives."

It was an assessment as awful as it was acute. Were the crisis confined to Cuba, swift, aggressive action would be the most obvious and effective option. But the crisis tangled Cuba with Berlin, and that made all the difference. Nevertheless, the attorney general continued: "If we do nothing, we will have problems in Berlin anyway. So, we have to do something."

At this, General Curtis LeMay, chief of staff of the U.S. Air Force and creator of SAC, the Strategic Air Command, wielder of most of America's nuclear arsenal, spoke up. Yes, he said, a blockade and political talks without accompanying air strikes and a ground invasion of Cuba would not simply fail to head off a world war: It would provoke one. Show weakness by hesitating to bring the hammer down on Cuba, and you positively invite the Soviets to take West Berlin. With this, LeMay reminded the president of what he himself had just said, that a Soviet move against West Berlin would mean nuclear war. Then, leaving this observation to hang in the air a moment, he invoked the burden of the past, observing that a blockade without an air strike and an invasion would be "almost as bad as the appeasement at Munich."

"I just don't see any other solution except direct military intervention right now," LeMay wrapped up, and suddenly the other chiefs joined in, insisting that failure to mount an immediate air strike and invasion would open the door to Soviet nuclear blackmail.

GOING PUBLIC

Kennedy thanked LeMay and the other chiefs and then sent them out of the room. Still adhering to the fiction of his public schedule, he flew to Chicago for a political appearance on October 20. When word reached him that yet more missiles had been discovered, including some of longer range, range sufficient to cover most of the United States, he pleaded a bad cold and returned to Washington. On Sunday, October 21, he met with EX-COMM and concluded, the new discovery notwithstanding, that an air strike still risked too much. Not only would it alienate allies, but because it would

kill perhaps as many as 20,000 Soviets and Cubans, it would also definitely provoke a massive retaliation, which would in turn require an even larger U.S. response. It would be *The Guns of August* in an atomic age.

On October 22, the president decided that it was time to bring the Cuban situation to Congress, but when he quietly met with Senate leaders, nearly to a man they clamored for an air strike. This moved Kennedy to bring the case directly to the American people at last instead. He secured television time on all three networks that very night.

> This government, as promised, has maintained the closest surveillance of the Soviet military buildup on the island of Cuba. Within the past week, unmistakable evidence has established the fact that a series of offensive missile sites is now in preparation on that imprisoned island. The purpose of these bases can be none other than to provide a nuclear strike capability against the Western Hemisphere.

He went on to declare his decision. It was a naval "quarantine"—he had been advised to avoid the word "blockade," because, under international law, a blockade was defined as an act of war. Kennedy continued:

All ships of any kind bound for Cuba from whatever nation or port will, if found to contain cargoes of offensive weapons, be turned back. This quarantine will be extended, if needed, to other types of cargo and carriers. We are not at this time, however, denying the necessities of life as the Soviets attempted to do in their Berlin blockade of 1948.

The American people did not know that LeMay and others had recommended an all-out attack and a full-scale invasion. They did not, therefore, understand that the "quarantine" was a step back from the abyss. Certainly, it did not look like one. The president put military alert status at DEFCON 3, two levels above normal and two below outright war. Fidel Castro responded by mobilizing all of his forces. On October 23, with the U.S. warships assembled along the quarantine line, new aerial reconnaissance revealed that a number of the missiles were now on their launchers. The phrase "hair trigger" suddenly seemed all too apt.

No one knew what would happen when the first Soviet ship reached the quarantine line. Would it stop? Would it admit a boarding party? Would it turn back? Or would it serve as the trip wire for world war by forcing the quarantine ships to fire on it? And would the counterattack come in the form of missiles from Cuba, or the Red Army marching into West Berlin, or an ICBM launch from within Soviet borders, or a combination of these? No one knew. Churches across the country filled as they had never filled before. The school day was interrupted by air raid drills in which students were instructed to "duck and cover" under their wooden desks.

Though packed with events, October 23 crawled by. Kennedy spoke hopefully to Secretary of Defense McNamara, telling him that he believed Khrushchev would order the cargo ships to turn back before they even reached the quarantine line. At the same time, he approved a plan to attack and destroy any Cuban surface-to-air missile (SAM) site that shot down one of the U.S. reconnaissance aircraft that were now making almost continuous overflights of the island.

It was on the following day, Wednesday, October 24, that several Soviet freighters closed in on the quarantine line at high speed. The showdown Kennedy did not believe Khrushchev wanted seemed imminent after all. Time stood still. Relief from the excruciating suspense came in the form of a radio transmission from a U.S. skipper on the line. The Soviet ships had stopped and were holding their positions outside of the quarantine perimeter. Dean Rusk, Kennedy's secretary of state, spoke: "We're eyeball to eyeball and I think the other fellow just blinked."

With a helpless world focused on the waters surrounding Cuba, Adlai Stevenson, U.S. ambassador to the United Nations, confronted Soviet Ambassador Valerian Zorin in the Security Council on October 25. Was his country installing missiles in Cuba? Stevenson demanded.

"Don't wait for the translation," the usually mild-mannered American snapped. "Answer 'yes' or 'no'!"

When Zorin tried to put him off with a vague promise that he would have his answer "in due course," Stevenson replied, "I am prepared to wait for my answer until Hell freezes over," then showed the reconnaissance photographs to the stunned Council. Against this backdrop, President Kennedy raised the U.S. alert level to an unprecedented DEFCON 2, one level below war.

As the public drama unfolded, the Kennedy administration used diplomatic back channels, including reporter John Scali of *ABC News*, who was on good terms with a highly placed Russian embassy contact, to communicate the president's willingness to reach a mutually satisfactory diplomatic solution. This approach produced on October 26 a telex from Khrushchev directly to the White House, offering to remove the missiles if Kennedy would make a public pledge not to invade Cuba. Yet even as this offer arrived, aerial surveillance revealed an increase in the pace of construction at the missile sites.

The president sent Robert Kennedy to meet secretly with the Soviet ambassador to the United States, Anatoly Dobrynin. He was to offer to remove U.S. missiles from Turkey (they were obsolete anyway) in exchange for the removal of the missiles from Cuba—though RFK was directed to specify that this quid pro quo had to remain secret. Dobrynin agreed to convey the offer to the Kremlin.

Incredibly, while these most delicate of negotiations were in play, the U.S. military staged a previously scheduled high-altitude nuclear test detonation in the Pacific, the Cubans shot down a U-2 (despite his resolution to respond by attacking the Cuban SAM site responsible for the attack, Kennedy withheld action), and, on October 27, another U-2 was caught blundering into Soviet airspace. Even worse, a second U.S. bomb test, this one of a thermonuclear device, was conducted in the Pacific.

As if these mishaps—some believe the nuclear and thermonuclear tests to have been the work of U.S. commanders at the highest levels, intent on forcing a showdown—were not bad enough, a second telex arrived from the Soviet premier, which seemed to retract much that had been offered in the first. This set off a frantic and complicated debate in EX-COMM, which President Kennedy cut short by declaring his decision to ignore the second telex and respond only to the first. On October 28, Khrushchev made a Radio Moscow broadcast. He announced that the missiles in Cuba were being dismantled.

SAVING HUMANITY

No decisions made by any American president were or have ever been of greater consequence than those of John F. Kennedy during thirteen days in October 1962. They preserved the international authority of the United States, they defended democracy, and they almost certainly saved humanity itself. In the nearer term, the outcome of the Cuban Missile Crisis enhanced Kennedy's reputation both abroad and at home, going a long way toward redeeming him from the blunders of the Bay of Pigs. Even as it improved JFK's standing, the missile crisis resolution drove a wedge between Castro and Khrushchev, beginning Cuba's drift away from the Soviets and toward engagement with the Chinese, thereby undermining the monolithic aspect of the so-called "Soviet bloc." As for Khrushchev, he was widely perceived among his Kremlin adversaries as having acted out of weakness, and he found himself inexorably driven from power.

In making the decisions, Kennedy both overcame the past—the burden of his father's reputation for appeasement, the postwar history of bitterness and distrust that existed between the United States and the Soviet Union—and learned from it, having taken to heart the lessons of *The Guns of August*. Kennedy understood that Cuba was bound to West Berlin and West Berlin was a trip wire tied to Armageddon. His approach to the Cuban Missile Crisis stands as a lesson in the critical importance of taking action only after understanding how the proposed action will affect the world beyond its immediate object.

CHAPTER 26

LYNDON JOHNSON PUSHES THROUGH THE CIVIL RIGHTS ACT

1964

RACIAL SEGREGATION WAS NOT LIMITED TO THE STATES OF THE OLD CONFEDERACY. During his term in office, President Woodrow Wilson had permitted segregationist employment practices in the U.S. Treasury and the U.S. Postal Service. By the 1940s, segregation had reached into the U.S. Capitol. In 1944, Rev. Adam Clayton Powell was elected to the House of Representatives for New York's 22nd Congressional District, which included Harlem. He was one of only two African American representatives in Congress (the other was William L. Dawson of Illinois) and the first black congressman from the North since Rutherford B. Hayes shut down Reconstruction in 1877.

In Washington, Powell found that an informal policy of segregation existed in the facilities reserved for members of Congress and their guests. He set about breaking the segregation barrier by patronizing the whites-only congressional barbershop, exercising in the whites-only congressional gymnasium, and inviting black constituents to dine with him in the whites-only congressional restaurant.

Representative John Rankin of Mississippi, a vehement segregationist, racist, and anti-Semite, denounced Powell's presence in Congress as a disgrace. In 1949 Rankin became notorious for using the word "nigger" on the floor of the House. When fellow congressman Vito Marcoantonio of New York called on the Speaker of the House to strike the offensive term from the record, Rankin shouted, "I said 'Niggra!' Just as I have said since I have been able to talk and shall continue to say." Powell baited Rankin by making a point of sitting as close as possible to the congressman; during one session of Congress, Rankin changed his seat five times in a futile attempt to get away from Powell.

In Congress, Powell styled himself "the irritant," because he berated both Republicans and his fellow Democrats for failing to ensure the civil rights of African Americans. He attached to bill after bill what became known as the Powell Amendment, calling on the federal government to cut off funds to any state that practiced segregation. In 1964 the Powell Amendment became law as Title Six of the Civil Rights Act.

ALL THE PRESIDENT'S REASONS

Lyndon B. Johnson was a Southerner, a Texan, but by the late 1950s he was moving away from his fellow Southern Democrats, siding more with Northerners like Powell and liberals who wanted to see a new bill that would put an end to segregation and guarantee the civil rights of African Americans in the United States. His reasons were complex. Johnson biographer Robert Dallek believes that as a poor boy from a hardscrabble corner of Texas, "Johnson identified with and viscerally experienced the sufferings of the disadvantaged."

Then there was the assassination of his predecessor, John F. Kennedy. Johnson suspected that Kennedy's support of civil rights legislation inflamed the segregationists and may have been a contributing factor in the murder of the president. Passing a civil rights bill would bring to fruition one of the noblest aspirations of the Kennedy administration. To paraphrase a line from JFK's inauguration speech, the torch had passed to Johnson, and he would not let it fall. Then there was the regional aspect of the issue. Racial attitudes in American were changing, and the South's adamant defense of segregation was isolating it from the rest of the country, making it a national pariah.

Passing a civil rights bill would bring to fruition one of the noblest aspirations of the Kennedy administration. The torch had passed to Johnson, and he would not let it fall.

Certainly justice also motivated Johnson. He was awkward, often crude, and indifferently educated compared to so many of his political colleagues. Although he was president of the United States, he was often mocked in the press as a rube; it stung, he resented it, and he had enough sympathy in him to identify with other disadvantaged Americans and want to help them.

The issue of civil rights was also personal. While traveling through the South, his personal cook, a black woman named Zephyr Wright, was barred from whites-only restaurants and hotels and could not even use a public restroom. He was still vice president when Johnson got into a verbal brawl on this topic with Senator John Stennis of Mississippi, a vocal opponent of any antisegregation legislation. Angry and shouting, Johnson told Stennis the humiliations Mrs. Wright and her husband endured while driving from Washington, D.C., to the Johnson ranch in Texas. "When they had to go to the bathroom," Johnson said, "they would . . . pull off on a side road, and Zephyr Wright, the cook of the vice president of the United States, would squat in the road to pee."

Finally, there was Johnson's outrage over one of the most notorious acts of domestic terrorism of the civil rights era: One Sunday morning in September 1963 members of the Ku Klux Klan detonated 122 sticks of dynamite inside a church in Birmingham, Alabama, killing four black girls, ages eleven to fourteen, and wounding twenty-two others.

Ever the master politician, LBJ was pleased to see that the country's adulation for the murdered Kennedy coupled with indignation over acts of violence committed by white supremacists in the South had tipped the poll numbers in favor of civil rights legislation. In the fall of 1963, 50 percent of Americans surveyed believed Kennedy was moving too fast in promoting civil rights legislation. By April 1964, 57 percent were in favor of Johnson's civil rights initiatives.

MASTER OF THE SENATE

Lyndon Baines Johnson's ancestors were pioneers who settled in Texas in the years before the Civil War. The future president was born in a small farmhouse on the Pedernales River in 1908. He grew up to be a tall, lean, gawky young man, but a great talker, a star of the local debate team.

In 1937 Johnson was elected to the House of Representatives, where he became a reliable supporter of Franklin D. Roosevelt's "New Deal" initiatives. He courted such influential congressmen as Speaker of the House Sam Rayburn as well as FDR's vice president, John Nance Garner. When he was elected to the Senate in 1948, he once again made himself pleasant and agreeable to senior senators, such as Richard Russell, the leader of conservative Democrats and arguably the most powerful man in the U.S. Senate. Johnson's deference was rewarded—he received a plum assignment to the Senate Armed Services Committee.

In 1952, when the Republicans won a majority in the House and Senate, Johnson was selected by his fellow Democrats as Senate minority leader. Two years later, when the Democrats recaptured the Senate, they voted Johnson Senate majority leader. Two Johnson biographers, Robert A. Caro and Dallek, argue that he was one of the greatest—if not the greatest—Senate majority leaders in American history. His trick was to gather as much information as he could about all the senators—what they believed in, what they wanted to accomplish, what they opposed, and what it would take to win their vote. Armed with this information, Johnson could persuade, wheedle, or intimidate almost any senator to vote as Johnson wanted him or her to vote.

REGISTERING TO VOTE IN SELMA, ALABAMA

In 1963 Selma, Alabama, was a small city of about 30,000 inhabitants. About 15,000 of Selma's black residents were eligible to vote, but only 156 of them were registered.

Members of the Student Nonviolent Coordinating Committee (SNCC)—college students, black and white, who held demonstrations throughout the South calling for an end to segregation—arrived in Selma in February 1963 to help the city's black residents register to vote. Some pastors of black churches refused to host the SNCC voting clinics, fearing a backlash from white supremacist organizations such as the Ku Klux Klan. Many of Selma's black residents were also uneasy about associating with the SNCC—Sheriff James G. Clark Jr., who described blacks as "the lowest form of humanity," routinely sent police officers to the clinics to take down the names of the attendees.

In spite of the anxieties of many of Selma's black citizens and the harassment of Selma police, SNCC organized a voter registration day on October 7, 1963. About 250 black men and women lined up outside the Dallas County Courthouse to register. Sheriff Clark was there, too, accompanied by his deputies and a photographer who took a picture of everyone in line, assuring them that their photographs would appear in the newspaper the next day. It was another form of intimidation—white employers might be inclined to fire a black employee who associated with activists such as the SNCC.

SNCC members who carried "Register to Vote" signs were dragged out of line and hauled off to the city jail. A SNCC worker who passed out water and sandwiches to the people standing in line was beaten by the police—so were out-of-town journalists and newspaper photographers who attempted to get anywhere near the prospective voters. Once the would-be voters reached the registrar's office they faced one more hurdle: They were required to fill out a four-page registration form. Registrars permitted only a handful of the 250 to fill out the lengthy application, and then rejected almost all of them on some technicality.

In 1966 journalists Rowland Evans and Robert Novak described what they called "the treatment," LBJ's unique method of winning a senator's support. "Its tone could be supplication, accusation, cajolery, exuberance, scorn, tears, complaint and the hint of threat," wrote Evans and Novak. "It was all of these together. It ran the gamut of human emotions. Its velocity was breathtaking, and it was all in one direction. Interjections from the target were rare. Johnson anticipated them before they could be spoken. He moved in close, his face a scant millimeter from his target, his eyes widening and narrowing, his eyebrows rising and falling. From his pockets poured clippings, memos, statistics. Mimicry, humor, and the genius of analogy made The Treatment an almost hypnotic experience and rendered the target stunned and helpless."

As early as 1956, Johnson had his eye on the White House, but in 1960 the Democrats were swept away by the handsome young senator from Massachusetts, John F. Kennedy. As a Roman Catholic, Kennedy suffered from a liability—no Catholic had ever been elected president, and anti-Catholic animosity was still widespread in America. To help him win the South, where Catholics were a tiny minority, Kennedy chose Johnson as his running mate.

After wielding considerable influence in the Senate, Johnson found the role of vice president frustrating. He had no power and no responsibilities other than what the president deigned to give him. But as head of the President's Committee on Equal Employment Opportunities, Johnson took a seemingly innocuous job and used it to carry the civil rights movement beyond the cautious comfort zone of the Kennedy administration. Historian Taylor Branch argues that Johnson's progressive position on civil rights took many in the Kennedy White House by surprise—they had assumed he was a typical Southern social conservative. But in a Memorial Day speech delivered in Gettysburg on May 30, 1963, Johnson revealed that on the subject of civil rights, he was ahead of his president.

"One hundred years ago, the slave was freed," Johnson told the assembled crowd. "One hundred years later, the Negro remains in bondage to the color of his skin. The Negro today asks justice. We do not answer him—we do not answer those who lie beneath this soil—when we reply to the Negro by asking, 'Patience'. . . Until justice is blind to color, until education is unaware of race, until opportunity is unconcerned with the color of men's skins, emancipation will be a proclamation but not a fact. To the extent that the proclamation of emancipation is not fulfilled in fact, to that extent we shall have fallen short of assuring freedom to the free."

Six months later, on November 22, 1963, while riding in an open car through Dallas, John F. Kennedy was shot and killed. Two hours later, aboard the presidential aircraft, Air Force One, with President Kennedy's widow Jacqueline Kennedy standing at his side, Lyndon B. Johnson took the oath of office as president of the United States. In the wake of the assassination, Johnson assured the stricken nation that he would accomplish President Kennedy's programs. In fact, Johnson would push through Congress a series of domestic programs far more ambitious than anything the United States had seen since the days of Franklin Roosevelt.

THE FIRST SUCCESSES

The civil rights movement of the 1950s and 1960s grew out of the migration of African Americans from the South to the industrial cities of the North in the 1920s, coupled with the return in the late 1940s of African American troops who had served during World War II in Europe. Black soldiers were surprised to find that there were no color barriers in England, France, Belgium, Italy, or Germany. Once back in the United States, many black veterans were unwilling to submit once again to racial discrimination.

In 1945, 1947, and 1949, the House of Representatives voted to abolish the poll tax, which obliged would-be voters to pay one or two dollars before they could cast their ballot. The purpose of the tax was to bar very poor blacks, whites, and Native Americans from voting. These bills died in the House because they were always voted down in the Senate.

Nonetheless, civil rights was making headway under presidents Harry Truman and Dwight Eisenhower, who ended racial segregation in the U.S. military and put an end to racially discriminatory hiring practices in the federal government.

Meanwhile, blacks and whites, led by the Rev. Dr. Martin Luther King Jr., were participating in marches, sit-ins, and boycotts to demand equal rights and equal protection under the law for all Americans.

Then, in 1954, in the case known as *Brown v. Board of Education of Topeka*, the Supreme Court ruled that segregated public schools such as those in Topeka, Kansas, were unconstitutional. "We conclude that in the field of public education the doctrine of separate but equal has no place," the justices wrote. "Separate educational facilities are inherently unequal."

In 1957 Congress passed a civil rights bill that had been introduced by the Eisenhower administration. The bill made it a crime to infringe upon the right of any American citizen to vote, and it created a civil rights division of the Justice Department to investigate attempts to intimidate voters or to discount their ballots.

In the South especially, resistance to these Supreme Court rulings and new pieces of legislation was often expressed in violence. Angry mobs attacked civil rights workers—white and black—who helped African Americans register to vote or challenged the laws regarding segregation in public facilities.

In 1962, when James Meredith, a black man, attempted to enroll at the all-white University of Mississippi, a wave of riots erupted around the campus that took the lives of two men and injured 375 others. The following year Medgar Evers, field secretary of the NAACP in Mississippi, was shot and killed outside his home. That same year William L. Moore, a white man from Baltimore, set off on a one-man protest march into the Deep South. He was carrying two signs that read "End Segregation in America" and "Equal Rights for All Men" when he was murdered along a highway in Alabama.

BLACK AND WHITE DEMONSTRATORS STAGE A "JUMP-IN" AT A SEGREGATED FLORIDA MOTEL POOL IN JUNE 1964. THE ANGRY MOTEL OWNER DUMPS TWO CONTAINERS MARKED "MURIATIC ACID" INTO THE POOL, CAUSING THEM TO FLEE.

Popperfoto/Getty Images

BREAKING BARRIERS: AFRICAN-
AMERICAN STUDENT JAMES
MEREDITH, ACCOMPANIED BY
FEDERAL MARSHALS, WALKS PAST
THE TAUNTS OF WHITE STUDENTS
AFTER HE ENROLLED AT THE
ALL-WHITE UNIVERSITY OF
MISSISSIPPI. A WAVE OF RIOTS AT
THE CAMPUS FOLLOWED, TAKING
THE LIVES OF TWO MEN AND
INJURING 375 OTHERS.

Time & Life Pictures/Getty Images

But civil rights activism was not limited to the South. Demonstrators in New York, Philadelphia, Chicago, and other major Northern cities called for an end to discriminatory hiring practices in skilled trades such as the construction industry.

THE BILL IN THE HOUSE

The civil rights bill that President Kennedy had convinced both Democratic and Republican leaders of the House of Representatives to introduce was not radical: It called for equal access to hotels, restaurants, theaters, housing, public transportation, public restrooms, water fountains, and all other public accommodations. It called for an end to racially segregated schools. It demanded equal employment opportunities. But it did nothing to end the discrimination and harassment black men and women encountered when they tried to exercise their right to vote. As president, Lyndon Johnson was determined to pass a bill that was much stronger than the one introduced by Kennedy.

On February 1, 1964, the civil rights bill, H.R. 7152, came to the House. Debate raged for nine days, and supporters of the bill had to beat back one hundred amendments intended to diminish the impact of the new legislation. On February 10, 1964, the bill passed the House by a vote of 290–130. Only eleven Democrats from the South broke ranks with their Southern colleagues to vote in favor of the legislation.

THE BILL IN THE SENATE

In March 1964 the House bill arrived in the Senate. Senator Hubert Humphrey of Minnesota and Senator Mike Mansfield of Montana—both Democrats—led the pro-civil rights faction in the Senate. They were opposed by Senator Richard Russell of Georgia, who led a group of eighteen Democrats and one Republican from the South known as the "Southern Bloc."

Russell relied on the filibuster to delay the civil rights bill from coming to a vote, but also to give Governor George Wallace of Alabama an opportunity to see what type of support he could attract for segregationist policies and defeating civil rights legislation outside the South. Wallace was one of the most outspoken proponents of segregation; during his 1963 inauguration speech as governor he had declared, "Segregation now, segregation tomorrow, segregation forever!"

In defiance of the Supreme Court's ruling in Brown, he tried to block four young black students from enrolling in an all-white school in Huntsville. He stood at the door of the Foster Auditorium, physically keeping two black students from enrolling in the University of Alabama, and only stepped aside when he was confronted by federal marshals backed up by members of the National Guard. If Wallace did well in the initial presidential primaries, Russell believed he could use those successes as proof that the country was not solidly behind civil rights legislation. As it happened, Wallace did best in three Northern states—Wisconsin, Indiana, and Maryland—where he garnered about 30 percent of the vote. But he won no primaries.

The Southern Bloc was fighting for its political life. The senators' constituents were overwhelmingly in favor of segregation. If these Southern senators compromised in the least with the pro–civil rights element in the Senate, they would almost certainly be voted out of office.

To sustain the filibuster, the Southern Bloc divided itself into three six-member teams. Each team would take an eight-hour shift; while one team held the Senate floor, the other two would have a meal, rest, and prepare for their next filibustering session.

Meanwhile, the nation at large was also following the civil rights bill closely. For example, Senator Everett Dirksen of Illinois estimated that he had received approximately 100,000 letters, telegrams, petitions, and phone calls from his constituents. And that was not counting the thousands of ordinary citizens who crowded into the Capitol in an effort to speak to their representatives personally about the bill.

And the Southern Bloc's filibuster dragged on—from late March when it began, through all of April, into May—until at last, after an impassioned plea by Senator Dirksen, on June 10, 1964, the Senate voted 71 to 29 to close the filibuster. By that date, the Southern Bloc had kept its filibuster going for fifty-seven days. A week later the Senate passed the civil rights bill by a vote of 73 to 27.

"THE LAW I SIGN TONIGHT FORBIDS IT"

The bill that passed the House and Senate was not perfect. It outlawed discrimination in all public accommodations, but it exempted private clubs. It called for an end to segregated public schools and authorized the attorney general to file suit against districts that refused to integrate their schools. State and local programs that received government funds were discouraged from practicing discrimination, but the bill did not penalize programs that failed to take the federal government's hint. Any business that employed twenty-five people or more was barred from discriminatory hiring practices, and the Equal Employment Opportunities Commission was established to review complaints. Finally, the Civil Rights Act of 1964 demanded free, open, and equal access to voter registration, but the bill backpedaled a bit when it failed to abolish the literacy tests that were used to disqualify blacks as well as poor whites from voting.

Nonetheless, President Johnson was pleased, even relieved, by the passage of the Civil Rights Act, but he worried that it might provoke violence and bloodshed in the South, not to mention the widespread defection of Southern whites from the Democrats to the Republican Party. In spite of the president's anxieties, his legislative aide, Lee White, urged him to hold a public signing ceremony. "It's so monumental," White told Johnson. "It's equivalent to signing an Emancipation Proclamation, and it ought to have all the possible attention you can focus on it."

On the evening of July 2, surrounded by more than a hundred dignitaries—including Dr. Martin Luther King Jr. and Attorney General Robert F. Kennedy—President Johnson signed the Civil Rights Act of 1964 into law.

Addressing the nation Johnson said, "We believe that all men are created equal—yet many are denied equal treatment. We believe that all men have certain inalienable rights. We believe that all men are entitled to the blessings of liberty—yet millions are being deprived of those blessings, not because of their own failures, but because of the color of their skins. The reasons are deeply embedded in history and tradition and the nature of man. We can understand without rancor or hatred how all this happens. But it cannot continue . . . Our Constitution, the foundation of our Republic, forbids it. The principles of our freedom forbid it. Morality forbids it. And the law I sign tonight forbids it."

Ironically, tragically, barely three weeks after LBJ signed the Civil Rights Act, American cities erupted in racial violence. That summer of 1964, riots broke out in Rochester, New York; the New Jersey cities of Elizabeth, Jersey City, and Paterson; and in Chicago and Philadelphia. Their causes were varied—charges of police brutality, of discriminatory housing and hiring practices, of high rates of poverty and unemployment. It was a bitter summer for supporters of civil rights, but the Johnson administration kept moving forward. In 1965 Johnson signed the Voting Rights Act, which made it illegal to require would-be voters to pass a literacy test. In 1967 he appointed Thurgood Marshall to the U.S. Supreme Court—the first African American named to the court. And in the Civil Rights Act of 1968 Johnson outlawed discrimination in housing.

IN THIS DECEMBER 4, 1964, PHOTOGRAPH, MARTIN LUTHER KING JR. HOLDS A PICTURE OF THREE CIVIL RIGHTS WORKERS WHO WERE SLAIN FIVE MONTHS EARLIER IN MISSISSIPPI BY MEMBERS OF THE KU KLUX KLAN, SOME OF WHOM WORKED FOR THE LOCAL SHERIFF'S DEPARTMENT. CIVIL RIGHTS WORKERS FACED VIOLENCE WHEREVER THEY WENT, ESPECIALLY AFTER THE PASSAGE OF CIVIL RIGHTS LEGISLATION.

Library of Congress

LBJ MEETS WITH CIVIL RIGHTS ACTIVISTS IN 1965. HIS REASONS FOR SUPPORTING CIVIL RIGHTS LEGISLATION WERE BOTH POLITICAL AND PERSONAL. WHILE TRAVELING THROUGH THE SOUTH, HIS PERSONAL COOK, A BLACK WOMAN NAMED ZEPHYR WRIGHT, WAS BARRED FROM WHITES-ONLY RESTAURANTS AND HOTELS AND COULD NOT EVEN USE A PUBLIC RESTROOM.

Lyndon Baines Johnson Presidential Library and Museum

LBJ'S LEGACY

More than forty years have passed since President Johnson signed the Civil Rights Act of 1964 into law. Americans who were not alive in the 1950s and 1960s can scarcely imagine the significance of that moment. The laws that kept blacks and whites apart everywhere from movie theaters to city buses, that locked black students out of state colleges and universities, that threw up obstacle upon obstacle to keep black men and women from exercising their right to vote, that even made it illegal for blacks and whites to drink from the same public water fountain—all these laws were swept away.

In the years that followed, more legislation was introduced to protect Hispanics, Native Americans, Asians, women, and persons with disabilities from discrimination. The old excuses of "custom," "tradition," or "states' rights" for denying certain types of persons their civil rights were no longer acceptable.

After the Civil Rights Act of 1964 came a host of ancillary legislation that banned discrimination based on race, ethnicity, religion, or gender; the implementation of these laws has not always worked perfectly, but by and large they have worked surprisingly well. And it has even seen successes that probably would have surprised President Johnson and Dr. King, not least being the morning in January 2009, when an African-American senator from Illinois took the oath of the office as president of the United States.

CHAPTER 27

LYNDON JOHNSON AND MEDICARE: "THE REAL DADDY OF MEDICARE"

1965

WHEN LYNDON JOHNSON WAS SWORN IN AS PRESIDENT AFTER THE ASSAS-sination of John F. Kennedy on November 22, 1963, he took a solemn oath to perform the duties of the chief executive of the United States, but Johnson was not the type of man who could remain solemn for very long—unless it suited him politically, that is.

He was easily the most colorful president since Teddy Roosevelt, another vice president thrust into the presidency by assassination, who took office in 1901. Like Roosevelt, Johnson was outsized. The fifty-five-year-old former Senate majority leader, used to wheedling, cajoling, and bullying his way to get what he wanted in Congress, now did the same on a larger scale in the White House. He micromanaged everything, from the growing war in Vietnam right down to minor repairs on his Texas ranch. Even his periods of rest, his vice president Hubert Humphrey wrote, were "controlled frenzy."

Johnson could be incredibly vulgar. Tales abounded of him dragging aides into the bathroom with him while he answered the call of nature. Once he urinated on a Secret Service agent's leg while making a pit stop in the Texas outback. (Supposedly the man said: "Mr. President, you are urinating on me." And Johnson answered: "I know I am . . . it's my prerogative.") Johnson taped more than eight hundred hours of conversations in the Oval Office; one such tape captures him browbeating the president of the Haggar Pants company into sending him several pairs of free slacks. Although he was completely devoted to his wife Lady Bird, Johnson, like John Kennedy before him, was a womanizer. Whereas Kennedy had had his nubile secretaries nicknamed "Fiddle" and "Faddle," Johnson had long-term affairs with two female associates dubbed "the chili queen" and "the dairy queen."

All of this might seem to add up to a portrait of an imperial and supremely egotistical president—and Johnson was that. But he was more as well. Like no other presidents—save, perhaps, for Abraham Lincoln and Franklin Roosevelt—he cared deeply for the plight of everyday people. He told biographer Doris Kearns Goodwin: "Some men want power simply to strut around the world and to hear the tune of 'Hail to the Chief' . . . I wanted power to give things to people—all sorts of things to all sorts of people, especially the poor and the blacks."

And one of things that Johnson gave us—which many take for granted today—is the medical insurance program for the aged known as *Medicare*. It has saved literally millions of lives since he first put pen to paper and signed it into law in 1965.

"A MOST SERIOUS DEFEAT FOR EVERY AMERICAN FAMILY"

The history of government-mandated health insurance programs is a long and controversial one (and still is, as the debates raging in Washington in 2009 attested). FDR's Committee on Economic Security (CES) originally created a government-run universal health insurance proposal to go along with the Social Security Bill of 1935, but dropped it because of the opposition of the American Medical Association (AMA) and private insurance companies. The president tried again in 1939 with the National Health Act, but this, too, was shot down for political reasons.

World War II intervened and it was not until 1948 that FDR successor Harry Truman attempted to push another national health bill through Congress. "The greatest gap in our social security structure is the lack of adequate provision for the nation's health," Truman said. "Our ultimate aim must be a comprehensive insurance system to protect all our people equally against insecurity and ill health." By the time Truman left office in 1953, this plan had been trimmed down from universal health care to a proposal to provide such health benefits only for those receiving Social Security.

The incoming Republican administration of Dwight Eisenhower effectively killed any attempt to institute national health care coverage, even one tied to Social Security, because of strong opposition from conservative Republicans and the AMA (which, in fact, cut its teeth as a lobbying organization on the national health care issue because it felt doctors would then have to accept much lower fees).

Even as popular a president as John F. Kennedy could not bring about passage of a health care bill tied to Social Security, a bill he called "Medical Care for the Aged." The bill failed to pass the Senate by only two votes, which angered Kennedy. He told a national television audience: "I believe this is a most serious defeat for every American family, for the 17 million Americans who are over sixty-five, whose means of support, whose livelihood is certainly lessened over what it was in their working days, who are more inclined to be ill, who will more likely be in hospitals, who are less able to pay their bills."

Kennedy vowed to pursue the issue vigorously, but his assassination intervened, leaving the matter in the hands of Lyndon Johnson. Johnson knew what he was up against. Conservative forces warned of "socialized medicine," a charge that frightened many voters during the cold war period. The AMA hired Ronald Reagan as its spokesman and organized a particularly effective grassroots movement called "Operation Coffee Cup," in which thousands of meetings were held across the country in the homes of women who were the wives of AMA doctors; these meetings were supposed to educate other women about the evils of government-sponsored health care for the aged and to get them to begin letter-writing campaigns to their congressional representatives.

Reagan, leaving his acting career for politics and newly switched from the Democrat to the Republican Party, fanned the flames of AMA alarmism in a recording that was played at every Operation Coffee Cup meeting:

> "Behind [Medicare] will come other Federal programs that will invade every area of freedom as we have known it in this country. Until one day, as [socialist] Norman Thomas said, 'We will awake to find that we have socialism.' And if you don't do this and if I don't do it, one of these days you and I are going to spend our sunset years telling our children and our children's children what it once was like in America when men were free."

MEDICARE BY THE NUMBERS

The Medicare program provides coverage for those over age sixty-five and, beginning in 1973, people with disabilities. The figures below show the growth of Lyndon Johnson's Great Society program.

2008
As of 2008, the year with the most up-to-date information, there were 45 million enrollees.

1960   1970   1980   1990   2000

1966
During the first year of the Medicare program, 19 million people were enrolled.

Source: www.cms.hhs.gov/MedicareEnRpts/Downloads/HISMI08.pdf

RETIRED SENIOR CITIZENS
SUPPORTING MEDICARE PICKET
OUTSIDE THE HOTEL AMERICANA
DURING THE AMERICAN MEDICAL
ASSOCIATION'S 114TH ANNUAL
CONVENTION. THE AMA,
CONSERVATIVE REPUBLICANS, AND
PRIVATE INSURANCE COMPANIES
ALL FOUGHT AGAINST THE BILL.
Library of Congress

"NUMBER ONE PRIORITY"

However, such anti-health-care proponents didn't realize what they were up against in Lyndon Johnson. His years as a senator and his time as vice president (though firmly pushed into the background by the Kennedy clan) had hidden his powerful populism and desire to help people.

In his first State of the Union address in January 1964, to a country and Congress still reeling from the shocking assassination of JFK, he spoke eloquently to the assembled senators and congressmen, telling them he wanted this 89th Congress "to build more homes, more schools, more libraries, and more hospitals than any single session of Congress in the history of our Republic." Johnson went on to declare a "War on Poverty," crusading on behalf of the 35 million Americans making less than $3,000 a year, insisting that he was offering not a "hand out" but a "hand up." Johnson's Economic Opportunity Act, sent to Congress in March, would enact such federal projects as the food stamp program, Operation Head Start, the Job Corps, and a domestic Peace Corps program (VISTA, which was envisioned by JFK but launched by Johnson and the creation of the Office of Economic Opportunity).

All of this infuriated Johnson's Republican opponents but made him a popular president. In 1964 he destroyed conservative Barry Goldwater during an especially dirty presidential campaign—Johnson, for all his altruistic sentiments, was master of the art of slashing his opponent's jugular. Victorious by more than 16 million votes—at that time, the largest winning vote margin in history—and with a two-to-one Democratic majority in each house, Johnson felt he had a mandate to go after the biggest plum of all in his "Great Society" campaign: Medicare.

Johnson biographer Robert Dallek writes: "For Johnson, there could be no Great Society—no improved quality of national life—without greater access for all Americans to health care." In 1964, Johnson decided to create a commission that would dedicate itself to finding effective treatments for heart disease, cancer, and stroke. Part of his desire to see this through was (typical of Johnson) personal—his family had suffered the ravages of strokes and cancer and he himself (a heavy smoker and drinker) had had a heart attack at the age of forty-six.

This desire segued into an interest in seeing a Medicare bill passed, especially after public opinion polls began to tell the president that a majority of Americans wanted some kind of national health insurance for the elderly. He told a reporter that Medicare was at the "top of the list" of "must" legislation to pass in 1965 and told Health, Education and Welfare Assistant Secretary Wilbur J. Cohen—the administration's man when it came to Medicare—that he must make it his "number one priority."

"YOU CAN'T TREAT GRANDMA THIS WAY"

When it came to Medicare, Johnson had just the right populist touch to defuse the objections of the AMA, conservative Republicans, and private insurance companies. His voice spoke right to the people. Oval Office tapes caught him casually telling Bill Moyers, his press secretary, that the administration needed to project a very simple reason behind wanting Medicare: "We've just got to say that by God you can't treat grandma this way. She's entitled to it and we promised it to her."

As put together by Wilbur Cohen and Wilbur Mills, the powerful Democratic chairman of the House Ways and Means Committee, Medicare would provide 60 days of hospital coverage, 180 days of skilled nursing care, and 240 days of home health care visits for Social Security beneficiaries sixty-five years of age and older. Payroll deductions and employer contributions would fund the program, but it would almost certainly need federal money as well.

The AMA and Republicans fought back. The AMA proposed a program called "Eldercare" that would provide fairly good benefits for those who qualified and who could afford to pay for it. Such a proposal, although it would leave a great many poverty-level seniors uncovered, might weaken the Democratic bill, so Mills suggested a compromise in which really poor people would qualify for an "expanded medical welfare program" administered by the states, to be called "Medicaid."

When told by Cohen that this version of the bill would cost the federal government an additional $500 million, Johnson exclaimed: "Five hundred million? Is that all? Do it. Move that damn bill out now, before we lose it!"

On April 8, the House passed the bill by a margin of 313–115 and it headed for the Senate. Its passage was by no means a foregone conclusion, because the powerful AMA still lobbied hard against it. When labor leader George Meany—whose AFL-CIO membership strongly supported Medicare—told the president that the AMA was a dangerous force, Johnson declared, in typical fashion, that he wasn't worried.

"George," he said, "have you ever fed chickens?"

Meany had to admit that he hadn't.

"Well," the president told him. "Chickens are real dumb. They eat and eat and eat and never stop . . . they start shitting at the same time as they're eating and before you know it, they're knee-deep in their own shit. Well, the AMA's the same. They've been eating and eating nonstop and now they're knee-deep in their own shit and everybody knows it. They won't be able to stop anything."

Johnson was right and Medicare passed the Senate on July 9. But, clever politician that he was, Johnson asked leaders of the AMA to come to the White House for a meeting in which he implored them to forget the past and support Medicare. At the same time, he appealed to their patriotic instincts by asking them to get physicians to work with the civilian population in Vietnam, where the war was growing daily. They agreed. Johnson praised them—profusely and publicly—and within two weeks the AMA reversed course and declared it would support Medicare.

WILBUR MILLS, THE POWERFUL DEMOCRATIC CHAIRMAN OF THE HOUSE WAYS AND MEANS COMMITTEE, WHO SPEARHEADED MEDICARE LEGISLATION. IT WAS MILLS WHO SUGGESTED A COMPROMISE TO THE EMBATTLED BILL IN WHICH POOR PEOPLE WOULD QUALIFY FOR AN "EXPANDED MEDICAL WELFARE PROGRAM" ADMINISTERED BY THE STATES, TO BE CALLED "MEDICAID."

Time & Life Pictures/Getty Images

"THE REAL DADDY OF MEDICARE"

On July 30, 1965, Lyndon Johnson led two planeloads of reporters and dignitaries from Washington to Kansas City, Missouri, where they landed and formed a limousine caravan to take them to Independence, about twenty minutes away. Independence was the birthplace and home of former president Harry S. Truman and it was also home to the Harry S. Truman Presidential Library.

With the instincts of a true showman and a great politician, President Johnson had decided to sign Medicare into law in the company of Truman, who, successor to Roosevelt, was the Democrat who had tried to fashion just such a program in the first place. Not only that, but Johnson had decided that Harry Truman, eighty-one years old, would become the very first American citizen to be enrolled in Medicare. After finishing his speech and signing the bill into law, LBJ turned to Truman, who was sitting next to him on the dais.

"They told me, President Truman, that if you wish to get the voluntary medical insurance you will have to sign this application form. And they asked me to sign as your witness. So you're getting special treatment since cards won't go out to the other folks until the end of this month." Johnson smiled at Truman. "But we wanted you to know, and we wanted the whole world to know who is the real daddy of Medicare."

Truman nodded, smiled in return, signed his name, and became the nation's first beneficiary of Medicare. But Truman and everyone else present—especially Lyndon

LBJ SIGNS THE MEDICARE BILL WHILE SITTING NEXT TO PRESIDENT HARRY TRUMAN, THE FIRST MEDICARE RECIPIENT IN THE COUNTRY, IN TRUMAN'S HOMETOWN OF INDEPENDENCE, MISSOURI. DECADES EARLIER, TRUMAN HAD TRIED TO FASHION JUST SUCH A HEALTH INSURANCE PROGRAM IN THE FIRST PLACE.

Lyndon Baines Johnson Presidential Library and Museum

Johnson—knew just who the real daddy of Medicare was: It was Johnson himself.

Lyndon Johnson had perhaps an even more extraordinary record in pushing through social legislation than Franklin Roosevelt did, especially considering that Johnson was in office for a term and a quarter, Roosevelt for three full terms and change. Civil rights reforms were a part of his Great Society, as were the Water Quality and Clean Air Acts and reforms to immigration policies. Unfortunately, the Johnson presidency was destroyed, in a very real sense, by the war in Vietnam, which Johnson did not start but in which he hopelessly enmeshed the American people.

However, of Johnson's many Great Society programs, Medicare has had the most lasting benefit and has been the most resilient to change. Ironically, by the time Medicare's old enemy Ronald Reagan took office in 1981, Medicare was firmly entrenched and extremely popular among America's senior citizens. In 2009, Medicare provided health care for 45 million Americans; enrollment may reach 77 million by 2031, when the baby boom generation is fully subscribed. (With the population aging at its current rate, there are fears that Medicare will eventually become unsustainable—but woe betides the politician who tries to pull the plug on it.)

The "sunset years" that Ronald Reagan had once lectured Operation Coffee Cup women about in 1964 had come to pass—and it's a safe bet that most of the women who sat listening to Reagan's golden tones then are now enjoying the benefits of Lyndon Johnson's Medicare in their golden years.

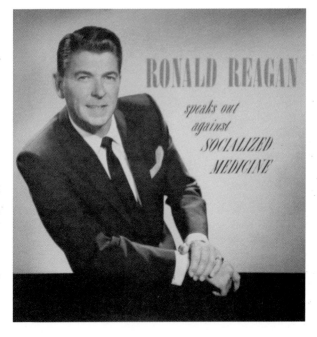

AN ANTI-MEDICARE AD BY THE AMERICAN MEDICAL ASSOCIATION FEATURES RONALD REAGAN, WHOM THE AMA HIRED TO LOBBY AGAINST THE BILL, SAYING SUCH A PROGRAM WOULD LEAD TO SOCIALIZED MEDICINE.

The Ronald Reagan Presidential Foundation and Library

CHAPTER 28

RICHARD NIXON VISITS CHINA, BEGINNING THE END OF A POLICY OF ISOLATION AND LAUNCHING A NEW ERA IN U.S.-CHINA RELATIONS

1972

GLENN COWAN WAS A VERY GOOD PING-PONG PLAYER, GOOD ENOUGH TO claim a spot on the U.S. team that competed in the 1971 31st World Table Tennis Championships in Nagoya, Japan. Few Americans took Ping-Pong seriously back then. It was a way to pass the time over a green table in a knotty-pine-paneled rec room, paddle in one hand, beer in the other. But Cowan took it as seriously as any committed athlete takes his or her sport.

He practiced with such intensity of focus that by the time he emerged into the Nagoya sunlight after one afternoon's session, the team bus was nowhere to be seen. It had taken off without him, and he stood as people who miss their bus always stand, blank and bewildered. A Chinese player—everybody took Ping-Pong seriously in China, which was one of the many things about China that Americans had yet to understand—leaned out the window of the Chinese team bus and motioned for Cowan to come aboard.

At the time, there were no official diplomatic relations between the United States and China. As far as the American government was concerned, Mao Zedong, chairman of the Chinese Communist Party, and Zhou Enlai, premier of the People's Republic of China, were pretenders to an authority that rightly belonged to the Nationalists exiled in Taiwan. American politicians and pundits routinely characterized China as no more than a "mad dog" among nations.

To Glenn Cowan none of this mattered that March afternoon. He'd missed his bus, and now he'd found another.

Through an interpreter who accompanied the Chinese team, Cowan chatted with the players, including Zhuang Zedong, a table tennis legend, three-time world men's singles champion, and, though he held no office, a high-profile political figure at home. Before Cowan left the bus, Zhuang reached into his bag, withdrew a silk-screen portrait of the Huangshan Mountains, and gave it to him. Cowan was carrying nothing to bestow in return, but before the Nagoya games were over, he had bought a T-shirt bearing a red, white, and blue peace-emblem flag below which was emblazoned the Beatles title and lyric "Let It Be." That was his gift to Zhuang.

It was a chance encounter, but also one of those accidents for which certain people, important people, had long prepared. Cowan did not know that in advance of the Nagoya games, Roy Evans, president of the International Table Tennis Federation, had been summoned to a meeting with no less a figure than Zhou Enlai, who wanted him to bar South Vietnam from the upcoming games. An uncomfortable Evans replied that he had no authority to issue such a ban, but, wanting to offer something friendly after saying no, he suggested to the Chinese premier that he invite some Western teams to visit China on their way home from Nagoya.

Between the Evans-Zhou meeting and the Cowan-Zhuang encounter, serious talk percolated up through the Chinese bureaucracy about inviting the American team for a visit. Just as the Chinese Department of Foreign Affairs was preparing to nip that notion in the bud, Zhou, together with Mao himself, let it be known that they thought such a meeting was a fine idea, and that is why, on April 10, 1971, nine American table tennis players crossed a bridge from Hong Kong (at the time a British Crown colony) to the Chinese mainland for a week of exhibition matches.

Most Americans still didn't pay much attention to the game, but they sensed that what it was bringing about between two implacable rival powers was surprisingly important. "Ping-Pong diplomacy," TV and the newspapers called it.

A little more than three months after the American players crossed the bridge, at 7:30 p.m. on July 15, 1971, President Richard M. Nixon appeared for three and a half minutes on all the national TV networks. He announced that he had accepted an invitation from Zhou Enlai to meet in Beijing for the purpose of seeking "normalization of relations between the two countries and also to exchange views on questions of concern to the two sides."

COLD WARRIOR RÉSUMÉ

If Ping-Pong seemed an unlikely overture to the normalization of relations between political, ideological, and military adversaries, Richard Milhous Nixon seemed an even more unlikely agent of the profound change in the diplomatic landscape that was about to materialize. He had been born in 1913 in Yorba Linda, California, to a Quaker mother and father who struggled to make a go of a lemon orchard and then, when that failed, labored to make a living from a grocery store and gas station in nearby Whittier. Dick Nixon earned a scholarship to Yale, but, even with tuition paid for, the family couldn't afford to send him so far away to school, so he enrolled instead in the local college, and then went on to Duke University Law School. He returned to Whittier after taking his law degree and practiced privately for a time. With the United States' entry into World War II, he moved to Washington, D.C., for a job in the Office of Price Administration before joining the navy in August 1942 as a logistics and cargo officer in the Southwest Pacific.

Nixon plunged into politics after the war, running in 1946 against Congressman Jerry Voorhis, a popular, five-term liberal Democrat. Nixon did not have to think very hard about how to conduct his campaign. Innuendo came naturally to him, and he used it to paint his opponent bright Red. Nixon seemed to revel in the bare-knuckles ugliness of the campaign and not only won election, but emerged with a high national profile as a youthful warrior in the war against Soviet communism.

He won, but even the voters who had elected him and admired his hard line against the Left didn't much like him. At the time, it hardly mattered. In 1948, he ran for reelection, boldly entering both the Democratic and the Republican primaries, both of which he won handily, so that there was no need to run in the general election. That was a move as unorthodox as it was typical of Nixon. The man could not abide losing, and he would do whatever needed doing to even the odds, stack the deck, and eliminate any chance of defeat.

It was also a move that got him noticed. The grandstand dual primary display, coupled with his precocious Red-baiting credentials, earned him a seat on the powerful and much-feared House Un-American Activities Committee (HUAAC), dedicated to rooting out communist infiltration in government, industry, and even Hollywood. He was earning his stripes as a "cold warrior," and he was carving out his niche in a Republican Party that was about to nurture the likes of Red-baiting Wisconsin senator Joe McCarthy.

On the fast track, Nixon next ran against Democratic representative Helen Gahagan Douglas, wife of the popular actor Melvyn Douglas, for a Senate seat in 1950. In this campaign, he escalated from innuendo to invective. Meaning to combine what he knew many voters would see as two negatives, Douglas's gender and her liberal politics, Nixon branded her as "pink—pink right down to her underwear." It was as outrageous as it was effective. Nixon sailed to victory.

Not without cost, though. California's liberal *Independent Review* covered the campaign and slapped Nixon with an epithet destined to dog the rest of his political career. "Tricky Dick," the paper called him. For now, however, Senator Nixon was a rising star whose velocity seemed unstoppable. In 1952, the Republican National Convention nominated him as Dwight D. Eisenhower's running mate in the hope that some of the senator's cold warrior patina would rub off on the candidate.

Nixon was nearly kicked off the ticket, however, when he was accused of hoarding a secret campaign "slush fund." Instead of assuming a defensive stance, Nixon confronted the accusations head-on with a speech televised on September 23, 1952, in which he admitted to the fund's existence, but denied that he had used it improperly.

He paraded his humble upbringing and protested that he was far from wealthy. As proof, he recited a list of his family's modest assets, pausing to underscore his wife's "respectable Republican cloth coat"—to be contrasted with the furs that presumably adorned the shoulders of Democratic wives—then ended with the single political gift he admitted to having accepted. It was, he said, a cocker spaniel puppy his six-year-old daughter, Tricia, had named "Checkers." Looking into the eye of the camera, he smiled: "Regardless of what they say about it, we are going to keep it."

THE ACCIDENTAL MEETING BETWEEN AMERICAN PING-PONG PLAYER GLENN COWAN, CENTER, WITH CHINESE PLAYERS IN JAPAN PROMPTED THE CHINESE TO INVITE THE AMERICAN TABLE TENNIS TEAM FOR A WEEK OF EXHIBITION MATCHES.

Associated Press

A smarmy tour de force, the so-called "Checkers speech" changed everything. For the first time in his political career, people almost liked Nixon. His place on the ticket was safe, and he and Ike won against Democrats Adlai E. Stevenson and John Sparkman in a landslide. After serving two terms as vice president, Nixon secured the nomination as the Republican presidential contender in 1960, only to lose by the narrowest of margins to the charismatic John F. Kennedy—who possessed the Ivy League pedigree that had eluded Nixon.

Seeking to keep his hand in politics, Nixon ran unsuccessfully for California governor in 1962 against incumbent Edmund G. ("Pat") Brown. This defeat embittered Nixon, eliciting from him a celebrated jab at the reporters gathered to hear his concession. Announcing his retirement from politics, he told the boys of the press that they would have reason to regret it. "You won't have Dick Nixon to kick around anymore," he sneered.

TRIANGULAR DIPLOMACY

Nixon did not retire, but he did step out of the spotlight to take up the practice of law in Manhattan, make a lot of money, and quietly remake himself. During the first phase of his career, he had spared no effort to brand himself as a single-minded anticommunist. Recognizing that the era of HUAAC and Joe McCarthy had passed, he reinvented his identity as a moderate conservative and reemerged in the Republican Party, which responded by nominating him as its 1968 presidential candidate. It was a convulsively turbulent year, marked by the assassinations of Dr. Martin Luther King, Jr. and Democratic hopeful Robert Kennedy, wracked by an increasingly strident anti-Vietnam War movement, and roiled by urban racial unrest.

White House incumbent Lyndon B. Johnson, mired in Vietnam—"his" war—withdrew himself early from the presidential contest, and the Democratic National Convention was deeply divided between an antiwar faction and the "mainstream" nominee, Vice President Hubert Humphrey, who vowed to see Vietnam to a respectable finish. Outside the convention hall, Chicago's lakefront erupted into riot; some three weeks earlier, in a convention as sedate as the Democrats' would be chaotic, Nixon and the Republicans had presented themselves as forces for stability. If this weren't enough to defeat Humphrey, candidate Nixon promised that he had a plan to end the Vietnam War, though he did not so much as hint at what it might be.

Following a narrow victory over Humphrey, Nixon did begin a phased withdrawal from Vietnam, incrementally reducing the number of U.S. ground forces in the country.

At the same time, however, he escalated the air war, intensifying the bombing of the North and expanding combat into Vietnam's neutral neighbors, Laos and Cambodia, in an effort to disrupt Viet Cong lines of supply into South Vietnam. In the meantime, he continued the peace talks that had begun at the close of the Johnson administration, sending his foreign policy adviser Henry Kissinger to Paris to wrangle with North Vietnamese foreign minister Le Duc Tho.

The way out was to end the war, which would appease the American Left, but to do so "with honor," so as not to alienate the American Right. He decided that as long as North Vietnam was tied both materially and ideologically to the Soviet Union and the People's Republic of China, no amount of bombing would beat it down. The only hope was to cut the country loose from the other powers.

But how?

Nixon believed that nations, like individuals, were motivated above all else by self-interest. He therefore decided to create a political, economic, and diplomatic reality in which the Chinese and the Soviets would see their self-interest as better served by friendly relations with the United States than by continuing to support North Vietnam. Yet the United States and the Soviet Union had been hardened ideological enemies since the Bolshevik Revolution of 1917 and, except for a period of forced alliance during World War II, were even more urgently at odds with one another from the mid 1940s on.

As for the People's Republic of China, it had come into being in 1949 after a bitter revolution-cum-civil war, and, from the beginning, its government, under the leadership of Chairman Mao Zedong, was absolutely dedicated to converting all the world to Marxism. Closed to the West, China was demonized, and when that demon acquired nuclear weapons beginning in the mid-1960s, the mutual distrust exploded into political paranoia.

And yet there was a glimmer of hope. From the late 1940s and through the 1950s, cold warriors such as Richard M. Nixon promoted the vision of a global reality divided between the West, which consisted of the United States and its allies, and a uniform, seamless "communist bloc," in which all communist nations, including China, were believed to take their orders from the Kremlin. It was a vision both threatening and yet, in its black-and-white simplicity, comforting. At the very least, most Americans believed they knew just where they stood.

But just as Nixon had been in the front ranks of those who promoted the "us versus them" model of world politics, so too, in the 1960s, he was among the first to see fissures in the communist bloc as relations between China and the Soviet Union

became increasingly contentious. To the surprise of those who still pegged him as the implacable cold warrior, President Nixon saw in this an opportunity to make the world a less dangerous place. With Henry Kissinger, he formulated what he called "triangular diplomacy." His objective was to play the Soviets against the Chinese, so that both would compete for improved relations with the United States and, in the process, abandon North Vietnam. What Nixon called "détente" with the Soviet Union (a status short of outright friendship but at least approaching rational cordiality) would in effect neutralize the USSR as a foe. All that remained was the task of "normalizing relations" with China.

BRAVE NEW NIXON

Launching this task was the subject of Nixon's speech on July 15, 1971. He knew those three and a half minutes of television would shake up the people who had helped him make his early political career. As he predicted, the right wing roundly condemned his overture to the "Reds." But Nixon believed the howls from the Far Right would serve to give him credibility with the American center and Left—and, equally important, with the Chinese. His willingness to break with the past and endure the conservative barbs would be perceived as proof of his sincerity.

Moreover, Nixon understood that his anticommunist record and reputation gave him unique license to approach China. A liberal Democrat who tried it would be opposed by everyone except other liberal Democrats, but no one could reasonably accuse Richard M. Nixon of being "soft on communism." Besides, Nixon had come to believe that reflexive right-wing protest against normalization of relations with China had become destructively obsolete. One after the other, nations were voicing their recognition of the People's Republic. Before long, the United States would find itself standing alone.

"Personally, I have never believed in bowing to the inevitable just because it is inevitable," Nixon wrote in his 1978 memoirs. "In this case, however, I felt that the national security interests of the United States lay in developing our relations with the [People's Republic of China]." In the back of his mind was the intention of doing what Truman, Eisenhower, Kennedy, and Johnson would not have dared—end the U.S. policy of blocking China's admission to membership in the United Nations.

DIPLOMATIC MINUET

The broadcast of July 15, 1971, hit the American airwaves and the American political consciousness with startling suddenness. Yet the decision behind it had actually been a long time coming. In 1967, before he was even a candidate for the presidency, Nixon had written in the journal *Foreign Affairs* about the importance of ending the isolation of China, and, as his inaugural address proved, the idea was never very far from his mind. From the steps of the Capitol on January 20, 1969, he proclaimed his wish to promote "an open world . . . in which no people . . . will live in angry isolation."

Just two weeks later, he instructed Kissinger to give "every encouragement" to the "attitude that the administration was exploring possibilities of rapprochement with the Chinese." The first public mention of the new policy came in the president's February 1970 "Foreign Policy Report to Congress," in which he called the Chinese a "great and vital people who should not remain isolated from the international community" and expressed his assessment that "it is certainly in our interest, and in the interest of peace

ALTHOUGH THE UNITED STATES HAD NO FORMAL DIPLOMATIC RELATIONS WITH CHINA, THERE WAS A NARROW PIPELINE TO THE CHINESE GOVERNMENT VIA WALTER STOESSEL JR., CENTER, THE U.S. AMBASSADOR TO POLAND, WHO OCCASIONALLY MET WITH CHINESE REPRESENTATIVES IN WARSAW.

Time & Life Pictures/Getty Images

PRESIDENT RICHARD NIXON AND
CHINESE PREMIER ZHOU ENLAI
RAISE THEIR GLASSES IN A TOAST
DURING NIXON'S LANDMARK TRIP TO
CHINA IN 1972. NIXON FORMULATED
"TRIANGULAR DIPLOMACY," WITH
THE OBJECTIVE OF PLAYING THE
SOVIETS AGAINST THE CHINESE, SO
THAT BOTH WOULD COMPETE FOR
IMPROVED RELATIONS WITH THE
UNITED STATES.

Time & Life Pictures/Getty Images

and stability in Asia and the world, that we take what steps we can toward improved practical relations with Peking." He intended the report as a signal to Congress and the American people that a new direction was in the offing, but, equally important, he knew that China's leaders would also read it. "Ping-Pong diplomacy" was still in the future. This was the first signal.

Although the United States had no formal diplomatic relations with China, there was a narrow pipeline to the Chinese government via Walter Stoessel Jr., the U.S. ambassador to Poland, who occasionally met with Chinese representatives in Warsaw. Two days after the "Foreign Policy Report" was issued, Stoessel's Chinese counterpart suggested that meetings between U.S. and Chinese diplomats be moved from Warsaw to Beijing. Less forthrightly, he let it be known that the government would "welcome" a "high-ranking American official" to lead whatever delegation might be sent to the Chinese capital. Stoessel communicated this breakthrough to Washington, and in March, President Nixon sent another signal in reply. He directed the State Department to end most restrictions on travel to China. In April, he ordered the relaxation of many trade restrictions.

It took the Chinese several months to respond, but when, in July 1970, the Beijing government released Roman Catholic bishop James Edward Walsh, who had been imprisoned by the communist regime since 1958, it was apparent that a thaw was under way. In October 1970, the president told an interviewer for *Time* magazine: "If there is anything I want to do before I die, it is to go to China. If I don't, I want my children to."

Nixon believed that opening U.S.-Chinese relations required a "diplomatic minuet," lest opponents to change in both countries put a sudden stop to the music. He sent Kissinger to China for secret talks, which set the stage for the invitation to the American table tennis team. The first act of "Ping-Pong diplomacy" was followed by a reciprocal visit of the Chinese team to the United States, and that in turn raised the curtain on the climactic act, President Nixon's trip to China during February 21–28, 1972.

A SAFER WORLD

Although the visit with Zhou Enlai and Mao Zedong did not yield the immediate dividend Nixon had hoped for—a route to "peace with honor" in Vietnam—it did sufficiently unnerve Kremlin leaders to motivate them to negotiate a favorable Strategic Arms Limitation Treaty (SALT I) and other agreements furthering U.S.-Soviet détente. Together with improved U.S.-Chinese relations, this surely made the world a safer place.

Not even Richard Nixon, however, could have predicted the magnitude of the long-term transformation that his visit to China set into motion. The opening of relations prompted the Chinese leadership to end its ideological, political, and economic isolation, which put the nation on an astonishingly fast track to what it is today: an industrial powerhouse and major trading partner with the United States. Whereas the Soviet Union disintegrated within years of the end of the Nixon presidency, giving way to a spasmodically capitalist state, China has remained a communist nation that is nevertheless a dynamic force in the world's capitalist economy.

Nations whose mutual welfare depends on the trade that exists between them rarely go to war, and so, despite profound differences in ideology, few Americans any longer feel the need to fear a "mad dog" possessed of nuclear weapons. Even so, although the world-changing economic rise of China has built many new bridges of commerce for the United States and the rest of the West, it also presents new challenges to an America long accustomed to being the planet's premier political and economic power.

SOURCES

CHAPTER 1

Hogeland, William. *The Whiskey Rebellion: George Washington, Alexander Hamilton, and the Frontier Rebels Who Challenged America's Newfound Sovereignty.* New York: Scriber, 2006.

Hunt, John Gabriel, ed. *The Dissenters: America's Voices of Opposition.* New York: Gramercy, 1993.

Lawson, John D., ed. *American State Trials: A Collection of the Important and Interesting Criminal Trails Which Have Taken Place in the United States, from the Beginning of Our Government to the Present Day.* F.H. Thomas Law Book Co., 1915.

Slaughter, Thomas P. *The Whiskey Rebellion: Frontier Epilogue to the American Revolution.* New York: Oxford University Press, 1983.

CHAPTER 2

Ambrose, Stephen E. *Undaunted Courage: Meriwether Lewis, Thomas Jefferson, and the Opening of the American West.* New York: Simon & Schuster, 1996.

"Lewis & Clark." Public Broadcast Service. www.pbs.org/lewisandclark.

"The Lewis and Clark Journey of Discovery." National Park Service. www.nps .gov/archive/jeff/LewisClark2/Circa1804/Heritage/LouisianaPurchase/ LouisianaPurchase.htm.

Peterson, Merrill D. *Jefferson: Writings.* New York: The Library of America, 1984.

Wilson, Gate. "Jefferson's Big Deal: The Louisiana Purchase," *Monticello Newsletter,* Spring 2003.

CHAPTER 3

Cunningham, Noble E., Jr. *The Presidency of James Monroe.* Lawrence: University of Kansas Press, 1996.

Dent, David W. *The Legacy of the Monroe Doctrine: A Reference Guide to U.S. Involvement in Latin America and the Caribbean.* Westport, CT: Greenwood Press, 1999.

Kenworthy, Eldon. *America/Américas: Myth in the Making of U.S. Policy Toward Latin America.* University Park: The Pennsylvania State University Press, 1995.

CHAPTER 4

Borneman, Walter R. *Polk, The Man Who Transformed the Presidency and America.* New York: Random House, 2008.

DeVoto, Bernard. *1846, The Year of Decision.* Boston: Houghton Mifflin, 1942.

Eisenhower, John S.D. *So Far from God: The U.S. War with Mexico, 1846–48.* New York: Random House, 1989.

Haynes, Samuel W. *James K. Polk and the Expansionist Impulse.* New York: Pearson Longmans, 1997.

Polk, James K. *Polk: Diary of a President, 1845–49.* Allan Nevins, ed. London: Longmans, 1929.

Schlesinger, Arthur M. Jr. *The Age of Jackson.* Boston: Houghton Mifflin, 1947.

CHAPTER 5

Boehringer, Carl H. "Meeting with the West." *American Heritage*, August 1963.

"Commodore Perry and the Opening of Japan." U.S. Navy Museum. www.history.navy.mil/branches/teach/ends/opening.htm.

Gallagher, Robert S. "Castaways on Forbidden Shores." *American Heritage*, June 1968.

Hale, William Harlan. "When Perry Unlocked the 'Gate of the Sun.'" *American Heritage*, April 1958.

"Millard Fillmore." Evisum, Inc. www.millardfillmore.org.

"President Fillmore's Letter to the Emperor of Japan." John Jay College of Criminal Justice. web.jjay.cuny.edu/-jobrien/reference/ob54.html.

Weisberger, Bernard A. "First Encounter." *American Heritage*, December 1991.

CHAPTER 6

Burlingame, Michael. *Abraham Lincoln: A Life.* Baltimore: The Johns Hopkins University Press, 2008.

Donald, David Herbert. *Lincoln.* New York: Simon & Schuster, 1995.

Guelzo, Allen C. *Lincoln's Emancipation Proclamation: The End of Slavery in America.* New York: Simon & Schuster, 2004.

Ward, Geoffrey C., with Ric Burns and Ken Burns. *The Civil War.* New York: Alfred A. Knopf, 1990.

CHAPTER 7

Davidson, Kenneth E. *The Presidency of Rutherford B. Hayes.* Westport, CT: Greenwood Press, 1972.

Dolan, Ronald E., ed. *The Philippines: A Country Study.* Washington, DC: GPO for the Library of Congress, 1991.

Foner, Eric. *A Short History of Reconstruction, 1863–1877.* New York: Harper & Row, 1988.

Franklin, John Hope. *Reconstruction after the Civil War,* 2nd edition. Chicago: University of Chicago Press, 1994.

Garner, James Wilford. *Reconstruction in Mississippi.* New York: Macmillan, 1901.

Lemann, Nicholas. *Redemption: The Last Battle of the Civil War.* New York: Farrar, Straus, and Giroux, 2006.

CHAPTER 8

Hoogenboom, Ari. *Outlawing the Spoils: A History of the Civil Service Reform Movement, 1883.* Champaign: University of Illinois Press, 1961.

Howe, George Frederick. *Chester A. Arthur: A Quarter Century of Machine Politics.* Norwalk, CT: Easton Press, 1987.

Reeves, Thomas C. *Gentleman Boss: The Life of Chester A. Arthur.* New York: Knopf, 1975.

Twain, Mark, and Charles Dudley Warner. *The Gilded Age.* New York: Modern Library, 2006.

CHAPTER 9

"Background Note: Philippines." U.S. Department of State. www.state.gov/r/pa/ei/bgn/2794.htm.

"Crucible of Empire: The Spanish-American War." Public Broadcast Service. www.pbs.org/crucible.

"The Destruction of USS *Maine*." Naval Historical Center. www.history.navy.mil/faqs/faq71-1.htm.

Dumindin, Arnaldo. *The Philippine-American War, 1899–1902.* www.freewebs.com/philippineamericanwar/filamwarbreaksout.htm.

Karnow, Stanley. *In Our Image: America's Empire in the Philippines.* New York: Foreign Policy Association, 1989.

Leech, Margaret. *In the Days of McKinley.* New York: Harper & Brothers, 1959.

Linn, Brian McAllister. *The Philippine War, 1899–1902.* Lawrence: University of Kansas Press, 2002.

McMorrow, Edward P. "What Destroyed the USS *Maine*—An Opinion." The Spanish-American War Centennial Website. www.spanamwar.com/Mainemo1.htm.

"The World of 1898: The Spanish-American War." Library of Congress, Hispanic Division. www.loc.gov/rr/hispanic/1898/intro.html.

CHAPTER 10

Harlan, Louis L., ed. *The Booker T. Washington Papers.* Champaign: University of Illinois Press, 2001.

Norell, Robert J. *Up from History: A Life of Booker T. Washington.* Cambridge: Belknap Press of Harvard University, 2009.

Smock, Raymond W. *Booker T. Washington: Black Leadership in the Age of Jim Crow.* Chicago: Ivan R. Dee, 2009.

Washington, Booker T. *Up from Slavery.* New York: Cosimo Classics, 2007. First published 1901.

CHAPTER 11

"'Disney Magic' cruise pays record Panama Canal toll." *Merco Press*, June 10, 2008.

"Interesting Facts." Panama Tours. www.panamatours.com/Pancanal/Canal_facts.htm.

"Panama Canal." Oracle ThinkQuest Education Foundation. http://library.thinkquest.org/27638/panama.html.

"TR's Legacy—The Panama Canal." Public Broadcast Service. www.pbs.org/wgbh/amex/tr/panama.html.

CHAPTER 12

Brinkley, Douglas. *The Wilderness Warrior: Theodore Roosevelt and the Crusade for America.* New York: Harper, 2009.

Hunt, John Gabriel, ed. *The Essential Theodore Roosevelt.* New York: Gramercy, 1994.

Morris, Edmund. *Theodore Rex.* New York: Random House, 2001.

Roosevelt, Theodore. *An Autobiography.* New York: Da Capo, 1985.

CHAPTER 13

Hart, Robert A. *The Great White Fleet: Its Voyage Around the World.* Boston: Little, Brown & Co., 1965.

Lord, Walter. *The Good Years: From 1900 to the First World War.* New York: Harper & Bros., 1960.

McKinley, Mike. "The Cruise of the Great White Fleet." Washington: Department of the Navy. www.history.navy.mil/library/online/gwf_cruise.htm.

Morris, Edmund. *Theodore Rex.* New York: Random House, 2001.

Russell, Francis. *American History of the Confident Years.* New York: American Heritage Publishing Co., 1969.

CHAPTER 14

Axelrod, Alan. *Selling the Great War: The Making of American Propaganda.* New York: Palgrave Macmillan, 2009.

Ferrell, Robert H. *Woodrow Wilson and World War I, 1917–1921.* New York: HarperCollins, 1986.

Kennedy, Ross A. *The Will to Believe: Woodrow Wilson, World War I, and America's Strategy for Peace and Security.* Kent, OH: Kent State University Press, 2009.

Thompson, John A. *Woodrow Wilson.* London and New York: Longman, 2002.

CHAPTER 15

Brands, W. H. *Traitor to His Class: The Privileged Life and Radical Presidency of Franklin Delano Roosevelt.* New York: Doubleday, 2008.

"The Historical Background and Development of Social Security." Social Security Online. www.ssa.gov/history/briefhistory3.html.

Morgan, Ted. *F.D.R. A Biography.* New York: Simon & Schuster, 1985.

Perkins, Frances. *The Roosevelt I Knew.* New York: Harper Colophon Book, 1964.

CHAPTER 16

Blum, John Morton. *From the Morgenthau Diaries,* vol. 3. Boston: Houghton Mifflin, 1959–67.

Churchill, Sir Winston. *The Second World War*, vol. 6. Boston: Houghton Mifflin, 1948–53.

Keegan, John. *The Second World War.* New York: Penguin Books, 1989.

Ketchum, Richard M. *The Borrowed Years 1938–41.* New York: Henry Holt & Co., 1997.

Kimball, Warren F. *The Most Unsordid Act: Lend-Lease 1939–41.* Baltimore: The Johns Hopkins Press, 1969.

Langer, William L., and S. Everett Gleason. *The Undeclared War, 1940–41.* New York: Harper & Brothers, 1953.

Mechem, Jon. *Franklin and Winston: Portrait of an Epic Friendship.* New York: Random House, 2003.

CHAPTER 17

Bennett, Michael J. *When Dreams Came True: The GI Bill and the Making of Modern America.* Washington, DC: Brassey's, 1996.

Brokaw, Tom. *The Greatest Generation.* New York: Random House, 1998.

Humes, Edward. *Over Here: How the GI Bill Transformed the American Dream.* New York: Harcourt, 2006.

Kiester, Edwin Jr. "Uncle Sam Wants You—to Go to College." *Smithsonian*, November 1994.

Olson, Keith W. *The GI Bill, the Veterans, and the Colleges.* Louisville: University Press of Kentucky, 1974.

CHAPTER 18

Brinkley, Douglas, and Townsend Hoopes. *FDR and the Creation of the U.N.* New Haven: Yale University Press, 1997.

Burns, James MacGregor. *Roosevelt: The Soldier of Freedom.* New York: Harcourt Brace Jovanovich, Inc., 1970.

Dallek, Robert. *Franklin Roosevelt and American Foreign Policy, 1932–1945.* New York: Oxford University Press, 1995.

CHAPTER 19

McCullough, David. *Truman.* New York: Random House, 1992.

Truman, Harry S. *Memoirs,* 2 vols. Garden City, NY: Doubleday, 1955–1956.

Truman, Harry S. *Truman Speaks.* New York: Columbia University Press, 1960.

Truman, Margaret, ed. *Where the Buck Stops: The Personal and Private Writings of Harry S. Truman.* New York: Warner, 1989.

CHAPTER 20

Ferrell, Robert H., ed. *Off the Record: The Private Papers of Harry S. Truman*. New York: Harper & Row, 1980.

McCullough, David. *Truman*. New York: Simon & Schuster, 1992.

Tusa, Ann, and John Tusa. *The Berlin Airlift*. New York: Atheneum, 1988.

CHAPTER 21

Ferrell, Robert H., ed. *Off the Record: The Private Papers of Harry S. Truman*. New York: Harper & Row, 1980.

McCullough, David. *Truman*. New York: Simon & Schuster, 1992.

"The President's Private War." Harry S. Truman Library & Museum. www .trumanlibrary.org/whistlestop/study_collections/korea/large/private.htm.

Toland, John. *In Mortal Combat: Korea, 1950–1955*. New York: William Morrow & Co., 1991.

CHAPTER 22

Ambrose, Stephen E. *Eisenhower: The President*. New York: Simon & Schuster, 1984.

Davies, Pete. *American Road: The Story of an Epic Transcontinental Journey at the Dawn of the Motor Age*. New York: Henry Holt, 2002.

Weingroff, Richard F. "The Man Who Changed America," Parts I & II. *Public Roads*. www.tfhrc.gov/pubrds/03mar/05.htm.

CHAPTER 23

Reeves, Thomas C. *A Question of Character: A Life of John F. Kennedy*. New York: The Free Press, 1991.

Sorenson, Theodore. *Kennedy*. New York: Harper & Row, 1965.

CHAPTER 24

Axelrod, Alan. *The Real History of the Cold War*. New York: Sterling, 2009.

Dallek, Robert. *An Unfinished Life: John F. Kennedy, 1917–1963*. Boston: Little, Brown, 2003.

Giglio, James N. *The Presidency of John F. Kennedy*. Lawrence: University of Kansas Press, 2006.

Shepard, Alan, and Deke Slayton. *Moon Shot: The Inside Story of America's Race to the Moon*. Atlanta: Turner Publishing, 1994.

CHAPTER 25

Dallek, Robert. *An Unfinished Life: John F. Kennedy, 1917–1963*. Boston: Little, Brown, 2003.

Giglio, James N. *The Presidency of John F. Kennedy*. Lawrence: University of Kansas Press, 2006.

May, Ernest R., and Philip D. Zelikow, eds. *The Kennedy Tapes: Inside the White House During the Cuban Missile Crisis*. Cambridge: Harvard University Press, 1997.

CHAPTER 26

Dallek, Robert. *Flawed Giant: Lyndon Johnson and His Times, 1961–1973*. New York: Oxford University Press, 1998.

"Major Features of the Civil Rights Act of 1964." The Dirksen Congressional Center. www.congresslink.org/print_basics_histmats_civilrights64text.htm.

Ward, Geoffrey. "Adam Powell and Malcolm X." *American Heritage*, July/August 1992.

Williams, Juan. *Eyes on the Prize: America's Civil Rights Years, 1954–1965*. New York: Viking, 1987.

CHAPTER 27

Dallek, Robert. *Lyndon Johnson and His Times, 1961–1973*. New York: Oxford University Press, 1998.

DeWitt, Larry. "The Medicare Program as a Capstone to the Great Society." www .larrydewitt.net/Essays/MedicareDaddy.htm.

"The Kennedy Assassination and the Transfer of Power: The LBJ Tapes." The Miller Center of Public Affairs, University of Virginia. www.millercenter.org/scripps/ archive/forum/detail/1847.

CHAPTER 28

Ambrose, Stephen E. *Nixon*, 3 vols. New York: Simon & Schuster, 1988–1991.

Dallek, Robert. *Nixon and Kissinger: Partners in Power*. New York: Harper Perennial, 2007.

MacMillan, Margaret. *Nixon and Mao: The Week That Changed the World*. New York: Random House, 2008.

Nixon, Richard. *RN: The Memoirs of Richard Nixon*. New York: Simon & Schuster, 1978.

Small, Melvin. *The Presidency of Richard Nixon*. Lawrence: University of Kansas Press, 1999.

ACKNOWLEDGMENTS

The authors would like to thank Fair Winds Press Publisher William Kiester, Developmental Editor Cara Connors, Project Manager Tiffany Hill, and Editorial Assistant Jennifer Grady. In addition, they would like to thank contributing writers Joseph Cummins and Alan Axelrod.

ABOUT THE AUTHORS

Thomas J. Craughwell is the author of more than a dozen books, including *How the Barbarian Invasions Shaped the Modern World, Stealing Lincoln's Body,* and most recently, *The Rise and Fall of the Second Largest Empire in History: How Genghis Khan's Mongols Almost Conquered the World.* He has written articles on history, religion, politics, and popular culture for the *Wall Street Journal*, the *American Spectator*, and *U.S. News & World Report*. He lives in Bethel, Connecticut.

Edwin Kiester Jr. has written more than 2,000 magazine articles and twelve books on subjects ranging from science to history. His most recent books are *Before They Changed the World, An Incomplete History of World War I,* and *An Incomplete History of World War II*. He lives in Essex, Massachusetts.

INDEX